Dispatches from the Balkan War
and Other Writings

# Dispatches from the Balkan War and Other Writings

Alain Finkielkraut

Translated by Peter S. Rogers and
Richard Golsan
Introduction and chronology
by Richard Golsan

University of Nebraska Press

Lincoln

Parts 1 and 2 of this book were
originally published as *Comment
peut-on être croate?* © Éditions Gallimard, 1992
Page 221 is a continuation of this page and
acknowledges the previously published articles in part 3.

Library of Congress Cataloging-in-Publication Data
Finkielkraut, Alain.
Dispatches from the Balkan War and other writings / by
Alain Finkielkraut; translated by Peter S. Rogers
and Richard Golsan; Introduction and chronology by
Richard Golsan. p. cm – (European horizons)
Parts 1 and 2 of this book were originally published
as "Comment peut-on être Croate?"–
CIP pref. Includes bibliographical references
and index. ISBN 0-8032-2003-0 (cl. : alk. paper)
1. Yugoslav War, 1991–1995. 1. Finkielkraut,
Alain. Comment peut-on être Croate?
English. 11. Title. 111. Series.
DR1313.F564 1999 949.7103–dc21
99-14268 CIP

# Contents

Translators' Acknowledgments      ix

Note on Translation      x

Chronology of the War in the Former Yugoslavia      xi

Introduction: French Intellectuals and the War in
the Former Yugoslavia      xvii

Part 1: *How Can One Be Croatian?: The Return of Ideology*

1. Let's Not Congratulate Ourselves      5

2. History's Poor Relatives      13

3. "I Am the Member of an Ancient Tribe . . ."      37

4. Indifferent Memory      42

Part 2: *How Can One Be Croatian?: Journal of a Disaster*

5. A Death Announcement      71
    *9 July 1991*

6. Words and War      78
    *4 October 1991*

7. The President Gives a History Lesson      80
    *12 December 1991*

8. "Ave Europa, Morituri Te Salutant"      83
    *10 December 1991*

9. A Dismissal of Charges      84
    *25 April 1992*

10. Sarajevo: Crimes against Humanity      85
    *10 May 1992*

# Contents

11. Past–Present      87
    *27 May 1992*

12. Sarajevo Twenty Days after François
    Mitterrand      90
    *21 July 1992*

13. The Boat Is Full      92
    *31 July 1992*

14. Bastards and Victims      94
    *3 August 1992*

15. Insults and Abandonment      96
    *9 August 1992*

16. Let's Not Add War to War      98
    *18 August 1992*

17. The French Exception      101
    *1 September 1992*

18. What Is a Nation?—Second Episode      105
    *September 1992*

19. "If This Is a Man . . ."      108
    *15 September 1992*

20. The Perfect Crime      111
    *15 October 1992*

Part 3: Writings on the Balkan Conflict, 1993–96

21. Introduction to Part 3      115

22. The Demands of the Day      18
    *16 December 1992*

23. Revisionism      120
    *15 January 1993*

# Contents

24. The Peacemakers:
    The Dream of Peace without Intervention
    Ends Up Prolonging the War                                    121
    *3 February 1993*

25. Two Europes                                                   123
    *February 1993*

26. The Inadmissible Frontier                                     129
    *18 March 1993*

27. Bosnia-Herzegovina: Without Shame                             131
    *21 May 1993*

28. The Injunction of Buchenwald                                  133
    *15 December 1993*

29. Vukovar, Sarajevo: Hitler's Posthumous Victory               139
    *1993*

30. The Crime of Being Born: Europe, Nations, War                148
    *February 1994*

31. Intellectuals, Politics, and War                             166
    *16 September 1994*

32. Will To Be Powerless                                          170
    *29 November 1994*

33. On the Uselessness of the Twentieth Century                  173
    *15 December 1994*

34. Forgetting the World                                          179
    *15 April 1995*

35. The Kusturica Imposture                                       182
    *2 June 1995*

36. Don't Let the Image of the Dead Bury the Dead               185
    *16 June 1995*

37. The King with No Clothes                                      188
    *26 July 1995*

# Contents

38. Of Men and Angels        192
    *20–21 August 1995*

39. Race in Opposition to the Nation        198
    *8 September 1995*

40. President Tudjman, Europe, and
    Bosnia-Herzegovina        204
    *5 October 1995*

41. The Politeness of Despair        207
    *14 September 1996*

42. Leaving the War: An Interview with
    Alain Finkielkraut        210
    *September 1996*

    Source Acknowledgments        221

    Index        223

# Translators' Acknowledgments

I would like to thank a number of people who have helped make this translation possible. First, my friend and cotranslator Peter Rogers generously shouldered the majority of the work on this volume and never once complained about my chaotic approach to things. Douglas Clayton, former editor at the University of Nebraska Press, was most supportive throughout the life of this project. My friends and colleagues Nathan and Françoise Bracher were most helpful in untangling translation difficulties I couldn't resolve myself. Thanks are also due to Patricia Brooke, who helped assemble the final manuscript. My own work on this project has been generously supported by the Center for Leadership Studies and its director, Arnold Vedlitz. Finally, and most important, my wife Nancy and my sons Jody and James saw me through as usual. My work on this project is dedicated to James and Jody, in the hope that in their lifetime they will see an end to the dreadful tragedies like the one Alain Finkielkraut describes so forcefully in these pages.

*Richard Golsan*

I am grateful to Joe Golsan for having suggested the translation and for help throughout the project. Terese Lyons and Kay La-bauve Rees read, questioned, and corrected many of my projected sentences. Any mistakes are my own. I also profited from the encouragement and criticism of Marlene Barsoum, Cassandra Mabe, Elizabeth McEvoy, Rick Mirabelli, Charles O'Neill, Josefa Salmón, Richard Snow, and Byron Wells. My work on the translation is dedicated to my sister Ellen Patrick Rogers.

*Peter S. Rogers*

The translators have, whenever possible, used published English translations of works that Finkielkraut cites in their French translation. A bibliographical reference for the published English translation has been provided in such instances. In all other cases, the translators have provided their own renderings of cited passages.

All ellipses used in the text, including those in brackets, appear in the original French publications; they do not signify an omission of text on the part of the translators.

# Chronology of the War in the Former Yugoslavia

*4 May 1980:* Death of Marshall Josip Broz Tito, ruler of Yugoslavia since the end of World War II.

*1986:* Slobodan Milosevic, former head of Beobanka, one of Yugoslavia's largest banks, becomes head of the Serbian Communist Party.

*April 1987:* Sent by Yugoslav president Ivan Stambolic to quell ethnic unrest in Kosovo, Milosevic takes advantage of a confrontation between ethnic Serbs and Albanian police to stir up, rather than reduce, ethnic tensions. His statement to Kosovan Serbs that the police "should not dare to beat them" assures him of Kosovan Serb loyalty and launches him onto the national stage.

*February 1989:* A massive strike by Albanian miners to stop the imposition of Serb rule in Kosovo is put down by the Serb government. To Milosevic's chagrin, the newly elected president of Slovenia, Milan Kucan, expresses his support for the miners, whom Kucan claims are defending Yugoslavia.

*May 1989:* Milosevic assumes the presidency of Serbia, having built strong support through the successful exploitation of Serb nationalist sentiment and an effective propaganda machine. The consecrating event of his assumption of power occurs on 28 June at a mass rally on the site of the historical Battle of Kosovo, where Milosevic arrives by helicopter to harangue a huge crowd in support of Serb nationalism.

*January 1990:* Hostile toward Milosevic's efforts to consolidate his power and toward his arguments for increased centralization in Yugoslavia, Slovenian delegates walk out of the Yugoslav Communist Party. Hope still exists in certain quarters, however, that new, multiparty elections will allow Yugoslavia to continue as a state.

*April 1990:* In Slovenia, a center-right coalition under the former Communist president Milan Kucan is elected.

*May 1990:* In Croatia, the Communists lose to the new nationalist HDZ Party, headed by Franjo Tudjman. Apart from adopting traditional Croatian symbols used previously by the fascist Ustacha regime during World War II, Tudjman also "demotes" the Serb population (approximately 600,000 people) from a "constituent people" to a "national minority." Henceforth Croatia will be known as the "the national state of the Croatian people." Milosevic quickly denounces Tudjman as a Ustacha agent and warns of a "new fascism" in Croatia.

*November 1990:* In Bosnia, election results generally fall along ethnic lines, although the vote is primarily anti-Communist in its inspiration. Twenty-eight percent of the voters do not vote for any of the ethnic parties. The Serb-Bosnian party is headed by the Sarajevo psychiatrist Radovan Karadzic. Alija Izetbegovic is elected head of the Muslim SDA Party. The three victorious parties form a coalition government, doomed shortly to fail.

*January 1991:* In a secret deal, Milosevic conveys to the Slovenian leader Kucan that Slovenia is free to leave Yugoslavia as long as Slovenia does not interfere with Serb ambitions for the rest of the country.

*March 1991:* Milosevic and Tudjman meet and agree in principle to the partitioning of Bosnia. After a tense and disruptive meeting of the Yugoslav presidency, Milosevic announces that Serbia will no longer recognize the presidency's decisions. (The presidency is the Yugoslav federal government; the position of president is itself occupied by a representative of one of the national groups on a rotating basis.) The Serbian Autonomous Region of Krajina declares its independence from Croatia. The first fighting between Serbs and Croats occurs at Plitvice, in the Krajina region of Croatia. One Serb and one Croat are killed. The JNA, or federal army, intervenes, ostensibly to stop the fighting, but the JNA is already squarely in Serbian hands.

*May 1991:* Serbs in the Krajina region of Croatia go to the polls to vote to join the Republic of Serbia. A week later, the rest of Croatia goes to the polls to vote for national independence. Conflict between ethnic Serbs and Croats has long been under way in several locations.

*June 1991:* Slovenia declares its independence from Yugoslavia. The JNA intervenes under confused circumstances, after the January 1991 meeting between Milosevic and Kucan. Some fifty men are killed during ten days of fighting.

*July 1991:* JNA troops withdraw from Slovenia, and full-scale war breaks out in Croatia between Croats and Serbs backed by the JNA.

*August 1991:* Aware of the grave danger facing the country, Franjo Tudjman creates a government of national unity in Zagreb, including all the major political factions. The Serb attack on the Croatian city of Vukovar begins. The city will fall in November.

*September 1991:* The UN declares an arms embargo on all of the former Yugoslavia.

*October 1991:* Siege of Dubrovnik begins.

*November 1991:* In an interview in the German newspaper *Frankfurter Allgemeine Zeitung*, French president François Mitterrand reminds his interlocutor that Croatia belonged to the Nazi bloc during World War II and that Serbia did not.

*December 1991:* The European Community, under pressure from Germany, announces that it will recognize Slovenia and Croatia.

*January 1992:* Cease-fire in Croatia negotiated by United Nations mediator Cyrus Vance. Serbia gains one quarter of Croatia's land mass, which it will lose in 1995.

*February 1992:* Bosnia-Herzegovina declares its independence from Yugoslavia. The Bosnian Serbs declare a separate state. Fighting spreads.

# Chronology

*April 1992:* Siege of Sarajevo by Bosnian Serbs begins. Bosnia is recognized by the European Community and the United States.

*May 1992:* Slovenia, Croatia, and Bosnia are admitted into the UN. The JNA releases command of one hundred thousand troops in Bosnia, effectively creating a Bosnian Serb army. The UN establishes an embargo against Yugoslavia (consisting now of Serbia and Montenegro).

*June 1992:* The European Community meets in London to discuss military intervention in Bosnia. On 28 June, François Mitterrand visits a besieged Sarajevo.

*July 1992:* International airlift to Sarajevo begins.

*August 1992:* Franjo Tudjman is reelected president of Croatia. *Newsday* reveals the existence of Serb concentration camps at Omarska and Brcko.

*September 1992:* Peace conference opens in Geneva. Lord Owen has replaced Lord Carrington as Europe's mediator in the conflict. Yugoslavia is dropped from the General Assembly by the Security Council.

*October 1992:* The UN resolves to investigate war crimes in the region.

*December 1992:* Milosevic is reelected president of Serbia.

*January 1993:* Mediators Cyrus Vance and Lord Owen propose a peace plan calling for division of Bosnia along ethnic lines into ten regions. The plan will be signed by Izetbegovic on behalf of Bosnia but rejected in April by the the parliament of the Serb Republic of Bosnia and by a referendum of Bosnian Serbs the following month.

*February 1993:* The UN Security Council establishes an international tribunal for war crimes in the former Yugoslavia. The tribunal will be inaugurated at the Hague in November.

*March 1993:* Bosnian Muslims and Croats begin to fight over Bosnian territories not seized by Serbs.

*September 1993:* After a series of failed initiatives to resolve the situation in Bosnia, the peace talks in Geneva collapse.

*December 1993:* Parliamentary elections in Serbia strengthen the hold of Milosevic and his Socialist Party.

*November 1993:* As perhaps the culminating act of fighting between Croat and Muslim Bosnians over the town of Mostar, the famous medieval bridge is destroyed by Croat artillery.

*February 1994:* Mortar shells fired by Serbs kill sixty people and wound some two hundred others at the downtown marketplace in Sarajevo. Spurred to action, NATO orders the removal of Serb mortar emplacements around Sarajevo. Karadzic complies on condition that Russian soldiers join the peacekeeping force. Four Bosnian Serb warplanes are downed for violating the no-fly zone.

*March 1994:* Under intense pressure from the United States, Croatian and Muslim factions in Bosnia sign an accord creating a Muslim-Croat federation and bringing an end to a year of fighting between the two groups.

*May 1994:* Five-nation contact group (with representatives from Russia, France, Germany, the United Kingdom, and the United States) proposes peace plan, which calls for a four-month cease-fire and the eventual partitioning of Bosnia. The Bosnian Serbs reject the plan in July. Apparently angered by this lack of cooperation, Milosevic severs ties with the Bosnian Serbs in August.

*October–November 1994:* Fighting around the Muslim enclave of Bihac triggers the largest NATO action of the war, an air strike of some sixty planes, which nevertheless fails to prevent further Serb air strikes against Bihac.

*December 1994:* Jimmy Carter ends peacekeeping mission with announcement of four-month cease-fire.

*April 1995:* After a plane bearing aid to Sarajevo is hit by gunfire, the UN calls a halt to further airlifts into the city.

*May 1995:* Croat troops and tanks launch an offensive to reconquer the Serb territory in Croatia. Serb appeals for help to Belgrade and Pale, capital of the Bosnian Serb Republic, are ignored. Rocket attacks by the Croatian Serbs against Zagreb kill several people but accomplish little. Meanwhile, in an effort to stop NATO attacks on their arms depots, the Bosnian Serbs begin taking UN peacekeepers hostage.

*July 1995:* Lightning Croatian attacks, ostensibly on behalf of the beleaguered Bosnian Muslims, result in stunning Serb reversals in Bosnia. On 11 July, Serb troops under General Ratko Mladic overrun the Muslim "safe area" of Srebernica. Several thousand Muslims are executed, apparently on orders from Mladic, while others add to the growing number of refugees.

*August 1995:* President Clinton vetoes congressional measure to lift arms embargo. With the aid of newly potent Bosnian Muslim troops, Croatian forces attack the Krajina region, and within days, the Republic of Serb Krajina collapses. On 28 August, two mortar shells kill thirty-eight people and wound many others in the Sarajevo marketplace. As a result, NATO's full military might is unleashed against the Bosnian Serbs for the first time, accompanied by a successful attack against Serb positions in western Bosnia by Croats and Bosnian Muslim forces.

*October 1995:* A general cease-fire in Bosnia is accepted by all parties.

*November 1995:* All parties meet in Dayton to hammer out a final accord. Bosnian Serb interests are represented by Milosevic. As a result of the accords, the new state of Bosnia was to consist of two parts, the Republika Srpska and the Bosnian Federation, the latter consisting of Croat and Muslim groups. A loose form of central government is envisioned, and all refugees are to be allowed to return home. Sixty thousand mostly NATO troops will act as peacekeepers in the region.

*Spring 1998:* Fighting between Albanian separatists and Serbian authorities increases in the province of Kosovo. Currently no solution to the conflict is in sight.

# Introduction

*French Intellectuals and the War in the Former Yugoslavia*

For French intellectuals, the 1980s were a period of relative "silence" on politics and international affairs. But in the early nineties they once again began to make their voices heard on a number of issues that would occupy public attention increasingly as the decade progressed.[1] Of particular concern to many of these intellectuals was the war in the former Yugoslavia, the brutality and horror of which were exposed daily in the media. The fighting in Croatia and later in Bosnia prompted cries of outrage in the press by many of France's leading philosophers, historians, and novelists. Calls for an end to hostilities, condemnations of one warring faction or the other, and, as the conflict continued, denunciations of inaction and even indifference on the part of the French government and the international community appeared regularly in the editorial pages of major French newspapers. Lengthy essays analyzing every aspect of the conflict fill the pages of the intellectual reviews and journals that are so much a part of the Parisian scene.[2] By 1995, the fervor and passions stirred by the Balkan conflict were such that many compared the impact of the war on France's intellectual elite to that of the Dreyfus Affair or the Spanish Civil War.[3] *L'engagement politique* was clearly back in vogue.

As one might expect, French responses to the conflict, initially very limited, intensified as the fighting spread and garnered increased media attention internationally. Moreover, given the complexity of the historical and political issues at stake in the Balkans, those who spoke out in France hardly agreed from the outset as to who the aggressors were or what the best solution to the conflict might be. In fact, many of those who took an initial stance in favor of one antagonist or the other or who espoused a particular remedy changed their minds as more information became available concerning the origins of the war and as the increasingly brutal actions of the Serbs came to light.

In an excellent essay on the history of these commitments, Frédéric Martel notes the initial signs of trouble in Yugoslavia in the late eighties and at the outset of the nineties – the growth of Serb nationalism, the brutal suppression in March 1991 in Belgrade of protestors demanding greater freedom of the press, the Serb refusal the same year to allow the Croatian representative to take his turn as president of the Yugoslav Federation – all went largely unnoticed by a Parisian intelligentsia still preoccuied with the Gulf War.[4] But in the summer of 1991, with the declarations of Slovenian and Croatian independence and the outbreak of hostilities, the intellectuals began to speak out. Alain Finkielkraut and Milan Kundera defended Slovenian independence in accordance with the principle of a people's right to self-determination. In October, a petition appeared in *Le Monde* signed by the distinguished historians François Furet, Marc Ferro, and Jacques Le Goff, as well as by Kundera and Finkielkraut, advocating French recognition of the legitimacy of Slovenian and Croatian claims to independence.

With the siege of Vukovar by the JNA – the Serb-dominated federal army – and the fall of the city in November 1991, the rhetoric became more charged. In editorial pages and elsewhere, writers and intellectuals began comparing the events in Yugoslavia to the worst memories of recent European history. In the Parisian daily *Libération*, the writer Annie Lebrun entitled her editorial on the destruction of Vukovar "Today Guernica is called Vukovar." The implicit comparison of Nazi destructiveness with Serb aggression would be a refrain French intellectuals voiced increasingly as the war continued.[5]

To the list of those who spoke out in opposition to Serb aggression against Croatia in the following months were added figures long familiar in the United States, such as the playwright Eugene Ionesco. Others less well known in this country but widely known in France included the "New Philosopher" André Glucksmann and Pascal Bruckner, Finkielkraut's former coauthor and a successful popular philosopher and novelist in his own right. In a commentary on the conflict, Glucksmann would extend the range of historical comparisons with the Second World War by comparing Serb aggression to that of the Japanese. Following the fall of Vukovar, Glucksmann published an article in *Le Monde* entitled "Un Pearl Harbor moral."

But not all those who spoke out in the first year of the conflict defended Slovenian and Croatian claims to self-determination while blaming the Serbs as the sole perpetrators. Fearful of a renascent nationalism in the region, Bernard-Henri Lévy, Jorge Semprun – the Spanish novelist, scriptwriter, and former minister of culture under Felipe Gonzalez (but a writer who has traditionally written in French) – the Nobel peace laureate Elie Wiesel, and the novelist Mario Vargas Llosa published in *Le Monde* in November 1991 a petition in which they stated that they did not wish to choose one "nationalism" over another in the war. They perceived the war as being essentially a "civil war," pitting "past against past, religion against religion, the dead against the dead," and noting that "the entire country risks sinking into an endless vendetta."[6] They also called on the "Yugoslav" people to settle their differences in the name of unity. As Martel explains, the petitioners were motivated in part by what they perceived to be strong cultural and political links between Franjo Tudjman's newly elected nation-

alist regime in Zagreb and Croatia's Ustacha – and Nazi-
affiliated – past.[7]

As the preceding remarks suggest, by the end of 1991
French intellectuals were divided into two camps over the
war: those who saw the Serbs as the aggressors and the
Croatians as the victims and those who held that both nationalities or ethnic groups were equally responsible for
the conflict. For the latter group – which, in general terms,
still held to the idea of Yugoslav unity and feared Croatian nationalism – the events of December–January 1991–92
brought good news and bad. On 29 November 1991, French
president François Mitterrand reminded his interlocutor in
an interview published in the German newspaper *Frankfurter Allgemeine Zeitung* that Croatia had been "part of the
Nazi bloc" during World War II. Mitterrand also stated his
belief that Serbia was not making war to conquer Croatia
but to protect Serb minorities there. This was music to the
ears not only of those who supported Serbia outright but
also of those who wished to reduce Serbia's culpability by
tarnishing any favorable reputation Croatia might enjoy. In
this fashion, any meaningful difference between the roles of
the two countries in the war could be discounted. This, in
turn, justified renewed calls for Yugoslavia unity.

If Mitterrand's statements were good news for those insisting on equal culpability among the warring factions and
calling for a new Yugoslav national unity, Germany's decision in December 1991 and the European Community's decision shortly thereafter to recognize Slovene and Croatian
independence were, by contrast, heavy blows. The historian
and former Communist Annie Kriegel, who would move
more and more toward the Serb camp as the war progressed, expressed strong regrets over these positions, arguing that Serb ambitions focused more on the maintenance of
a "Lesser Yugoslavia" than on a "Greater Serbia." Moreover,
the process of fragmentation in Europe into smaller and

smaller nations, undesirable in itself, would only accelerate as a result of these decisions.

For his part, Elie Wiesel lamented the recognition of Croatia, arguing forcefully in an article in the political review *Lignes de Fond* that since World War II, Croatia's national aspirations had been linked to the "hatred of the other" associated with the Ustacha regime. That regime, he continued, had been an "unconditional ally" of the Nazis, and the atrocities committed in its name occasionally surpassed those of the Germans themselves. Unlike Kriegel, during the course of 1992 Wiesel would slowly redirect his hostility toward the Serbs; in early 1993 he announced that he had in effect been duped by their propaganda.

The renowned sociologist Edgar Morin followed a similar trajectory, entertaining – at least initially – serious reservations about Croatian independence and expressing his belief that a renewal of Ustachan fascism was a genuine threat. As to the origins of the conflict, Morin argued that the "arrogant politics" of Milosevic and Tudjman were equally responsible. These views, articulated in early 1992 in two successive articles in *Le Monde* jointly entitled "The Yugoslav Agony," also implicitly challenged the position that the small nations like Slovenia and Croatia had the right to self-determination. At what point, asked Morin, did one stop? What of the smaller "nations" within those nations, which, according to the same principle, likewise had a legitimate claim to self-determination? By March 1993, however, Morin's position had changed. He now saw Serbia, previously yoked in its "arrogant politics" to Croatia, as representing a new and greater threat to the degree that it embodied a new ideology Morin labeled "Total Nationalism."[8]

With the outbreak of war in Bosnia in the spring of 1992, the *engagement* of France's intellectual elite vis-à-vis the conflict expanded in scope, while the issues at stake underwent significant changes. As Martel notes, many of those who opposed Croatian and Slovenian independence as a dangerous expression of ethnic nationalism did not encounter the same difficulty in the case of a multiethnic Bosnia.[9] For many, Bosnia came to represent an idealized, peacefully diverse, and cosmopolitan state that fully exemplified Europe's "communal" values. Although the realities of the situation were more complex, Bosnia's fate came to symbolize for a large number of intellectuals the fate – and future – of Europe itself. The nation's sovereignty and integrity therefore had to be defended at all costs. Disagreements remained over conceptions of nationhood and citizenship, dating from the war in Croatia. But inaction on the part of the international community and especially of France itself as regards the war in Bosnia provoked among virtually all the intellectuals a strongly indignant response that served to unite them in spite of their differences.

The revelation in the summer of 1992 of the existence of Serb concentration camps and of the full horror of "ethnic cleansing" intensified this indignation. Although the debates over Maastricht temporarily drew attention away from the conflict in Bosnia, by the end of 1992 the war once again took center stage. On 21 November, a demonstration beginning at the Place du Panthéon and winding its way to the Place Montparnasse brought together a large group of well-known writers, historians, philosophers, and other public figures, who marched under the banners "1991: Vukovar. 1992: Sarajevo. 1993: . . . ?" and "This time, we will not be able to say that we did not know." A petition signed in association with the demonstration included the names of intellectuals like Paul Ricoeur, Pierre Vidal-Naquet, and Jean-Pierre Azéma as well as those of Cardinal Decoutray, a leader of the French Catholic Church, the politicians Jacques Toubon and Alain Carignon, and the movie directors Patrice Chéreau and Roman Polanski. Names on the petition already associated with French activism regarding the conflict were those of Finkielkraut, Bruckner, and Morin. The demonstration and the signing of the petition, moreover, proved to be one of the most visible activities of the group known as the Sarajevo-Vukovar Committee.

The demonstration at the Panthéon constituted in many ways a watershed event that accelerated public indignation over the war in Bosnia and encouraged a number of intellectuals to assume ever more prominent roles. Foremost among these was Bernard-Henri Lévy, whose resources and influence as arguably France's most visible public intellectual resulted in a number of highly visible (if occasionally somewhat ridiculous) efforts on behalf of the embattled Bosnians. On 21 December 1992, with a group of colleagues, Lévy organized a public meeting at the Mutualité hall, a building already memorable for earlier meetings by the Parisian intellectual elite in the service of various political causes. At that meeting, Lévy announced his intention to purchase arms for the defenders of Sarajevo. Shortly thereafter, he was instrumental in bringing Bosnian president Alija Izetbegovic to Paris to request support for his besieged nation, a visit that accomplished little.[10]

Lévy had also been instrumental in convincing François Mitterrand to go to Sarajevo in June, a visit that had resulted in the temporary reopening of the airport so that humanitarian supplies could get in. (Finkielkraut refers to this visit in several of the essays included here.) In 1993 – like one of his heroes, André Malraux, who during the Spanish Civil War had made a memorable film adaptation of his pro-Republican novel *L'Espoir* – Lévy began filming his documentary *Bosna!*, which was released to widespread public acclaim in April 1994. Finally, in May 1994, a number of *intellos* led by Lévy proposed the creation of a pro-Bosnian list for the European parliamentary elections. This maneuver did more to divide the French Socialist Party, and to a certain degree the organizers themselves, than it did to help the Bosnians.[11] Lévy's last-minute decision not to vote in the election disconcerted his colleagues and lent credence to those who claimed that these intellectuals had only been seeking the spotlight in the first place. For Frédéric Martel at least, what had begun as a noble defense of the Bosnian people two years before ended, at the outset of summer 1994, as a joke.[12]

But Martel's conclusion is premature, although not inaccurate in its pessimism. As Finkielkraut's essays here and those of other intellectuals confirm, the French intelligentsia continued to speak out vehemently on Serb aggression and to call for international intervention in the conflict right up to the time of the final cease-fire and the signing of the Dayton Accords. More important perhaps, the agitation of the intellectuals – and the creation of the Bosnian list for the European elections – did force a number of politicians to deal with the issue and, in some cases, to take a strong stand in favor of Bosnia. Such was the case of the Socialist leader and one-time prime minister Michel Rocard. As events reached their climax in the summer of 1995, the new French president, Jacques Chirac, took more forceful steps than had his predecessor in bringing about an end to the conflict, although, if Bernard-Henri Lévy is to be believed, this was certainly not due to pressure from the intellectuals.[13] Moreover, for Lévy at least, the cessation of hostilities and the successful conclusion of the Dayton peace accords did not mark a victory for those who had agitated so long for international intervention on behalf of the Bosnians and against Serb aggression. Instead, it marked the tragic defeat of the cosmopolitan ideal that Bosnia embodied – and something more as well. Lévy concludes his Bosnian diary with the following entry, dated 28 December 1995: "Defeat of Bosnia? No. The debacle of Europe."

A similar pessimistic, indeed apocalyptic tone also characterizes Alain Finkielkraut's commentaries and dispatches on the conflict gathered here in book form. As the preceding remarks suggest, of the intellectuals mobilized by the conflict, few committed themselves as early or played as continuous a role as did Finkielkraut. Already in 1991, long before many of his colleagues followed suit, Finkielkraut was writing editorials in *Le Monde* and *Libération* and giving interviews in the press in an effort to make his compatriots come to terms with the growing disaster to the east. In 1992, these early commentaries on the Balkan conflict were gathered together and published as a book under the title *Comment peut-on être croate?* (*How Can One Be Croatian?*) These texts comprise parts 1 and 2 of the present volume. Following publication of that book, Finkielkraut continued to write opinion pieces for the Parisian dailies (mostly *Le Monde*) and to publish essays and interviews in intellectual reviews assessing the implications of the military, political, and diplomatic developments in the region. One of the latter essays, originally published in Finkielkraut's own journal, *Le Messager Européen*, was expanded and published in pamphlet form in 1994 under the title "Le Crime d'être né: L'Europe, les nations, la guerre" ("The Crime of Being Born: Europe, Nations, War"). The majority of these texts are included in part 3 of the present volume.

In the foreword to *How Can One Be Croatian?* Finkielkraut alludes to many of the major themes and issues that recur regularly in his reflections on the Balkan conflict. The first of these is what he perceives to be the moral bankruptcy of humanitarian efforts in the region, and indeed of the humanitarian spirit itself in its recent manifestations. For Finkielkraut, humanitarian efforts mask a real and terrible indifference to the actual cost of the fighting in terms of human lives, since these efforts are carried out *in place of* more serious and beneficial attempts to stop the massacre and find a political solution to the conflict. Moreover, because humanitarian aid casts all those it helps in the role of hypothetical victims, it fails to distinguish between real perpetrators and real victims. Thus Serbs, Croatians, and Bosnians are all the same. Not only does this perspective exonerate the Serb aggressors in advance, but it perpetuates for Finkielkraut one of the more widely held prejudices concerning the Balkan region – that *all* Balkan peoples are essentially bloodthirsty brutes who gladly kill one another on the slightest pretext.

A second concern expressed in many of the texts gathered here is the problematic role that history and memory play – or fail to play, as the case may be – in efforts to understand the conflict and to come to terms with the real issues at stake. How is it, Finkielkraut wonders, that in a Europe haunted by the memory of Nazism and claiming to remain vigilant to avoid its recurrence, one can fail to recognize a renewal of Nazism's worst excesses in Serb-sponsored acts of genocide? Rather than acknowledging these crimes for what they are, Europe and its leaders dismiss them as inconsequential incidents occurring on the fringes of the continent. But then, as Finkielkraut also bitterly reminds his readers, for the large and powerful European nations, these small countries are fundamentally insignificant. They are therefore perceived as existing essentially outside history.

In France, the problem is compounded by an obsessive "duty to memory" where Vichy and its crimes are concerned. Caught up in what Finkielkraut derisively refers to as a form of national "navel contemplation," contemporary France pays more attention, for example, to the difficulties involved in bringing the former fascist *milicien* Paul Touvier to justice for murders committed fifty years ago than it does to the atrocities perpetrated daily in the former Yugoslavia.[14] While assuming the role of activists when it comes to rectifying past injustices that cannot in fact be undone, the French consistently reveal themselves to be both blind and impotent in confronting real crimes in the present.

Finkielkraut is most sharply critical, however, of those

who offer selective readings of Yugoslavia's past in order to justify both misleading interpretations of the current situation and irresponsible political choices vis-à-vis the fighting. The title *How Can One Be Croatian?* is in itself an ironic barb. It is aimed at those who point accusingly at Croatia's fascist past during the Second World War in order to suggest Croatian responsibility for the current conflict, or to imply that even if the Serbs are responsible for war in the nineties, one should still feel no sympathy for the Croatians or assume that their cause is the more just one. The worst offender along these lines, given his 1991 remarks to the German press, is former president François Mitterrand, whom Finkielkraut pointedly criticizes in the essays here. For his part, Finkielkraut considers Croatia's bid for independence from the Yugoslav federation absolutely justified, a position he maintains in his writings on the conflict well before and after the publication of *How Can One Be Croatian?*

At the heart of Finkielkraut's pro-Croatian stance, as he indicates on numerous occasions, is a belief in the rights of small countries in Europe to independence and self-determination. As the epigraphs to both *How Can One Be Croatian?* and "The Crime of Being Born" suggest, the disappearance of these small countries is linked in the recent European past to the triumph of authoritarian ideologies and totalitarian regimes. The epigraph appearing at the outset of part 1 of *How Can One Be Croatian?* – entitled, appropriately, "The Return of Ideology" – is a quote from Friedrich Engels: "I am authoritarian enough to consider the very existence, right in the middle of Europe, of such small, primitive peoples to be anachronistic." Similarly, the epigraph to "The Crime of Being Born," taken from Pierre Drieu la Rochelle's wartime journal and dated 15 May 1940, reads: "No more Holland. The number of small obsolete countries is shrinking in Europe."

The irony, for Finkielkraut, is that in a supposedly post-fascist, postcommunist Europe, the mere existence of these small, ethnically based countries to the east is considered antithetical to the future of a unified, cohesive, and peaceful Europe because these countries supposedly represent a rebirth of new and lethal forms of nationalism. In fact, as the title of the 1992 conference "Europe or the Tribes" (held in Paris and dealing with the Yugoslav conflict) suggests, the choice, for the organizers at least, was perceived as being one between a unified "European" civilization and a hodgepodge of small, barbaric nation-tribes. Having been ascribed the status of primitive, indeed prehistoric peoples by the title of the colloquium itself, the inhabitants of the newly independent East European nations are, as Finkielkraut suggests, all the more easily lumped together as "all those Southern Slavs!" To comprehend the absurdity and offensiveness of such a perspective, Finkielkraut asks what the Western European reaction would be to an Eastern European who, when asked about the history of Franco-German conflicts, dismisses the entire issue with "They're all just Franks!"

Finally, Finkielkraut reserves some of his sharpest barbs for the media that daily floods us with horrific images of one conflict, famine, or catastrophe and then, just as quickly, drop the first disaster in order to move on to a new one. Overwhelmed by this endless stream of images, the television viewer is at once anesthetized by them and detached from them, despite their apparent proximity. Living *everywhere* simultaneously through these images, the television viewer – that is to say, modern humankind or "planetary man" – in reality lives *nowhere* at all. We simply beam into one situation or crisis through the television screen and then beam back out just as easily. The reality of the events themselves leaves no trace on us, nor are we truly affected by what we witness – for example, the very tangible sufferings of the people of Sarajevo. As Finkielkraut caustically remarks, the latter are not merely "the telespectators of their own suffering." They actually bleed and die.

As a thinker and writer, Alain Finkielkraut is nothing if not controversial. It is not surprising, therefore, that in dealing with a subject as hotly contested as the war in the former Yugoslavia, and especially in taking a staunchly pro-Croatian line, Finkielkraut should come under fire for his views. As he notes in his introduction to part 3 of the present volume, many of those who disagreed with his pro-Croatian stance referred to him derisively as "Finkielcroate." Some were more explicit in their condemnations. Claiming to defend the rights of "all nations, all ethnicities, all the peoples of ex-Yugoslavia," Edgar Morin condemned Finkielkraut's position in a 1992 article in *Le Monde* that, ironically, echoed the position of those who wished to condemn Croatia for its past, a position that Finkielkraut, in his turn, had criticized: "Alain Finkielkraut has taken a stand in favor of unlimited recognition of the sovereignty of a Croatia whose democracy is fragile and limited, which has embraced a most disquieting past from the perspective of its Serb minorities. The latter were the victims of Ustacha massacres from 1941 to 1945, and they avenged themselves at the end of the last World War." [15] In a dossier entitled "Bosnia, the War of the Intellectuals" published by the Parisian daily *Libération* after the conflict in the former Yugoslavia had ended, the British-American historian Tony Judt, a self-professed admirer of Finkielkraut's, lamented the fact that Finkielkraut "committed himself in a situation about which he was not fully knowledgeable, and ended up being exploited . . . in serving as the guarantor of a questionable authority (in Croatia), that he would not support were it in power in France." [16]

While his critics may be right that Finkielkraut idealized, at least to a certain degree, Croatia's bid for independence, and that he underestimated the ultranationalist leanings of some of its leaders, he was certainly not wrong in denouncing early and forcefully Serb aggression as the principal source of the conflict.[17] In this regard, testimony to Finkielkraut's foresight can be found in the belated conversions of some of his critics. In any case, Finkielkraut's purpose in writing these articles and editorials – these "dispatches" from the Balkan conflict – was not so much to give history lessons or write position papers as it was to stir the West to act to stop the worst bloodbath in Europe in fifty years. The writings gathered here speak well of Alain Finkielkraut's commitment, perseverance, and eloquence.

*Richard Golsan*

NOTES

1. For discussions of the "silence" of the French intellectuals in the eighties, their recent efforts to redefine their roles, and their various political commitments in the nineties, see the special issue of *L'Esprit Créateur* (vol. 37, no. 2 [summer 1997]).

2. Bernard-Henri Lévy's *La Règle du Jeu* and Alain Finkielkraut's now-defunct *Le Messager Européen* regularly ran analytical essays, polemics, and editorials on the conflict, as to a lesser degree did more established reviews like *Esprit, Les Temps Modernes*, and *Le Débat*. Editorialists such as Jacques Julliard also wrote regularly about the war in the pages of large-circulation weekly magazines like *Le Nouvel Observateur*. Julliard's prolific writings on the conflict have been published in book form under the title *Pour la Bosnie* (Paris: Seuil, 1996).

3. For these comparisons, see Emmanuel Wallon, "La Guerre de Sarajevo a vraiment eu lieu," *Les Temps Modernes* 587 (Mar.–Apr.–May 1996): 374–99.

4. Frédéric Martel, "Pour servir à l'histoire de notre défaite: 'L'Élite intellectuelle et morale' française et la guerre en ex-Yugoslavie," *Le Messager Européen* 8 (1994): 127–54.

5. The Basque town of Guernica was destroyed by twenty-one German and three Italian bombers on 26 April 1937.

6. The text of the petition is published in Bernard-Henri Lévy's diary of the conflict, *Le Lys et la cendre* (Paris: Grasset, 1996), 68–69.

7. Martel, "Pour servir à l'histoire," 131–32.

8. Morin's writings on the conflict have been published in book form under the title *Les Fratricides: Yugoslavie-Bosnie 1991–1995* (Paris: Arléa, 1995).

9. Martel, "Pour servir à l'histoire," 136.

10. For Lévy's account of Izetbegovic's visit, see *Le Lys*, 133–37.

11. For a discussion of the Bosnian list and its impact on French politics at the time – and on the Socialist party in particular – see Sylvie Pierre-Brossolette, "BHL: Les Leçons de l'imprécateur," *L'Express*, 2 June 1994, pp. 23–24.

12. Martel, "Pour servir à l'histoire," 151.

13. In *Le Lys et la cendre*, Lévy describes a visit he made with Finkielkraut, Julliard, and others in late June 1995 to see the new president about the Bosnian conflict. According to Lévy, the visit was a total fiasco and accomplished nothing. See pp. 420–23.

14. A *milicien* was a member of the collaborationist police in France. For details of the Touvier case, see my *Memory, the Holocaust, and French Justice* (Hanover NH: UPNE–Dartmouth Books, 1996). More recently, Finkielkraut has made similar remarks concerning the trial of Maurice Papon for crimes against humanity for his role in the deportation of Jews from Bordeaux during the Occupation. See "Papon: Trop tard," *Le Monde*, 14 Oct. 1997.

15. Morin, *Les Fratricides*, 39.

16. Tony Judt, "La Faute à Voltaire?" *Libération*, 14–15 Sept. 1996.

17. For an excellent account of the reemergence of Croatian nationalism and its relation to the country's Ustacha past, see Marcus Tanner, *Croatia: A Nation Forged in War* (New Haven: Yale University Press, 1997). For the reemergence of ultranationalism in Croatia, see Chris Hedges, "Fascists Reborn as Croatia's Founding Fathers," *New York Times*, 12 Apr. 1997.

Dispatches from the Balkan War
and Other Writings

# PART ONE

# How Can One Be Croatian?

## *The Return of Ideology*

I am authoritarian enough to consider the very
existence, right in the middle of Europe, of such
small, primitive peoples to be anachronistic.
FRIEDRICH ENGELS

*Why are you supporting the Croatians? What has gotten into you anyway? Are you looking for some cause to support? Do you smell a rat? Are you paid by the Vatican? Do you have to* chercher la femme?

This book, born from my astonishment before this astonishment, tries to shed a little more light upon the paradoxes of an epoch – or of an elite – that is humanitarian but indifferent to carnal humanity, antiracist but stupefied that one could be Croatian, haunted by Nazism but blind to what resembles it the most, worried about Europe but that, all the while deploring the war in the Balkans and hoping strongly for peace, considers the ethnocide undergone by Croatia and Bosnia-Herzegovina to be minor events of the European adventure.

The first part of this book questions the reasons behind this will not to know. "Let's Not Congratulate Ourselves," written in August and September 1991, appeared in issue number 5 of the *Messager Européen*. "History's Poor Relatives" is a new version, updated and completely redone, of an interview that appeared in issue 55 of *Politique Internationale* (International politics). "I Am the Member of an Ancient Tribe . . ." is the text of my talk at the international colloquium "Europe or the Tribes," held at the Chaillot Palace in Paris on February 27–29, 1992. "Indifferent Memory" was written for this book.

Written throughout the conflict, the articles in the second part were, in each case, inspired by the distance between the event and the way, with some few exceptions, it was taken in by France, Europe, and the New International Order. In some way these texts constitute the journal of our disaster and are now published so that the scandal of *the* truth, as Bernanos would have said, might not sink into oblivion.

# I

# Let's Not Congratulate Ourselves

A man, in a large town, walks quickly. Nervous, worried, and glum, he doesn't notice anything or anyone: he simply walks along. Suddenly shouting voices get his attention. He raises his head and on the other side of the street he sees a group of people arguing. Intrigued, he crosses the street, approaches them, and listens. A little later, he grimaces and continues his walk, crying out to the quarreling people, "You're bothering me to death!" *Verdrei mir nicht dem Kopf*, says the Yiddish that has left us this profound story.

The same bad humor, the same impatience, the same exasperation have characterized the reaction of the French media to what we have agreed to call the Yugoslav crisis. They noticed people arguing, approached them, and listened with mike and camera in hand. And then they shouted, "You're bothering me to death!" They found that this manner of discussion came from mental retardation. The Balkan specificity of the conflict has been underscored with a kind of enraged contempt and undifferentiated disgust for all involved. Forget about finding out who attacked or was attacked in what has been called and today is still condescendingly referred to as "interethnic" confrontation. The antagonists have never had a right to the political distinctions that hold for the rest of Europe. These people are all the same, they are all animals. Just like the "Negroes" in colonial discourse, the Slovenes, Croatians, and Serbs are all the same. They are the interchangeable representatives of the same bestiality.

This is not the first time the small nations of Central Europe have been dealt such treatment. In 1938, the contempt of the civilized toward the savage played a role in the abandonment of Czechoslovakia that was at least as important as was political cynicism or fear. As Emmanuel Terray has quite justly recalled, and in a timely fashion, the spirit of Munich was not only cowardly but arrogant.[1] In response to or rather echoing Goering, who had referred to Prague's leaders as if they were "dwarfs or ridiculous Pygmies about whose origin we know nothing and who let themselves trouble a people of great culture," Chamberlain declared to the House of Commons, though in a much more refined style, "How horrible, how fantastic, how incredible that we should be reduced to digging trenches and putting on gas masks because of a quarrel in a distant land that has come about between people about whom we know nothing." And the journalist Stéphane Lauzanne reflected a widespread feeling among the French elite that France should not have "to carry with outstretched arms this or that unknown amalgam of diverse races in the Balkans."

For some time the "Balkans" had been a synonym for "Africa," and we placed Bohemia there with the same geographical casualness as we do with Slovenia today.

Out of order, you may object. It's a false analogy. For journalism's anger against Yugoslavia is not racist but, on the contrary, imbued with and even drunk on antiracist feelings. We're reproaching the belligerent not for being *other* but for crying out, "Death to the others!" and for reproducing on a small scale the types of behavior that Europe, learning lessons from Hitlerism, had decided once and for all to outlaw on its territory; it is not to be Pygmies, but it is to belong to Le Pen's Front National and, Ustachis here, Chetniks there, chauvinists everywhere, to *immure* themselves in this communitarian adherence at the very time when we have the destruction of the Berlin Wall and the free movement of persons and goods in Europe.

And in order to emphasize the contrast with Munich where Goering held sway, the writer Peter Handke has just given, with the rejection of the national claims which are today set forth in Yugoslavia, the triple guarantee of his Slovene origin, his status as a cosmopolitan artist, and *last but not least*, his German bad conscience.

But what does Peter Handke say in this "Conte du neuvième pays" (Tale of the ninth country), which today serves as a reference to the French *Verdrei mir nich dem Kopf* in regard to Yugoslavia? He begins in these terms: "All sorts of reasons have been evoked for the declaration of a separate regular State called the 'Republic of Slovenia.' But for me to be able to differentiate them in my mind, I must first be able to see them: the substantive 'reason' cannot, in any case, for me anyway, have any value except in relation to the verb 'to see.' And I see no reason, none whatsoever – not even Greater Serbia's famous Panzer communism – to create the State of Slovenia; nothing but an accomplished fact. In the same way, I see no reasons to advance for the creation of the Croatian State." [2]

It would probably be frivolous to place before Peter Handke's eyes the outcome of a referendum by the people themselves concerning their self-determination. True democracy, in effect, combines the principle of the people's sovereignty and the idea expressed by Péguy in an issue of the series Cahiers de la Quinzaine, titled none other than *De la raison* (On reason), that "the people are not the sovereign of reason." [3]

One person may thus be right against everyone else. The problem is that Handke's "reason" is exclusively made up of subjective impressions and estheticizing nostalgia: "For me Slovenia has always belonged," he writes, "to Great Yugoslavia." The Yugoslavian part of Slovene history, however, only begins in 1918, but what does that matter! The "for me" here takes care of any proof, the "I" of genius is reason unto itself and disqualifies as mere whims or guises of egoism the very reasons Slovenes and Croatians give for their declarations of independence.

The Slovenes and Croatians did not, however, act lightly or capriciously, as Handke would have it. And contrary to the allegations or insinuations of the French journalistic leadership, neither have they taken history in the wrong direction, by choosing the nation – that is to say, partition – as opposed to federation – that is to say, unity – at a time when the law of the peoples' solidarity is imposed upon the European conscience and allows the national to bloom into the supranational. They have seen Serbia answer the claims of the Albanians from Kosovo (who make up between 80 and 90 percent of the province's population) with the installation of a colonial regime: dissolution of the Parliament; Serbization of the police to allow for a more efficacious repression; the establishment of a government under orders from Belgrade; the temporary interdiction of Albanians in secondary education; dismissal of all professors refusing to abide by this decision; etc. They have seen the increasing stranglehold of the local Serb power upon diplomacy, the army, finance, and the federation's political police. In short, they have noted the (re)constitution of a Serboslavia instead of and in place of the Yugoslavia that Tito had subjugated to his iron rule and which he took with him to the grave. And after asking in an atmosphere of indifference and even of general hostility for a confederation of sovereign states (the very thing that is being set up with everyone's approval in the former USSR), the Slovenes and Croatians concluded that democracy was possible only within a national framework and, for the nation, only outside of Yugoslavia.

No autocentrism in this gesture. These small nations do not take themselves as ends in themselves. Their objective is not to be rid of all foreign influence. What animates them is not a refusal to live any longer in a plurinational space but instead the desire that Handke hates so much, and yet that is so legitimate: the desire to belong to Central Europe, and the desire, in leaving Yugoslavia, simply to join Europe immediately. We accuse them of being turned in on themselves, when they succumb to the call of the sea. What, in effect, is the construction of Europe for Croatia and Slovenia, if not precisely the end of "Balkanization" – that is, finally the realizable possibility of being integrated as free nations into a communitarian unit, instead of being pawns in the hands of imperialist rivals?

From India to the United States, certainly nothing is worse than the splintering of societies into piecemeal communities or hostile and closed tribes. But a little attention, memory, and *a little wracking of one's brain* would be enough to understand that the Yugoslav problem is not comprehensible in those terms. By reducing the conflict to a phenomenon of allergy or mutual exclusion and by turning each person into the "other" of one's enemy instead of trying to understand the motives, forms, and "political" stakes of this enmity, the media generously betrayed their mission to inform and instead walked hand in hand with our diplomacy's aloofness. The antiracism of the first gave a kind of moral cloak to the will of the second not to tamper with the borders set up by the Treaty of Versailles to counter German influence, and to save the Soviet empire, by avoiding any bad example from Yugoslavia.

With heart and aloofness mixed, the *status quo ante* was defended, as though it were a question of a federal system defined by the transfer of national competencies to common institutions rather than of a hegemonic system characterized by one nation's predominance. We have called the military invasion a "civil war" and let "Serbia lead, with the decisive help of a supposedly 'federal' army, a cruel operation of pure and simple conquest at Croatia's expense"[4]: a grand premiere in a Europe where institutions have rested since 1945 on "the repudiation of war as an instrument of national expansion."[5]

French thought never ceases to congratulate itself on being cured of communism, reconciled with democracy, un-compromising on the rights of man, and free of ideologies that not long ago still simplified reality in the most outrageous fashion. This is not a reason, however, to be proud. There is nothing here for currying favor. Never has Zola's remark been more apt: "Let's not congratulate ourselves." Though communism is dead, it has nevertheless handed on to its detractors a hate for any complexity as well as the rejection of a pluralistic world.

In 1848, Paris was the home for the Springtime of Peoples. Those who dreamed of replacing a dynastic Europe with the United States of Europe looked to France, the second homeland of all patriots, and the headquarters of a revolution that wanted to combine freedom within with freedom without, civil and political rights with national independence.

Today Paris no longer has this influence. Whether it invokes economic constraints, individualism's irresistible progress, or the pain of a recent past, the thought that unfolds there no longer has room for the nation. And when it is a question of condemning the putsch of the Kremlin Apparatchiks, personalities as unquestionable as Jacques Attali, president of the European Bank for Reconstruction and Development (EBRD), Pierre Joxe, minister of defense, and Elie Wiesel, winner of the Nobel Prize for Peace, state their solidarity with the "Soviet people," that is to say the homogeneous entity, the historical community of a new type, Russianized and normalized, which has been broken up in the name of freedom, in Vilnius and in Yerevan as it has been – or such is the hope – in Leningrad or Moscow.

But of course we were not born yesterday. We know, as Istvan Bibo has written, that "following a cataclysm or an illusion," the nation's cause may be separated from that of freedom. We know that the national community's reappropriation of a country is not necessarily always accompanied by freedom of the individual. Vigilance is therefore necessary. Numerous rounds of territorial litigation, finding scapegoats to blame for shortages, the persecution of minorities, the fascist retraining and xenophobic bidding on the part of administrators of the old party eager to remain or to return to power, blaming the Jews for the 1917 Revolution and its consequences, the rehabilitation of national figures who collaborated in the Nazi "crusade" against Bolshevism, "the convulsionary fear of seeing freedom threaten the nation's cause": all these scenarios are possible and some are already being carried out.[6]

But if it is true that nations, beyond their cultural, historical, and climatic differences, should be subjected to the same democratic rules, democracy, for its part, needs a body, a land, a particular city so as to be something more than the power to go to a different television channel or to choose between several brands of deodorant. And to those who – in our age of a single Market, economic concentration, world music, and culinary cosmopolitanism – dismiss as anachronistic or barbarian the aspirations of the small European nations to exist on the world stage as subjects with full rights, there is no better nor more just answer than these lines from *Vues sur l'Europe* (Views on Europe), the book André Suarès wrote to denounce the Nazi danger during the dark days of the 1930s: "I proclaim the greatness of small nations. They alone are on the scale of man. Large empires are only on the scale of the species. Small nations created the city, morality, and the individual. Large empires have not even conceived their necessary law or dignity. The empires have quantity; quality marks the small nations. . . . Humanity's destiny is bound up with these divine small societies. Man holds strongly onto God; and God has created a man and not crowds. Variety characterizes this creative hand. Nature itself is not pleased with mass production. A world faithful to the Creator's thought tends toward harmony and not unison. A single note, arrived at by the destruction and ruin of all the others, makes the musical genius shudder."[7]

NOTES

1. Emmanuel Terray, "Munich: Un Anniversaire oublié," *Le Genre Humain* 18 (1988).

2. Peter Handke, "Le Conte du neuvième pays: Ma Slovénie en Yougoslavie," *Libération*, 22 Aug. 1991, p. 17.

3. Charles Péguy, *De la raison*, in *Oeuvres en prose complètes* (Gallimard, Pléiade Edition, 1987), 1 : 838.

4. Paul Fabra, "Un Faux pas en amène un autre," *Le Monde*, 3 Sept. 1991, p. 24.

5. William Pfaff, "Europe Can't Afford to Tolerate a Serbian Grab," *New York Herald Tribune*, 8 Aug. 1991, p. 4.

6. Istvan Bibo, *Misère des petits Etats d'Europe de l'Est* (L'Harmattan, 1986), 115.

7. André Suarès, *Vues sur l'Europe* (Grasset, 1991), 306–7.

# 2

# History's Poor Relatives

*Politique internationale* (PI): What are the political, intellectual, and moral reasons that have committed you so strongly in the conflict which, for more than a year, has been tearing up Yugoslavia?

AF: In the days following 13 December 1981, all our intellectuals had denounced at once the coup d'état in Poland and the complacency or temporizing of French politics. Let's remember the unanimously indignant reaction to the declarations made by Claude Cheysson, then minister of foreign affairs, "Of course, we shall do nothing." During the years that followed, we spared no support for the Polish struggling for their freedom. Had Slovenia and Croatia benefited today from the same fervor that just recently supported Poland, I probably would not have given this cause so much of my time and energy. The aggression had to reach Bosnia-Herzegovina for us to see a little sympathy toward the victims. But neither the war imposed on Croatia, the razed villages and cities, the occupation of a third of its territory, nor the displacement of populations, not one of these atrocious facts shocked anyone who had been moved to act because of the state of siege imposed upon Poland. And I wondered why. My commitment was born from this double scandal: the scandal of invasion and the scandal of indifference. Faced with the indifference of those in power and of the majority of intellectuals, I experienced a feeling of helplessness and surprise.[1]

PI: What kind of surprise?

AF: Hannah Arendt defines totalitarianism as a composite of Ideology and Terror. As its name indicates, Ideology consists in submitting history to the logic of a single idea. "Ideology," writes Hannah Arendt, "treats the series of events as though it obeyed the same law as the exposition of its 'idea.' If ideologies presume to know the mysteries of the entire historical process as well as the secrets of the past, the labyrinths of the present and the uncertainties of the future, it is due to the logic inherent in their respective ideas."[2] As for Terror, it is, so to speak, Ideology's secular arm. It breaks reality's resistance to its decrees by deciding, for example, to eliminate classes, which – Ideology affirms – have already served their purpose. Ideology renders the verdict and Terror carries out the sentence.

We can continue this analysis made at the end of the Second World War by noting that with the partitioning of Europe, Ideology and Terror gradually went their separate ways. In the countries where Terror was rampant, Ideology has not held on; popular wisdom has made it fly into pieces, and those whom we didn't yet call dissidents dismantled its mechanism; common sense refused to look for reality behind appearances as propaganda would have it do, and Czeslaw Milosz wrote *La Pensée captive* (*The Captive Mind*). On the other hand, in the countries Terror spared, Ideology has been very powerful. A terrible phenomenon has come about: instead of meeting with understanding in Western Europe, the survivors of Terror came up against rock-hard realities. The most outstanding intellectuals rejected them with the arguments and vocabulary that back home were the prerogative of their own bureaucrats. Fleeing Stalinist Poland for France in 1951, Milosz felt he had truly been placed in quarantine: "It is rather sad, for a poor guy who has never had any fortune but his skin and his pen, to be pictured in the press as a spoiled bourgeois fleeing his socialist country. I was not spared such compliments, and that period was quite difficult. . . . The Hegelian intellectuals will never understand the consequences their quibbling had on the level of human relations, and what an abyss they created between themselves and the inhabitants of Eastern Europe, informed about Marx or not."[3] And let's never forget how Kravchenko was pilloried in *Les Lettres Françaises*, which accused him of not having himself written *J'ai choisi la liberté* (*I Chose Freedom*), a damning eyewitness account about the Soviet concentration camp world, of being immoral, drunken, a traitor to his country, bought by the U.S. Secret Service, and finally of having published a web of lies. "Is there *a spirit of Vichy* in this book?" Maître Nordmann asked Vercors during the trial for defamation brought by Kravchenko against the communist weekly. Vercors answered soberly, "Yes."[4]

The twentieth century's specificity lies not in tragedy – all times have known tragedy – but in the *nightmare*; that is, in the very denial of tragedy. To the lived horror of tragedy is added the questioning of its reality. "The Trojan war *did not take place*," such is our own century's proper contribution to the history of terror.[5]

I had hoped that with the collapse of communism, such a situation would no longer be possible. Well, I have recognized that, in spite of communism's collapse, the twentieth century's nightmare has not come to an end and that the Croatians can testify to the fact. I have defended them with all the more passion since they have doubly suffered: on the one hand they have been attacked, and on the other, they have seen the truth of their suffering either denied or slandered. Camus said that "to name things badly was to add to the world's misfortune." This "consciousness of words" made him Milosz's *brotherly partner*, one of the very rare Western intellectuals, the latter tells us, "who held out his hand to me . . . whereas others avoided me as though I were a victim of the plague and a sinner against the Future."[6] Today there are hardly any more priests of the radiant future, but where can we find another brotherly Camus for the Miloszes of Zagreb and Vukovar? We Westerners, we have celebrated the triumph of our values while adding to Croatia's misfortune.

When I am asked why I have taken sides in this conflict, I answer that that is not the real issue but rather, "How can it be that the nightmare of the twentieth century can survive the fall of the Berlin Wall?"

PI: Don't you think politicians give in too easily to a kind of fascination with the status quo, especially the French leaders who insisted on supporting the Yugoslav federation while it no longer even existed?

AF: That's true. Politicians, and in particular those who govern, would have wished for the fall of communism to trouble nothing in the world order.

They sang the praises of freedom but were not ready to pay the price. Then when they realized that "hodgepodge," as Péguy has said, "is the very name of freedom," they decided to side with order.[7] And that's an understandable position: the Holy Alliance, born of the Congress of Vienna, did not want order for the sake of order, but order for peace, and Metternich fought against liberal ideas because, in his eyes, they threatened to plunge Europe into mortal chaos. But the scandal peculiar to the Yugoslav affair is that order was desired while leaders were pretending to defend freedom. Our government played on both registers while protecting itself behind the political and moral artifice of the rights of minorities.

PI: In what way was this argument used?

AF: In June of 1991, two nations "disassociated" themselves from the Yugoslav federation according to a constitutional right and after freely deciding at regular election time. A democratic Europe could hardly reject a process which, at this point, was in conformity with its demands. There was still the question of minorities. The French government and the European commission on arbitration it created, presided over by Robert Badinter, threw themselves into examining

the problem. They did so even though the Croatian Republic had guaranteed the rights of Serbs and other minorities
in the first articles of its constitution, even though this guarantee had been confirmed several times, even though a number of Serbs had chosen to be Croatian citizens and defend
their country, even though the Croatian government had requested, repeatedly, that European commissioners come to
Croatia to see for themselves, even though the Serbs of Krajina did not clash with Zagreb authorities over their rights as
a minority but to contest their minority status in a free Croatia. Milan Babic, their president, made the point clearly:
"The Serbs of Krajina cannot accept a plan which would reduce them to the rank of an ethnic minority." And the Serb
autonomists ended up by ratifying the agreements on the
termination of military operations signed in Sarajevo on
2 January 1992 between Serbia, Croatia, and the army, when
they received Belgrade's assurance that, far from reestab-
lishing the *status quo ante bellum*, the arrival of the United
Nations forces would consolidate their power.

Thus the refusal by a minority to recognize the majority
has been turned into its opposite, and our purist jurists have
accomplished this prodigy: we support in the name of minority rights those Serbs who defend, with the help of the
federal army and therefore against a much weaker enemy
than themselves, their right not to be a minority anywhere
on Yugoslav soil.

PI: On what do you base your support of the legitimacy
of Croatian national claims?

AF: Read your history books. Croatia is an old nation that
emancipated itself even before those who were to become
French liberated themselves from Frankish control. "Trpi-
mir, who reigned from 845 to 864, bore the title of *dux Croatorum* (this is the first mention of "Croatians" as such); in
925 Tomislav (910–928) took the title of *rex Croatorum*,
which the Pope recognized."[8] And during the time that the

personal union with Hungary and the reign of the Haps-
burgs lasted, Croatia kept the attributes of a state with its
*ban* (governor) and its *sabor* (parliament). Furthermore,
Croatia answers perfectly to Otto Bauer's definition: "The
nation is the body of men united by a community of destiny
in a community of character." Briefly, in order to justify its
aspirations to a sovereign existence, Croatia can simultaneously lay claim to the ancient right of the state and the modern right of nationalities.

The intellectuals and political leaders who talk about the
Croatian people as though they were a "tribe" thus show
their profound historical ignorance. An ignorance that the
form taken by the war should have dispelled, if only they had
eyes with which to see. Serb aggression was aimed not only
at the industrial and military power of Croatia. It was directed against its very Europeanness. While the European
elite was worried about the Croatians' "tribalism," Europe
was losing in Croatia its Baroque and Roman churches as
well as its Venetian palaces.

PI: Why have the claims for nationhood by an old European nation been so ignored by their fellow Europeans?

AF: Because we have taken Yugoslavia to be an old nation
whereas it is only a recent and chimerical idea. That idea has
two versions: the first, Herderian, would have the Southern
Slavs form a spiritual community by virtue of the similarity
of their languages; the second version, a Marxist one, would
have these peoples unite together in order to form the reign
of Man on earth and, among men, the reign of equality.

We have known for some time already that this second
dream is deceptive, but by replacing it purely and simply
with the liberal idea (that is to say, the rights of man allied to
a market economy that is more or less corrected by society's
protection) and by having Europe defend it, that is the other
lie – the panslavic lie – which we no longer have the means
of identifying.

After seventy years of Yugoslav experience, Croatians and Slovenes apply to the Serbs the remarks Czech writer Karel Havlicek once directed toward the Russians more than a century ago: "The Serbs, they say in substance, call Slav all that is Serb in order to be able to name Serb all that is Slav."[9] And they add, "We believed in Yugoslavism, we even invented it. The inaugural session of the first Yugoslav academy was held in Zagreb, 31 July 1867, and there it was said, 'There is no longer any river or mountain separating Serbs, Croatians, Slovenes, and Bulgarians.'[10] But at our own cost we have learned that this southern variety of Pan-Slavism is a myth, that it has served to cover up Serbia's expansionism, and that promiscuity within the same state has not erased the differences between Slavs of the East and Slavs of the West."

Today's liberals make fun of the Slavic soul. The cultural difference between Western and Eastern Europe is as outmoded and artificial for them today as it was for yesterday's Marxists. Now that everyone looks at the same television shows, aspires to the same form of well-being, and recognizes the superiority of Western societies, we end up living in one big world. Hasn't Serbia chosen a rich relative, an "American Uncle," in the person of Milan Panic in order to solve its problems and have a new beginning? If divisions arise in spite of this unanimity among people, it means that irrationality still exists and that history is not protected from a crisis, a breakdown or regression. For the Europeans we have become, the partitioning of Yugoslavia is the most striking form of this regression or of the power of the irrational.

In the chapter of his book *Une autre Europe* (Another Europe) dedicated to what his compatriot Joseph Conrad calls the *incompatibility of temper* of Russians and Poles, Milosz makes the following observation: "The twentieth century, panicking before the follies of nationalists and racists, tries to fill the abyss of time with production statistics and a few names of politico-economic systems; it refuses to study further the texture of becoming where no thread should be omitted."[11] *Une autre Europe* was written in the 1950s and Milosz was then probably criticizing the reduction of history to the struggle between communist and capitalist systems. Now the opposition between democracy and totalitarianism has replaced it and occupies our thoughts. But the remark still holds true: the same reductionism is at work; the same blindness prevails. In spite of pictures, in spite of the news, our commentators doggedly continue to qualify as a *civil* war or as a *fratricidal* war a war of aggression that, in Dubrovnik or elsewhere, is fought to ensure the destruction of any architectural presence of the West on Slavic land.

Ignorance also has more conjectural reasons due to Yugoslavia's privileged political status, on the Left as on the Right, during the period of the two blocks. On the Left, Yugoslavia benefited for a long time from a positive image because of the challenge it had given Stalin, because of its worker management and its place in the movement of nonaligned nations. The Yugoslav experience allowed all those disappointed with the Soviets not to abandon all hope in the revolution.

As for the Right, without supporting the regime, it carefully handled Yugoslavia because, in keeping with the containment policy set up by the West, Tito's country was an essential piece. There was no need to know the domestic realities of a country whose foreign policy so openly defied Soviet hegemony.

P1: How did the European blindness, the inner workings of which you have just shown, manifest itself?

AF: Oscar Wilde relates that on the day following the Crucifixion, "when darkness covered the earth," Joseph of Arimatheia saw "kneeling on the hard rocks of the valley of Desolation . . . a young man who was naked and crying." Joseph told him that after such an event, he was not sur-

20

prised to see such great sorrow. And the young man answered, "I am not crying for him, but for me. I also changed water into wine, and I cured a leper and gave sight to the blind. I even walked on water and expelled demons from those who were living among tombs. I fed the hungry in the desert where there was no food, and I raised the dead from their tombs; and, at my command, and before a large crowd, a sterile fig tree dried up. I have accomplished all that this man did, and yet you have not crucified me." [12]

This strange and moving appearance of a man who did everything that Christ did but who did not have the latter's career invites us to be suspicious of History. Some events enter into history or into the historical, and others that are just as intense or valuable count for absolutely nothing to anyone. Acceptance into the grand narrative of nations is a question of chance. Thus the Prague Spring was, in our comprehension of the totalitarian phenomenon, of capital importance. Three years later, a similar movement in Zagreb was born: it came from civil society and, as in Prague, it had the participation and protection of the Party's reformers. As in Prague it brought together political reform and the cultural reconquest of both national and European identity. And as it did in Bohemia, it realized the same dream of deprovincialization and life out in the open. Writers played a major role and, like the Prague Spring, the movement was brutally interrupted. As in Prague, the Party was purged, spokesmen for the revolt were imprisoned or forced into exile, and Croatia was roughly and durably brought back into line. [13] Well, we know nothing about that springtime. We have not retained it to symbolize the miracle of renewal and its suppression in the countries of real socialism. "I have accomplished everything this man did, and yet you have not crucified me." The Croatians who came to France to speak about the experience they had gone through found themselves in a vacuum. "We can't do that to Tito," was what the directors of the major leftist papers said to justify the rejection of the Croatians' articles. Some texts did appear in several journals, but the news remained confidential. Had it been passed along, we probably would still have had some misunderstanding. Milan Kundera needed a lot of obstinacy and patience to tear the Western intellectual away from his "proverbial egocentrism" and have him understand that Prague Spring *was not* a Czech avatar of Paris' own May 1968.[14]

Yet hearing Zagreb and Croatia named did not lead to better understanding. And had we been more familiar with these names, our "proverbial egocentrism" would have been kept from tribalizing this war or from transforming Croatians into the Corsicans of Yugoslavia.

PI: Would you say that this error in appreciation can be imputed to the Left as a whole?

AF: I don't think you can yet speak of the Left in the singular. Solzhenitsyn and other dissidents have managed to divide the Western Left into two: a Third World Left dedicated, despite having been proven wrong repeatedly, to preserving a Marxist reading of History, and an antitotalitarian Left, affected by the shipwreck of communism and trying to rethink the world all over again. But these two inimical Lefts have crossed each other and even come together in order to condemn the dismemberment of Yugoslavia.

The Third World Left cannot imagine how the position of the West, in certain places on earth, can be weak, unstable, and threatened. For the West is, by definition, riches and power, the middle class on a planetary scale, the North that – having colonized and despoiled the South – now tries to protect itself from it. Applied to Yugoslavia, the theory translates into the following terms: the two northern republics wanted to leave the federation for purely material reasons, reflecting the Lombard leagues, which dream of no longer having to be responsible for the misery and corruption of the Italian Mezzogiorno. In other words, this Left stigmatizes the egoism of the Croatians and Slovenes, their cruel lack of solidarity with the republics and disadvantaged provinces of Yugoslavia, in spite of the fact that the Slovenes' democratic movement began by showing its support for the Albanians of Kosovo Province. And the Bosnians and Macedonians, other poor people, other southerners, have themselves seceded and they refuse, in turn, to continue to support at their own expense the privileged cast of the industrial-military complex. As the Slovenian university professor E. Haldnik-Milharcic wrote in July 1991, "Yugoslavia is not a state that must call upon the army to safeguard its integrity; today it is rather an army that needs a state in order to exist."[15]

The antitotalitarian Left finds Yugoslavia's demise repugnant because it lives on the illusion that the fewer nations there are, the more democracy there is.

PI: How do we distinguish good national causes from bad ones? Do we have any criteria to sort them out?

AF: Democracy is precisely the criterion. Nationalism's destructive force should not make us lose sight of the fact that the nation is also the framework in which the experience of democracy has been able to thrive. Since the mode of the *city state* no longer holds and that of *empire* is undemocratic, the nation – until this can be disproved – and only the nation allows for full participation in political life. "Don't fear the nations!" is what Bronislaw Geremek tells the antitotalitarian Left, which sees their resurrection as the supreme peril of the postcommunist age.[16] In effect, the true question is not whether democracy will get the better of the nation (that would be asking it to get rid of its very foundation) but, according to Istvan Bibo's ever relevant words, whether the democratic version of national feeling will win out over antidemocratic nationalism ("this fearful monster of political evolution in recent times"[17]), whether the causes of individual and community will converge or whether they will come into conflict, whether the affirmation of national sovereignty will go together with the defense of public liberties or whether citizens will be asked to surrender their rights to examine and their independence to the state, briefly whether democracy will be perceived as the best system for the nation or as an attack upon its integrity and the cause of its problems.

PI: What do you think of the thesis whereby the free expression of nationalisms would endanger European unity?

AF: "Virgin Europe is engaged to the handsome genius Liberty; they embrace one another lovingly, they savor their first kiss," wrote Heine in 1844 – that is, at the first quivering of the peoples' Springtime. Will it be necessary, for Europe's construction, to break off this engagement and grant freedom only to those European peoples who have always embraced it?

It is true that the detractors of national movements which trouble posttotalitarian Europe feel they are fighting not freedom, a value they revere, but *identity* politics run amok. In this case, it is "the one who says it who is it": this accusation reveals the large nations' own sense of identity, their decidedly hopeless egocentrism. Slovenia, Croatia, Macedonia, and Bosnia-Herzegovina no more exist for a Frenchman, be he a researcher or an intellectual, than did the Baltic countries before 1990. The rest of us citizens from the large nations have received, in things historical, a Mickey Mouse education. In our vision of the world, the small nations on the confines of Europe are quaintly picturesque and vaguely ridiculous entities that the planet in no way needs as business has always been carried on without them. So we react with disbelief and disgust when these frogs want to become as big as the oxen that we are.[18] "Serb aggression, imperialism, fascism, communism, Serb barbarianism," writes Annie Kriegel, "have been raised to an ontological status responsible for breathing life (and death) into realities – Croatia, Bosnia-Herzegovina, and tomorrow Macedonia in spite of Greek protests – which, without them, would not exist." [19] Croatia does not exist for me, therefore its existence is a matter of manipulation and fantasy. One would have to be a full citizen of Great History, a permanent member of the *Weltgeist*, to think in such a way and, declaring that a thousand-year-old state does not exist, quietly affirm that Europe is complete without Croatia.

PI: It is nevertheless said that nationalism is now making closed and gloomy societies out of the "small Eastern European nations" which are giving in to their demons . . .

AF: Such an assertion is all the more ludicrous since the only way for captive nations to open up is precisely for them to win their sovereignty: "Every movement that aims at national emancipation has an 'autocentric' component (turning in on self, exaltation of one's roots, etc.) but also a significant cosmopolitan component (the desire to enter into *direct* relation with the world, to have the right to be influenced according to one's *free choice* by others and to be able to influence them)." [20] In an empire, the nostalgia of the world nurtures national sentiment, for you understand very quickly that to enter into the "political cosmos" you must yourself form a "polis," a free and independent city. Didn't we have to wait for the end of the Soviet Union for Latvia, Estonia, and Lithuania to become a part of the world once again?

PI: But then why today do some so readily oppose cosmopolitan values to all forms of national affirmation?

AF: I wonder whether contemporary liberalism is not more impoverished than nineteenth-century liberalism. Then liberals celebrated the Springtime of the peoples. National belonging entered into the composition of freedom, and cosmopolitanism was symbolized by the friendship between Michelet, citizen of a nation whose existence was unquestioned, and Mickiewicz, representative of a nation whose right to existence had been ridiculed. Today's liberalism, the one that overthrew totalitarianism and that is claimed by both the Right and the Left, conceives of no other freedom than that of a consumer and entrepreneurial society. So to today's liberalism any national aspirations appear to be pathological.

This attitude reveals not only that Michelet has been forgotten ("Europe is not some fortuitous grouping, the simple juxtaposition of peoples, but rather a grand harmonic instrument whose every string is a nation that represents a tone") but also that the large nations of Europe have relapsed into their provincialism. Mostly, however, this attitude reveals the common *paneconomics* shared both by Marxism and the ideology that has replaced it. For Marx and his disciples, with the notable exception of the Austro-Marxists, the nation was a moment of History and was supposed to die when it had completed its mission: "For the great revolutions that await man," writes Anton Pannekoek in response to Otto Bauer, "the technical and scientific conquest of the entire earth and its development into a magnificent dwelling for a race of lords (*ein Geschlecht von Herrenmenschen*) happy and proud of its victory and which has become master of nature and its forces, for these grand accomplishments – which today we can hardly imagine – the borders of states and peoples are too narrow and limited. The community of destiny will unite all humanity into one community of idea and culture."[21] Marx is dead, but in the eyes of his gravediggers, the economy still determines man's fate. Judging the nation to be outdated or even "incestuous," they also thought that democracy was going to replace the empire in the very forms it left behind.[22] And they punish in the name of nationalism a desire to be free that does not fit the unidimensional idea they have of freedom.

PI: We are nevertheless seeing a rise in the extreme Right in Eastern Europe. How do you interpret this?

AF: I think it's dishonest to treat all national identity movements as though they were fascist and to warn against national populism every time you hear the word *nation* pronounced. Such eagerness is eminently suspect: it lets those partisans and profiteers of the totalitarian system who have only recently converted to democracy make us forget, to the advantage of the new planetary threat, the *disaster* with which they were associated. There is something intolerable in seeing the very ones who placed the lid so tightly on the peoples of the other Europe invite us, now that it has been removed, to shout in horror when confronted with this boiling kettle. The ex-nomenclaturists and ex–fellow travelers exaggerate, with malicious joy, nationalism's dangers, for they see in it the justification of their past Sovietism or Yugoslavism.

However, we still need to be vigilant for several reasons. First, most of these countries, leaving communism tired and drained, have no democratic traditions. The second reason is economic: whatever its political tradition, a devastated and poor country always has the tendency to look for a scapegoat. Since the solution for such penury is quite far away, those who claim that to get out of it, you only have to get rid of foreigners necessarily meet with the backing of the people most harshly affected. The third reason for being vigilant arises from the shameless instrumentalization of World War II and of communism's anti-Nazi struggle: "The Slavic hour has struck on the European clock. . . . Only those who, consciously or not, play into Germany's hands will deplore it or be worried by it. Great Russia saved the Slavs from servitude or destruction and so today it is understandable for them to show Russia their gratitude by coming together under its aegis." This editorial in the Parisian newspaper *Le Monde* for 17 April 1945 says it all.[23]

On the one hand, the conquerors of the vile beast – Soviets or Yugoslavs – have experienced so many losses and made so many sacrifices in order to bring it down that they feel they should get a reward. On the other hand, the beast is still kicking, the proof being found in the scheming of those who oppose their plans. In 1968, when the Warsaw Pact armies intervened in Czechoslovakia, Brezhnev, the head of the Kremlin, told Dubcek, the leader of Prague Spring: "Your country finds itself in the zone where Soviet soldiers got a foothold during the Second World War. We made great sacrifices for that result, and we are not going to give it up. Your borders are also our own and, because you do not want to obey us, we feel threatened. In the name of all the dead of the Second World War who sacrificed themselves for your freedom, we have a right to send you soldiers, so that we can feel truly secure within our borders. Little does it matter that, in one way or another, someone should threaten us directly. It is a question of principle independent of all external contingencies. . . . Our soldiers have come as far as Elba and, since then, that is where our border is, the Soviet border."[24] Thus the doctrine of limited sovereignty found its justification in the struggle against Hitlerism. In Yugoslavia, the principal actors in the Zagreb Spring were accused of being Ustachis; that is, of wanting a return to the Croatian Independent State granted in 1941 by the Axis powers to Anton Pavelic and his party.

In a country such as ours, you can denounce the fascist threat by calling upon the past. This is much more difficult in countries where propaganda has taken over the past and itself invoked it, evoked it, and commemorated it ad nauseam. There communism has for a long time compromised the struggle against fascism, for it has lied too much under the protection of its slogans. So we shouldn't be surprised that Zagreb's municipal government has, in the face of strong opposition from the Croatian intelligentsia, renamed the former "Square of Victims to Fascism" as the "Square of the Croatian Sovereigns." By doing this it was not showing a dubious appreciation for fascism but rather a profound distaste for language of antifascist coinage. Nothing, however, would be more dangerous than to throw away antifascism with the coinage.

I don't know how to define Europe. I do know it was the theater for two catastrophes, which will forever bear the names of Hitler and Stalin. Are they mutually exclusive or can they be taken together? Does the obsessive fear of one necessarily lead to the neglect or relativization of the other? How can we turn these "two sorrows of Europe," to use the admirable expression of Elisabeth de Fontenay, into only one community of fate? That, more than any monetary union, is the great challenge Europe must now face.

PI: A parenthesis apropos of Nazism and anti-Semitism: what do you tell those who reproach you for your support of a blatant anti-Semite, the Croatian president?

AF: "For its president Croatia has a man who claims that the Jewish Holocaust never existed." Indeed, this is repeated in all the editorial offices from London to Melbourne. Where would Franjo Tudjman have asserted such a thing? In his Faurissonian book entitled *Déroute de la vérité historique* (The defeat of historical truth).[25] Has anyone read the book? No. Serbia's propaganda services translated fifteen pages of a work that has five hundred and sent them to the principal governments and world media. In France the government took it upon itself to inform the media. In these fifteen pages, does Tudjman question the reality of the extermination of the Jews? No, he goes into a critical analysis of the different sources relating to the number of victims. Basing his argument on, among other sources, the testimony of Anton Ciliga (the author of one of the very first books on the Soviet camps: *Pays du mensonge déconcertant [Russian Enigma]*), he writes that until 1944 the internal administration of the Ustachi camp in Jasenovac was in the hands of Jewish prisoners who often behaved terribly; and finally, he holds something against Israel's Jews for in turn practicing a politics of genocide toward the Palestinians.

That's enough, you tell me. Of course, but doesn't a respect for facts that one holds up to every revisionism require you to look at the text itself and verify the accusation? Such a reading would have been very enlightening. You would have seen that the book's title is not *Déroute de la vérité historique* but *Les Terres désolées de la réalité historique: Traité sur l'histoire et la philosophie du mal et de la brutalité (Horrors of War: Historical Reality & Philosophy)*. You would have seen that the author dedicated it "to the memory of my father, my brother and my mother-in-law, who perished on the arid lands of history" (under the blows of Communists and Nazis), and that the extermination process of the Jews during the Second World War is described in detail. You would have taken into account how much the translation we do have, at once fragmentary and faulty, alters and even denatures the meaning Tudjman gave to his endeavor. While his book is an examination of the genocides that have taken place in history and a reflection on the philosophies that made them possible, it is also a warning against the danger of any manipulation regarding the number of victims.

PI: On the contrary, doesn't the danger consist in attacking the phantoms of the past and recounting the dead?

AF: I often hear it said that Yugoslavia is dying from an excess of memories, each one rehearsing the Ustachi-Chetnik conflict that no longer has any right to exist. In reality, the Yugoslav problem is not one of memory but, quite the contrary, that neither memory nor history has its rightful place and that only myths hold sway. Were we to believe the official word from Belgrade, Ustachi fascism would have made victims of somewhere between seven hundred thousand and a million and a half Serbs. If we cling to this last estimate, there would have been more Serbs killed by Croatians than there were victims on all Yugoslav soil between

1941 and 1945! But this incredible number obviously aims at making the first number (700,000) seem reasonable. The two great historians of this question – the Serb Bogoljub Kotchovitch, and the Croatian Vladimir Zerjavic – place at about three hundred thousand (334,000, according to Kotchovitch; 295,000, according to Zerjavic) the number of Serbs killed during this period in Croatia and Bosnia, whether they were exterminated by the Ustachis, whether they were victims – in one or the other camp – of the civil war between the Chetniks and Tito's partisans, or whether they were killed while fighting with German troops.

So if Tudjman would have the dead recounted, it isn't in order to excuse the massacres for which the Pavelic regime is guilty but rather to put an end to the chain of violence and quash this *logic of victimization* that drives the Serbs to justify their present hegemony with their past suffering. From this point of view, his book is premonitory. Unfortunately, he doesn't avoid generalizing his own experience and so, in some ways, imputes Serbia's behavior to Israel. Zagreb's Jewish community did indeed protest against these slips at the very time of publication. But one must realize that Tudjman's book played no role in the only two electoral campaigns that ever occurred in Croatia (in 1990 and 1992) and that, during the last electoral vote, the party which is more or less inspired by the Ustachis and which again circulated the latter's emblems obtained 5 percent of the vote, that is, half as much as the National Front in France – and this despite the loss of a third of the territory and the problems posed by a massive influx of refugees. And so to conclude from Tudjman's book that present-day Croatia is fascist and anti-Semitic is to fall into the revisionist trap set up by Serb propaganda for international consumption.

Serbia falsifies the past by saying that Croatians were all Nazis and that Serbs were all in the Resistance; it falsifies the present by saying that Croatians remain a "genocidal people," and hides behind this double falsification the first racial war Europe has known since Hitler. To put it in a nutshell: *the Nazis of this story have wanted to pass themselves off as Jews*. And they have spared no pain to do so. As an article that appeared on 31 July in the Belgrade newspaper *Nin* shows, General Alexandre Vassiljevic, chief of counterespionage services of the Yugoslav army, organized right at the outset of the war the attack against the building of Zagreb's Jewish community with the sole aim of accusing Croatians of the crime and thus bringing forth tangible proof that they were and remain more than ever Ustachis. It was worth their trouble since Elie Wiesel, conscience of the Jewish world and Jewish conscience of the world, still affirmed at the time of Vukovar's destruction: "The historical nature of Croatian claims, linked to similar claims of the Ustachi Regime of Ante Pavelic during World War II, leads us inexorably back to the hatred for the other. Let us remember that Zagreb was between 1941 and 1945 an unqualified ally of Nazi Germany, and that the atrocities it committed often surpassed those of its masters in Berlin. The collapse of communist regimes has visibly awakened the old demons, allowed phantasms of exclusion to return to center stage, the phantoms of the 1930s with their irrational ethnic hatred again to assume control over part of the European population."[26]

Were I not myself Jewish, perhaps I would not have been so eager and insistent in defending Croatia, as you have noticed. But because, as Péguy has said so admirably in *Notre jeunesse* (Our youth), "the more we have our past behind us, the more (precisely) we have to defend it to keep it pure," it seemed to me indispensable not to bequeath to Serbia the blessing of Jewish memory, and not to let the dead, whose guardian I feel I am, be enlisted by the present practitioners of "ethnic cleansing."

An anecdote to close with: on 11 September 1992, at the Holiday Inn built in 1984 for the Winter Olympic Games, the Jews of Sarajevo commemorated the five-hundredth anniversary of Spain's expulsion of the Jews. Muslims and Croatians from Sarajevo's religious, economic, cultural, and political world attended the event in great numbers. "We are living a time of contrasts," declared President Alija Izetbegovic in his inaugural speech, "a contrast between good and evil, a contrast between friendship and hate, one pitted against the other. This sweet celebration in the middle of a devastated city is yet another contrast." While the orchestra played Sephardic music, some bullets hit the hotel. Where did these shots come from? From an old Jewish cemetery situated on a hill overlooking the city and which had become, since the beginning of the siege, one of the favorite positions of the Serb snipers, who have pulled out the tombstones to hide behind.[27]

PI: The collapse of communism deprives democracies of one certainty: having to fight an enemy. Can we now live without enemies?

AF: I wouldn't ask the question that way. Democracy has enemies, but the unfortunate thing is that we don't know how to recognize them. When a conflict flares up in posttotalitarian and postimperialist Europe, we only see *hatred* in it and this hatred, as in the case of divorce, prevents us from seeing any difference between the antagonists. The more atrocious the aggression, the more barbarian the aggressed himself appears to us. The loss of the enemy is not what is agonizing in our new world order but the loss of political judgment and the psychologizing of everything.

PI: Where do you stand in the debate that Francis Fukuyama's book has started? Is history really over?

AF: If, for what it's worth, we had actually finished with communism, we would not be seeing, cited to praise its fall, the Hegelian-Marxist schema of the end of History. And the place left vacant by the revolutionary cry "Tomorrow, shaves will be free" would not be immediately replaced without any form of procedure or of deconstruction by liberalism's "Today, you will have to pay, but no one will get hurt!"[28]

If, moreover, the democratic idea had in fact won out over its rivals, we would not feel such a violent aversion to a people's national awareness, nor would we abandon "the defense of this strong and legitimate feeling of belonging to a natural community to extremist sympathies of the national-populist type."[29] For there is not only no wrong in "living in a national history, inscribing oneself in the reality of a culture and of a language, and feeling oneself in solidarity with a people's destiny," but it is the only way of being truly a citizen.[30]

Those who have contempt for such feelings conceive the nation as a service, and no longer as a city. That is why, and we saw this when discussion on the reform of the Nationality Code took place in France in 1987, they vehemently protest against the idea of requiring the children of immigrants to adhere freely to the national community. Does one adhere to a service? No, one uses it. Or in other words: one is a consumer. Today's rejection of "national sentiment" is in reality nothing more than the substitution of the consumer for the citizen. If there is a democracy today, then it is, as Paul Thibaud writes, "an irresponsible democracy, a democracy of plaintiffs who affirm the rights of man while evading political commitment; that is to say, the idea that the proclaimed ideal (the fulfillment of every man) is not a right that can be guaranteed but a collective task."[31]

PI: Do you think this fading interest in the democratic idea is perceived by those who direct French foreign policy?

AF: It was in France that, for the first time, a nation took responsibility for the experiment in democracy. So the French nation appeared for a long time to be the democracy par excellence. France gave captive nations a reason to dream.

Today by supporting Serb imperialism and by reducing to the maneuverings of a renascent Pan-Germanism the indissolubly national and democratic aspirations that have come to light in Slovenia and Croatia, France has put an end to the French dream of other nations. It has thus twice broken the pact that it had itself sealed between nation and democracy. While democracy, freed from its debt to nationalism, dissolves into consumerism, the instigators of the nation's foreign policy, cleared of any democratic mission, give in to the vertigo of absolute cynicism.

NOTES

1. Certainly there were the dissenting voices of François Fejtö, Annie Le Brun, Pascal Bruckner, Jacques Julliard, Rony Brauman, Michel Polac, and Alexandre Minkowski, but what could they do but note that they could do nothing?

2. Hannah Arendt, *Le Système totalitaire* (Le Seuil, 1972), 217.

3. Czeslaw Milosz, "L'Interlocuteur fraternel," in *Preuves: Une Revue européenne à Paris* (Julliard, 1989), 389.

4. Nina Berberova, *L'Affaire Kravchenko* (Actes Sud, 1990), 36.

5. This is an allusion to Jean Giraudoux's play written in 1935, *La Guerre de Troie n'aura pas lieu* (The Trojan War will not take place). *Trans.*

6. Milosz, "L'Interlocuteur," 389.

7. Charles Péguy, *De la situation faite au parti intellectuel dans le monde moderne devant les accidents de la gloire temporelle*, in *Oeuvres en prose*, 2:704.

8. André Sellier et Jean Sellier, *Atlas des peuples d'Europe centrale* (La Découverte, 1991), 146.

9. Havlicek's sentence, which this one imitates, is quoted and commented upon by Milan Kundera in "Un Occident kidnappé ou la tragédie de l'Europe centrale," *Le Débat* 27 (Nov. 1983): 11.

10. Franjo Racki, quoted by Louis Léger, "Les Slaves en 1867, Agram et les Croates," *La Revue Moderne* (Paris), 1868, p. 28. I owe this reference to Mile Pesorda, poet and editor from Sarajevo, now a refugee in Zagreb.

11. Milosz, *Une autre Europe* (Gallimard, 1980) 148.

12. Oscar Wilde, *Le Maître*, in *Oeuvres* (Stock, 1977), 2:512.

13. See Neven Simac, "Un Printemps occulté," *Le Messager Européen* 6 (1992).

14. Milan Kundera, preface to *Miracle en Bohême* by Josef Skvorecky (Gallimard, 1978), vii.

15. Quoted by Francois Fejtö, *La Fin des démocraties populaires: Les Chemins du post-communisme* (Le Seuil, 1992), 387–88.

16. Bronislaw Geremek, "N'ayez pas peur des nations!" *Commentaire* 57 (spring 1992): 59–62.

17. Bibo, *Misère des petits Etats d'Europe de l'Est*, 71.

18. An allusion to "La Grenouille qui se veut faire aussi grosse que le boeuf" (The frog that would like to become as big as the ox), La Fontaine's fable dealing with people who are never satisfied with their condition in life. *Trans.*

19. Annie Kriegel, "Le Monde dans un triste état," *Le Figaro*, 8 July 1992, p. 2.

20. Milan Kundera, "Réponse à une enquête sur la question nationale," *La Règle du Jeu* 3 (Jan. 1991): 232.

21. Anton Pannekoek, "La nation et le prolétariat," in Georges Haupt, Michael Lowy, and Claudie Weill, *Les Marxistes et la question nationale, 1848–1914* (François Maspero, 1974), 298.

22. Gérard Miller, "Au-delà de l'inceste," *Vu de gauche* special issue (Sept. 1992).

23. Quoted by Jean-François Revel, *Comment les démocraties finissent* (Pluriel, 1988), 293.

24. Quoted by Zdenek Milynar, *Le Froid vient de Moscou: Prague 1968* (Gallimard, 1981), 314–15.

25. Robert Faurisson became famous in France in the late 1970s in denying the existence of the Shoah, the Holocaust. *Trans.*

26. Elie Wiesel, "Nommer l'exclusion et la haine comme l'ennemi," *Lignes de fond* 2 (Jan. 1992): 92.

27. Blaine Harden, "At Jewish Fete, an Ethnic Array of Sarajevo Elite," *International Herald Tribune*, 12–13 Sept. 1992.

28. An allusion to Théophile Gautier, "Ici l'on rasera gratis demain." *Trans.*

29. Geremek, "N'ayez pas peur," 60.

30. Geremek, "N'ayez pas peur," 60.

31. Paul Thibaud, "L'Europe: Essai d'identification," *Esprit*, Nov. 1991, p. 60.

# 3

# "I Am the Member of an Ancient Tribe . . ."

I am the member of an ancient tribe, more ancient than our old Europe. I am a Jew, born of Jewish parents, and as such I benefit from the clause of *jus sanguinis*, the law of return, which allows me to return to Israel. In no way do I intend to use this right, since for me France is not just a country of convenience but my political, cultural, and linguistic homeland. But I wouldn't want this right of return taken away from me. And, without making a big fuss over it, I also don't want to deny my Jewish identity. It is problematic; it creates difficulties for me with non-Jews and sometimes with my fellow Jews. Relatively speaking, however, I will take as my own Hannah Arendt's response to Gershom Scholem, who, after she had published her book on the Eichmann trial, reproached her for not loving the people of Israel. Love, Hannah Arendt said, is a feeling that is too *personal* to apply to a people (one loves faces, not groups), and she adds that there is something much too *narcissistic* in loving one's own nation. This criticism of the heart, or of the misuse of the heart, implies no detachment: "I have always regarded my Jewishness," writes Hannah Arendt, "as one of the indisputable factual data of my life, and I have never had the wish to change or disclaim facts of this kind. There is such a thing as a basic gratitude for everything that is as it is; for what has been *given* and was not, could not be, *made*; for things that are *physei* and not *nomo*. To be sure, such an attitude is prepolitical, but in exceptional circumstances – such as the circumstances of Jewish politics – it is bound to have also political consequences."[1] Between this *gratitude* that I, for my part, have also known, and Europe, I had never – until to-day – noticed any antagonism.

And here I am called upon to choose. Either high principles or respect for what is given. Either the spiritual or the corporal. Either values or gratitude. Either justice or my mother. Either universality or the consciousness of a particular destiny. Either openness or heritage. Either tolerance or fidelity. Either Europe: riches, tranquility, and disembodiment or chaos, frenzy, and a tribal earthquake.[2]

Will this double allegiance be forbidden from now on? I don't question for a second the militant and demanding love for things Jewish on the part of those who organized the colloquium "Europe or the Tribes"; still, it is sad to see this kind of alternative repeating the pattern of the coercive manner of thinking typical of a quiet brand of anti-Semitism.

And it is not only as a Jew but as a European that I don't recognize myself in this ultimatum. As Hannah Arendt has written: "Impartiality came into the world when Homer decided to sing about the deeds of the Trojans no less than about those of the Acheans, and to exalt the glory of Hector no less than that of Achilles." In this sense Europe is Homer's daughter. This doesn't mean it is free of all ethnocentrism. Like any civilization, it tends to judge others according to its own values and tradition, and – since it has decided to enter the modern age – according to its own technical acumen and machinery. But Europe has the gift for ridiculing this attitude and seeing the other also, the foreigner – savage or barbarian – as a challenge to me, of recognizing a hostile intent, and not just seeing feathers among these tribes.

Conversely, when one says: "Europe or the tribes," one only sees feathers on those who today defend their identity. Faced with dissidence and upheaval in Budapest, Prague, or Warsaw, which were *indissolubly cosmopolitical and patriotic*, we never wondered how one could be Hungarian, Czech, or Polish. By contrast, the ideology of our so called posttotalitarian and postideological age breaks with the heritage of Homer and connects up again with the malevolent prejudices of Marx and Engels. In 1849 they wrote:

*The Czechs, among whom we would include the Moravians and Slovaks, although they differ in respect of language and history, have never had a history of their own. Bohemia has been chained to Germany since the time of Charles the Great. The Czech nation freed itself momentarily and formed the Great-Moravian state, only immediately to come under subjection again and for five hundred years to be a ball thrown from one to another by Germany, Hungary, and Poland. Following that, Bohemia and Moravia passed definitively to Germany, and the Slovak regions remained with Hungary. And this historically absolutely nonexistent "nation" puts forward claims to independence?*

*The same thing holds for the Southern Slavs proper. Where is the history of the Illyrian Slovenes, the Dalmatians, Croats, and Shokazians? Since the eleventh century they have lost the last semblance of political independence and have been partly under German, partly under Venetian, and partly under Magyar rule. And it is desired to put together a vigorous, independent, viable nation out of these tattered remnants?* [3]

And faced with the Springtime of the Peoples, faced with the claims of these "rickety" nations, of "these tender flowers of nations," Marx and Engels unhesitatingly defend the Germans and the Hungarians. For "in history, nothing has been accomplished without violence and harsh brutality." For Marx and Engels, who are Hegelians, anything may be done by historical peoples, by the peoples History has chosen. But since Marx and Engels are also revolutionaries, they think that these great nations themselves lose nothing for waiting. Once their mission has been accomplished, they will disappear as well since, according to the Marxist perspective, the nation is an illusory and transitory reality, which hides the class struggle beneath the calm exterior of a community of individuals. Stated differently, Marx and Engels accuse the nation and the bourgeois democracy of the same thing: elections and nations are two variants of one and the same trap for fools, of the same forgetfulness of a fundamental antagonism. Beyond Hegel, they give History the mandate to supersede and dominate both the nation, through internationalism, and formal democracy, through real democracy.

We have seen the result: the nation has been superseded into the empire, and the bourgeois democracy into totalitarian rule. Inheriting this double disaster, the nations of what Ivan Djuric calls "the Yugoslav space" wish to escape from both imperialism and totalitarianism.

In speaking of the tribe, we recast this eminently *political* conflict as an *ethnic* one. The word *tribe* is therefore not only odiously paternalistic: it is a smoke screen that paralyzes thought and action, because in this war unfolding entirely on Croatia's soil, it makes us incapable of distinguishing the aggressor from the aggressed. For the first time in Europe since 1945, a city, Vukovar, with forty-five thousand inhabitants, was sacked and completely destroyed: stronger than the pictures that paraded on our television screens, the smoke screen word *tribe* placed the victims of this monstrosity in the same category as the guilty.

Today, it isn't so much tribalism that threatens us as the word *tribe*. If we want to be truly European, and truly post-Marxist, we have to get rid of it, we must wake up from the ethical sleep into which it has plunged us. We have to remove the screen between the event and us, between truth and us, so as to discern in the Yugoslav space – as in the conflict that opposes tiny Armenia to Azerbaidjan – imperialism and aspirations to freedom. At that point we will finally be able to act. Then perhaps European patriotism will be born. If, on the other hand, we persist, contemptuous and impassive, in speaking the language of the tribes, Europe will come about,

Europe will be constructed but, and please forgive the solemnity of my words, it will definitively have lost its soul.

NOTES

1. Hannah Arendt's letter can be found in *The Jew as Pariah: Jewish Identity and Politics in the Modern Age*, ed. Ron H. Feldman (New York: Grove Press, 1978), 245–71; quoted from p. 246. *Trans.*

2. The last is an allusion to a repeated verse of Charles Baudelaire's poem, "L'Invitation au voyage": "Là, tout n'est qu'ordre et beauté, luxe, calme et volupté" (There, all is order and beauty, riches, calm and voluptuousness). *Trans.*

3. *Marx and Engels: 1848–49*, vol. 8 of *Karl Marx, Friedrich Engels: Collected Works*, (New York: International Publishers), 367, 370. *Trans.*

# 4

# Indifferent Memory

On 15 June 1992, the "1942 Vél d'Hiv Memorial Committee" sent a petition signed by the most important members of the Parisian intelligentsia to President François Mitterrand. The petition demanded of Mitterrand that on 16 June, the fiftieth anniversary of the Vél d'Hiv (Winter Velodrome) roundup, and in his capacity as head of the French Republic, he make a symbolic gesture and officially recognize the Vichy regime's responsibility for the persecution of and crimes committed against the Jews of France.[1]

When questioned during his annual television interview covering the Bastille Day celebration as to his intended answer to the petition, President Mitterrand declared that the French State did not have to assume Vichy's crimes, because "the French State, I dare say, just does not exist." There was the Republic that liberated the Jews, and there was Vichy, which abolished the Republic in order to found a government of exclusion: "So, do not ask this Republic to account for anything; it has always done what it had to do."

At the end of the interview, the reporters raised the question of Yugoslavia and asked the president whether, faced with the patent failure of the international community to bring Serbia to its knees by economic sanctions, it wasn't necessary to think of using military force: "Must we wage war as we did against Saddam Hussein in the Persian Gulf?" "Those are merely words," the head of state answered. Then, after listing the diplomatic initiatives taken by France since the beginning of the hostilities, he gave his analysis of the conflict: "Over there," he said, "we have minorities who live in terror, who have no defense, who have no guarantees, and who have no international status." So the European Community has done the wrong thing by switching priorities. They first recognized the sovereignty of the republics that wanted to separate themselves from Yugoslavia and only afterward did they concern themselves with the security of the minorities and guarantee them an international status. "And then," the president added, "there is Serbia's desire to annex territories inhabited by Serbs." But fulfilling this desire would constitute, in his eyes, less an aggression than it would a problem and even a "problem that almost has no solution," since there are no clear borders between these different minorities and, in any case, the existing ones are not recognized by the community of nations. "It is very difficult to determine where this type of interior border stops – and interior borders of this sort violate international law anyway." And President Mitterrand's third argument: "The Croatians do the same thing, always against poor Bosnia-Herzegovina." Conclusion: war is not on today's agenda. What we must do is maintain and, if need be, accentuate the embargo's pressure on *all* the protagonists so as to convince them to replace shells and machine guns with peaceful discussion: "That is why I have called for an international conference. This international conference will certainly take place. One day people will come around to France's opinion. It would nevertheless be better to speed up the process."

The president's refusal to make any gesture to commemorate the 1942 roundup in the Winter Velodrome got the press talking. Well-known French reporters and moral leaders reacted. Yet others echoed the president's argument and declared unacceptable the affirmation of the Vél d'Hiv committee that "the French state is responsible today for all that was done in the name of France." Still others put forward the fact that "it was the Parliament of the Popular Front, elected in 1936, that offered France to Pétain and his collaborators four years later" and that, if the Republic as such is not responsible, it was nonetheless government employees and top administration who promulgated the Anti-Jewish Statutes and then participated in the Final Solution.[2] In other words, beyond the constitutional opposition between the Vichy regime and the Republic, the French nation must answer for its own continuity.

Yet François Mitterrand's remarks about the war in the former Yugoslavia have not received any reaction or commentary whatsoever, except for a harsh editorial in the newspaper *Le Monde*. The French press, still thrilled over the trip the president of the Republic and his minister of humanitarian action had taken to Sarajevo, was happy to simply make note of and summarize France's position. The justification for this stance, however, is hardly self-evident; that's the least one could say of it. First of all, it took strange liberties with the truth. It is not quite true to say that the recognition of sovereign states preceded that of minorities. From the time of the Slovenian and Croatian declarations of independence to their admission as truly independent nations, Europe waited ten months. This was the time needed for the commission on arbitration (over which the French jurist Robert Badinter presided) to determine whether or not respect for minorities figured adequately in the legislative and constitutional texts of those republics seeking to be recognized by the member states of the European Community. As for Bosnia-Herzegovina, it obtained its entrance ticket into the international community after it had organized a referendum at the request of the commission on arbitration and after a majority of voters had answered yes to the question: "Are you in favor of a sovereign and independent Bosnia where all the citizens and peoples of this State, Muslims, Serbs, Croatians and members of other peoples who inhabit it, are equal by right?" To pretend that the Croatians are doing the same thing as the Serbs "with this unfortunate Bosnia-Herzegovina" is to ignore the fact that, from the start, the plan of Greater Serbia included all of Bosnia. If then the Croatians had not prepared themselves for war, if they had not resisted Serbia's forces, if they had not defended their homes and their villages, they would have been chased from them in as great a number as the Bosnian Muslims who have, moreover, for the most part, found refuge in Croatia.

Second observation: there is hardly any difference between the analysis of the president of the French Republic and the one made in Belgrade. By raising the question of minorities as a crucial problem of the former Yugoslavia, François Mitterrand takes as his own the reasons put forward by Serbia for going to war. By insisting on talking about the interior borders *after* Europe's recognition of Croatia and Bosnia-Herzegovina, he dismisses the obstacles placed by law to prevent the realization of Serbia's objectives. And by saying: "They are all the same!" he exonerates Serbia of its guilt.

We should remember that this happened on 14 July 1992. The conflict had been going on for more than a year. Massacres about which we then knew nothing had occurred. We did not know that, in a concentration camp near Brcko, some seventy-five miles to the north of Sarajevo, the Serbs killed, by groups of fifty, three thousand Muslims, men, women, and children, once they had occupied the city. But we did know that the politics of "ethnic cleansing," carried out openly and with impunity, had already uprooted more than a million and a half people. We have seen the pictures of Vukovar in ruins. And every day we now see Serbia's sharpshooters take potshots in Sarajevo. In spite of this *terrifying spectacle*, the declarations made by the president of the Republic in favor of Serbia go almost unnoticed.

"We must learn to look our past squarely in the face." That is the oft-repeated refrain of those who shape public opinion since three judges of the Court of Appeals in Paris dismissed the case of the collaborator Paul Touvier for crimes against humanity.[3] It has to be this way to protect the memory of our dead and for our children. It is necesssary for the memory of the victims and to prevent "it" from ever happening again.[4] And yet, when, for the first time since 1945, an event takes place in Europe which is not "it" but which has something to do with "it," which is not industrial extermination but a war that is openly inspired by a racist doctrine and that deliberately appeals to mass murders, this event – while it is definitely regrettable – seems to be exotic and secondary. And no sentinel of memory would think of reproaching France with being implicated. Enjoined to take responsibility for Vichy and to assume its shame, the president of the French Republic did not have to account, on the other hand, for his active and current complicity with Greater Serbia's plan and implementation of ethnic cleansing. We did not ask him to explain himself. He even evaded, in spite of the outrageous remarks he took to be self-evident, the burden of producing his reasons. And he did this despite the attention being given to Vichy – a horrific policy that not only gave way to force, as others had, but granted it every right – and it caused no scandal. Nor did Mitterrand's penchant at every opportunity to take the opposite view of that espoused by Germany while at the same time singing the praises of the European Community. Nor did the president's fear of change or his knee-jerk loyalty to old alliances as well as his blatant inability to judge reality as it is. Past errors, in short, blinded us to those occurring in the present.

Of course, we are not talking about the same error. The current French government did not participate in the crimes perpetrated in the former Yugoslavia. It simply backed them up with its diplomacy and speeches, and it has been most vigilant in keeping the crimes from being truly punished. Still, there has been crime and complicity; namely, the very sort of behavior to which a true meditation on the Second World War would have made public opinion definitively resistant.

So what is the source of the sentinels' blindness? How do we explain that it should be precisely the Sisters Ann, so ready to detect in any change of the right to asylum the portents of absolute horror, who saw nothing coming? Should we accuse memory itself and the keen remembrance of the abominations perpetrated by the Ustachis in the "independent" state that Mussolini and Hitler had subcontracted to them?

In 1956 the Soviets had already used such an argument to justify their suppression of the uprising in Budapest. "It's fascism," they said, "that we have come to fight. The revolt against the Party and the people's government was hatched by those nostalgic for the alliance with the Nazis to reestablish a nefarious dictatorship in Hungary." More generally, Soviet propaganda continued to hammer away at the theme that *the war was not over* and that other Hitlers, namely the enemies of the October Revolution and socialism's fatherland, had taken over from him. "Among the victims of the Second World War, one is missing: fascism," wrote Ilya Ehrenbourg. "It survived 1945. Certainly, it had known a period of malaise and decline, but it has not died."[5] In other words, Germany had hardly been defeated when antifascism began to serve Ideology – that is, to serve the Manichean division of society and History. The bad camp was not simply reactionary; it was henceforth vengeful, Fascist, and Nazi.

In 1956, in spite of the fascination that the dualist and even gnostic vision of History exerted on intellectuals, Nagy's Hungary was not mistaken for Horthy's. No matter how much Roger Garaudy and others condemned "the attack made by the reaction and fascism," the trap was thwarted, and he was not believed.[6] How could it be that we had to wait for the fall of communism for Garaudy to become credible again and for the trap finally to work?

A picture published in the press and shown on television on 21 July might perhaps help us solve the enigma. It depicts

47

Vaclav Havel, the dissident president, on the day following his resignation. He had been walking in the streets of Prague and had swapped his formal suit and tie for jeans, a T-shirt, and a jacket, which he has casually thrown over his shoulder. He had become an ordinary citizen again so that he would not have to ratify the partition of his country. He is, in this first image of his new life, no more Czech than he is Slovak: he is *cool*. And for the television news program commentator who discusses the photo with some feeling, there is little room for doubt: this is precisely the quality that, along with Havel himself, the Europe of postcommunism is in the act of proscribing.

The disappearance of Brezhnev's mummies was to ring in a new era: a time when one would experience less rigidity and the rejection (which, if not worldwide, at least true for our continent) of definitive summons, inflexible memberships, solemn thoughts, and prescribed roles. But hope was betrayed, because democracy did not show up at the appointed time. Blue jeans did not defeat the mummies, but rather hymns and flags did. National and ethnic identities did not melt with the general thaw but, rather, the ideological ice of the police state that covered them did. In short, without realizing it and probably at the expense of the dissident president, we saw in Vaclav Havel's photograph the symbol of a change in epoch and an unkept promise. The love of ties and the land dismisses the spirit of liberty, and the artisans of fragmentation and the fanatics of borders get rid of the cosmopolitan president, the politician in espadrilles. The hero with soles of wind leaves the scene in the hands of Slovaks, Czechs, Serbs, Macedonians, Moldavians, Ossetians, Georgians, Armenians, Azeris, and so on ad infinitum, all of them victims of the same partisan fever, all of them clinging to their own being, bound to their difference and intent upon building a wall around their little plot of land. Once there was *a* Wall, today there are a *thousand*, and it is quite naturally in the Balkans that this *balkanization* assumes the most furious and fiercest shape.

Our ancestors used to wonder, "How can one be a foreigner?" Now our contemporaries who have learned, or so they believe, from the experience of barbarity wonder *how one can be an autochton*. So we find grouped together, among the signatories of the petition to the president of the Republic asking for the persecutions and crimes of Vichy against the Jews to be officially recognized, a number of people who, during the siege of Vukovar, held out this new idea of the Other to all the protagonists of what they called "the explosion of hate in Yugoslavia."[7]

But from the first question to the second, there is only apparent progress. The person who wonders how he can be a foreigner coincides at this point with his being, and he holds on so tenaciously to his manners and is so completely captive to his sense of identity that he ignores himself as belonging to humanity or to a particular civilization. In his eyes, he is but one humanity: his own. Those who speak a language he does not understand or who do not share his customs are other than man because they are other than him. A prisoner of his attachment to a group, confined to his place, he experiences every difference as a difference of kind, even and especially the tiniest one that separates him from his neighbor. The person who does not understand how one can be an autochton congratulates himself for hating the hate of the Other and for denouncing the foreigner's expulsion. In fact, he expresses the very same xenophobia. He can quote Rimbaud – "Je est un Autre" (I is an Other) – or Holderlin – "Nul sans ailes ne peut connaître le Plus Proche" (No one without wings can know the One Most Near); he confuses the world with his world and humanity with his humanity. Simply put, his world is no longer his place but the system immediately linking him to all possible places. Even before being present to his own people, he enjoys his "telepresence" in the entire world.[8] "From his modest cottage or manor, every person can pretend to communicate immediately with any part of the globe and enlarge his mental universe throughout the entire world, while every bit of information and the announcement of every event can sweep completely across the planet."[9]

Modern man is thus a man of the entire world, but this does not mean he has no prejudices. The global village is his village. The videosphere is his fatherland. Detached, at the outset, from his natural surroundings, he tends to naturalize the environment without borders that progress has fashioned for him. Far from opening up his mind, his wings obsess him. *Hardwired* today as once he was *rooted*, he cannot conceive that one can humanly live outside the networks of communication and consumerism in which he evolves. This is why he looks at the autochton as a peasant and at this peasant as the bizarre and disturbing reminder of a prehuman species. Since everything, in his view, exists here and now, and since all identities are, under the name of differences, exchangeable, available, and offered for consumerism, people from some other place, the wogs, the "unhealthy," are, for him, those who do not play the game of exchange and who claim to be attached to a history, a land, and a community. Because he has conquered distance and telecommands reality, he believes he is free from the superstition of place and emancipated from his birthplace and its traditions. Because he is on earth as he is in space, he thinks he enjoys some distance from the bloody convulsions that cover the earth. Just as his blue jeans and sneakers indicate, he wants to be mobile, tolerant, and open. In reality he is only tolerant toward those who dress the same way; he is so taken up in the planetary telecity that for him any other form of rootedness appears to belong to a barbarian world. Today's question, "How can one be Croatian?" is simply the one asked in the past, "How can one be Persian?" but inscribed in a world where now the technical order imposes its evidence in the place of tradition.

The proof of the continuity between these two states of astonishment is found in the word that has been used and still is used by all the elite – political, intellectual, and media – to designate the different actors of the Yugoslav conflict. This word, which we have already come across, is the word *tribe*.

Ever since Boas and Lévi-Strauss, anthropology had gotten us out of the habit of thinking condescendingly about tribes. We have granted them the more civilized or more evolved character of societies with a national form. Yet we have forgotten our lesson, and self-complacency rules again. But, paradoxically, it has found its second breath in antifascism and in the contemporary denunciation of racism – at the price, it is true, of a slight displacement. One used to judge the tribe from the nation's summit; now the tribe is the nation, and the inhabitants of the legitimate great nations, of the indisputably great nations, of the undeniably great nations, sum up the fierce claims to an identity of the small nations of postcommunist Europe by quoting a phrase used to advertise Levi's jeans: "One day freedom will end up by going to everyone." From now on, "civilized" will mean *postnational*. And it matters little, in such a context, that the members of these nations have expressed their opinion and voted to leave the Yugoslav "federation." This choice no longer has the right to be respected. Recently an ethnic theory defining the nation by a set of unconscious and involuntary characteristics, and which lays claim to peoples and populations in spite of their protests, has confronted an elective theory, which, while taking into account historical, cultural, and linguistic factors, does not give them the last word. This theory affirms with Mazzini that "the fatherland is above all the conscience of the fatherland," and with Fustel de Coulanges that "the fatherland is what one loves," and with Renan it confers an absolute priority upon the clearly expressed desire to live together. Today this very same desire is qualified as ethnic or tribal as soon as it drives men to enter into a particular history in order to have it endure. In light of this new evolutionism, the difference between popular consent and all forms of imposed sovereignty becomes blurred. Of course, democracy is not itself denounced or contested. We never appreciated and recognized democratic values so unanimously as when the totalitarian truth of communism was brought to light. But what is celebrated under this name is no longer the sovereign state, it is no longer the nation enjoying the once transcendent powers to deliberate and decide, it is no longer the people liberated from all foreign, dynastic, or despotic supervision. Democracy, for its current participants, is the possibility afforded to individuals progressively to free themselves from national supervision and constraints.

So it is useless for Croatians to invoke the right of nations to self-determination. By choosing self-determination, they have opted not for freedom but for the prison *of the* people. They have retreated into their identity instead of openly embracing the consummation of differences.[10]

Only Bosnia-Herzegovina avoids the odium attached to the aspiration of nationhood. Why? Precisely because it is not a nation but a national imbroglio, because it is not a place but a crossroads, because it is not perceived as a community of destiny but as an entanglement of histories, because one does not see in it a world but a microcosm of circulation on the earth. In reality, there probably is a Bosnian identity. But, to the extent that they suppose this identity to be nonexistent, the neodemocrats of the technological age like Bosnia and support it to the detriment of its colleagues stuck in their magma or in their nationalist aspirations. Relying formerly on the principle of nationalities, the democrats used to uphold the right of nations to constitute themselves into cities, and, in return, the right of cities to question and modify the national heritage. In the present democratic perspective, homogeneity is an unpardonable sin, and only [multiethnic] Yugoslavias, little or big, have the right to exist.

One day we shall have to write the history of the Yugoslav dream in the East: a dream of self-management as opposed to the centralization and economic plans of communism; a dream of nonalignment as opposed to factional politics; finally the dream of a kind of Hapsburg cosmopolitanism instead of the world's division into nations. "Just like the word 'Austrian,' the word 'Yugoslav' has something of Musil's imaginary," writes, for example, Claudio Magris in *Danube*. "It refers to the abstract power of an idea more than to its accidental realization in the concrete; it is the result of a subtraction, the element which remains once the national characteristics have been removed, it is what everyone has in common but which cannot be identified with anyone."[11] After Marx, Musil: from the Liberation to our day, from the revolutionary utopia to the criticism of the Revolution, the Yugoslav dream has often changed its form but it has never been interrupted.

And what the supporters of the postnational democracy today reproach the peoples of the Yugoslav "mosaic" with is that they have interrupted the critics' dream and failed to conform to the latest conception these critics have of the way Yugoslavia ought to be. What these critics hold against them is that they have ceased to be Habsbourgeois when everyone, they think, is becoming just that. They are setting up borders when the need to abolish them is imperative; they are Croatian or Slovenian or Macedonian when we are all "black-white-beurs."[12] In a word, they are succumbing to the "virus of fragmentation" – to use Maurice Duverger's elegant coinage – while, by the very fact of technoscience, as much by its promises *as by its threats*, there is just one com-

munity of destiny on the earth: the one that unites all the
members of the human species to one another.

On this point, in effect, ecology does not contest anything
but rather confirms the observation technology has us make
of places and things. It opposes the value of Life to the value
of Development and the well-being of health to that of consumerism, but then, in turn, it pushes back the inherited divisions and the plurality of worlds into humanity's prehistory. Ecology proposes to save us from technology, but just
like technology it makes the *impossibility of having borders* the
only way to salvation. Whether it be a question of still pro-
gressing in our mastery or of overcoming that mastery, of
getting the whole planet to come to reason, or of solving
problems that have become worldwide, from now on it is
the responsibility of Humanity, as though one person, to
take things in hand: "Father Earth is in danger. We are in
danger, and the enemy, we finally discover today, is none
other than ourselves."[13]

Anachronistic Croatians! They are "politically correct"
neither for the biosphere's citizens nor for those of the
videosphere. They have effectively decided to live with borders, while Doctors for the Environment, not to forget
Games, Pharmacists, Reporters, and Democracy itself, indeed all that is good in our day, do not or should not have
any borders. ("President without Borders" is the headline
one of the large morning papers used to hail, as it should,
François Mitterrand's trip to Sarajevo). In short, they de-
Yugoslav themselves at the very moment when humanity
recognizes in Yugoslavia the form of its maturity and the
image of its future. Their unpardonable crime, in other
words, is that they are simply not *good contemporaries*.

The "secessionists" might very well plead their case in
quoting the memorandum written in 1986 by sixteen members of the Academy of Sciences and Arts of Belgrade, stress-
ing the following: that ever since Tito's death, Serbia had

been and continued to be engaged in an ongoing reconquest of Yugoslavia; that it unilaterally suppressed Voïvodine's and Kosovo's autonomy while maintaining – for its own advantage – their right to vote in federal elections; that at the time of the first free elections organized in Yugoslavia, the Communists lost power in Slovenia, Croatia, Bosnia-Herzegovina, while it was only necessary for them to do some window dressing to win in Serbia; that Croatians and Slovenians proposed the replacement of the former federation with a confederation of six sovereign republics, each one endowed with its own currency and national army but bound to a common market built on the European model of the time; that faced with the Serb refusal of such a solution, with a heavy heart they decided upon "disassociation"; that they did not then declare war on Serbia but that the federal army, of which they were the main financial backers, invaded them after confiscating the majority of their arms; and that this war, finally, did not aim to protect the rights of the Serbs living outside Serbia but to annex territories and, according to the instigators themselves, to gather Serbs living outside Serbian borders into the bosom of a "Greater Serbia" purged of all foreign presence, physical as well as cultural.[14]

However you might argue it, this type of defense is useless. The sentence has already been given. Even if the Serbs have their faults, the "secessionists" have immediately been disqualified because they refused or did not recognize what Edgar Morin calls "the role vital for the future of the principle of association at the level of our continent and also, beyond, at the level of our planet earth."[15] They are guilty of having decided on separation and dismemberment; that is, to mention Edgar Morin again, barbarianism and death.[16]

And when, getting to the bottom of things, they insist that they are fighting Serbia to defend their national identity and their belonging to the West, they seem, in the eyes of official Westerners, to be even more guilty. When they say that their nation is the vernacular declension of their Westernness, the particular translation of a larger history marked by Catholicism, the Renaissance, the Reformation, the Counter-Reformation, and the Enlightenment, they only dig themselves in a little deeper. When they announce that what dies with Yugoslavia is Pan-Slavism (the romantic idea whereby, beyond the schism between Rome and Byzantium, beyond the ancient division between Europe's East and West, all Slavic peoples were the scattered members of one great nation), they give themselves the coup de grâce. When, quoting Karel Havlicek's words on his return from Russia, they declare that the experiment with a state begun in 1918 "extinguished the last spark of panslavic love in them," that "Slavs do not form a nation," and that the "name Slav is and must ever remain a purely scientific and geographical entity," they are accused of thinking themselves superior and of *holding simultaneously different racisms* while adding the haughtiness of the civilized to the anxiety of identity.[17]

Culturally you want to situate yourself in Western Europe, one retorts, but in fact, by putting up a *cultural barrier* between the Serbs and yourselves, and by giving them an insurmountable otherness, you betray the true European spirit. What effectively characterizes Europe, at least when it does not let itself be taken up with its riches, development, and power, is to think against itself and not to think or to think oneself against the Other. It is, therefore, to see in the Other one other possible self. "Our tradition," writes Eric Weil, "is *the* tradition that ever questions its own validity," which means that European thought transcends its borders instead of being imprisoned in them, and it relativizes them instead of essentializing them.[18] In short, the Europe you call for is the Europe of *nail files* and of disdain. In the grand confrontation of which History is today the theatre between the associative forces and the forces of dissociation, the good

Europe, the Europe worthy of its name, takes, against all walls, the decision for "an audacious opening of conscience to other men, other nations, and other cultures."[19]

Our best antitotalitarian, antiracist, and ecological minds flatter themselves for having refused all Manicheanism in the Yugoslav conflict. In fact, those who have led a war of ethnic purification in Yugoslavia and those who have suffered it have backed up against a Manichean vision of History, actively and radically blind to history such as it occurs, detached from concrete experience and in no way affected by the sorrow of men or by that caused by the rocks they have thrown at one another's backs.

Ideology has not died with communism; it has simply made itself at home, with arms and traveling bags, with communism's victorious opponents. All the traits that appeared to characterize totalitarian thought are found in the present manner of thinking about History: politics reduced to a simple alternative – formerly "socialism or barbarianism," now "association or barbarism," indifference to what happens in the name of what is supposed to happen, the subservience of the event to theory, the stranglehold of generalization over the particular, and thrusting a meaning upon reality that no denial can shake nor exception succeed in troubling or weakening.

Ideology has removed this European war from us, and it has even ejected it out of our time and space. The force of the word *tribe* has relegated the sacking of the national and European patrimony of Croatia, the pillage of cemeteries and monuments to the dead, the burning of the botanical garden at Trestno and the park at Lokrum, the destruction of the museum of Croatian medieval art at Split, or the bombing of the cathedrals in Sibenik and Osijek, the churches Saint Anastasia and Saint Chrysogonus in Zadar or Saint Blaise in Dubrovnik to the column, "News from the Amazon Forest." The unaltered power of "the modern era's pseudo divinity called History" has covered with the skins of beasts the actors in the conflict, and it has transformed "memoricide" committed *hic et nunc* by Serbia into a kind of fiery war.[20] Better still, or worse: as in the most somber moments of Stalinism and its vertiginous distortions of reality, the Croatians have been accused of wanting to push Serbia outside of civilization at the very time when *their* civilization was the object of bombing, when *their* monuments became the primary targets, and when the Serb army razed, with methodical savagery, all the places that had given body to the Western tradition on the question of self and the examined life. Punished for having betrayed the Slavic cause for the benefit of the Latin world, attacked as a people and as a world, the Croatians were immediately accused of ethnocentrism by that world's official spokesmen, once they set forth claims for that world. The more they were condemned as Westerners, the more they were rejected by the West.

Learning the news (which later turned out to be false) about the fire at the Louvre during the uprising of the Paris Commune, Nietzsche, it seems, cried. A few weeks after the annihilation of Vukovar and the bombing of Dubrovnik's historical center, Edgar Morin declared to *Globe* magazine, "Let us consider the case of Yugoslavia. If it falls to pieces, you increase the risk of seeing new East-West divisions after the schisms between Rome and Byzantium, the Christian world and the Ottoman world, then the iron curtain. On the one hand, the Catholic Croatian-Slovenian bloc would join the West and, on the other, one would cast the Serbs, the orthodox, and the Islamized out of a decent Europe."[21] This is the height of Ideology: since Slovenia and Croatia threw up to Serbia their firm mooring in Western civilization, they could only logically (that is, by analogy with the National Front) have the same attitude toward the "Islamized" of Bosnia. Five hundred thousand of them have, since then, fled to Croatia from the "ethnic cleansing" carried out on them by the Serbian army.

Recalling in his acceptance speech for the Nobel Prize his life as a *zek*, Solzhenitsyn wrote: "In exhausting camp marches, rows of lanterns lighting the columns of prisoners in the darkness of subzero nights, more than once we felt in our throats what we would have liked to shout out to the whole world, if only the world could have heard some spokesman from among us." And he added a little later, "When the external pressure lessened, our outlook and my own outlook broadened, and gradually, if only through a peephole, the 'whole world' could be seen and discerned. And, surprisingly for us, that 'whole world' turned out to be something quite different from what we had expected it to be. . . . When it came to a swampy bog, it exclaimed: 'What a divine and lovely lawn!' When it encountered stocks made of concrete that were going to be placed around the necks of prisoners, it exclaimed: 'What a lovely necklace!' And where unquenchable tears poured forth for some, others danced to lighthearted music." [22]

The Berlin Wall has fallen, but its world has remained our own. While some, in Osijek or Sarajevo, have shed innumerable tears, others, so close and so far, have distractedly cried out, "Oh! those Yugoslavs," and they have stopped dancing to the rhythm of light music only to talk about the treaty of European Union with slogans such as: "We have had our fill of wars," or even "Let Europe live so that peace might live!"

It is true that the humanitarian bond between the theatre of operations and us has never been broken. First planes and then trucks brought food and medication to the besieged cities; corridors were created to rescue civilian populations, and when it was deemed necessary, the United Nations hurried in troops to protect the convoys. Without choosing a side, without worrying about knowing who was hurt or why, it was a question of answering the plea of misery. The French minister of humanitarian action said at the time of one of his many quick visits to the front, "Their nationality does not interest me. If they are Croatians, Serbs, or other, that does not interest me. What matters is their suffering."

This philosophy of extreme urgency apparently reflects the will to be finished with Ideology and selective compassion: after expressing its sympathy to the weak but only if they were progressive Palestinians and anti-Americans, *the heart refuses to be the dupe of the spirit any longer*. From now on it pities all victims and, from Yugoslavia to Somalia, flies to help them without distinction or points of view established a priori. But appearances lie: the humanitarian refusal to take into consideration the meaning men give their existence bears the mark of Ideology. Under the regime of the "without distance" and "without borders," all identities are anachronistic, and all worlds merge. But what is man without his belonging to a world? Nothing more than a set of corporal functions, nothing more than the organic and anonymous Life that throbs in him. Long live life! This is the war cry, or rather the cry for peace, for the global village, and it is the grand tautology that constitutes the supreme value of the cabled planet.

Humanitarian action represented real progress until the day when the humanitarian conquered the monopoly of morality and action. Now this mercy is merciless. The other side, in effect, of its concern for suffering is its disdain for everything in life that is not reduced to Life in the biological sense of the term. It is an Olympian indifference with respect to peasant humanity.

The indifference has, however, suffered some exceptions. The salesman of ideological sand has not, in spite of his planetary vocation, closed everyone's eyes at the same time on our earth-planet. While France wavered between the abhorrence of tribes and the celebration of its humanitarian prowess, German public opinion went to bat for the new republics before showing any feeling for their dereliction. Germany left its doors wide open for the refugees of Bosnia and Croatia, refugees whom France, the fatherland of the Rights of Man, had turned down.

Without going so far as to speak of the Fourth Reich, as does Belgrade's Propa-Ganda, the French watchmen of antifascism were quick to detect in this solidarity the return of the old *MittelEuropean* or Pan-Germanic demons. They have seen Germany, after half a century of political dwarfism, connect to its imperialist past and reconstitute its zone of influence by destroying Yugoslavia. However, after looking into it, we see that it is not nostalgia for power that inspired the German population's behavior but the memory of suffering and desolation: "The Germans know as do few other peoples in the world what it is to lose one's country and be on the run," declared the minister of the interior. And this inhabitant of East Berlin who stood up as a candidate to receive the uprooted people said, "My parents were refugees after the war, and when they were desperate and hungry, a person who had heart helped them." We can probably deplore the fact that, after the wrong it had done, Germany should refer itself at the start to the hurt it suffered and to its own refugees, victims first of the war and then of communism. Yet we must see the old demons where they are – that is, in the attacks against the homes of Bosnians and Croatians and not in the fact of offering them hospitality. We must realize that the double ordeal of destruction and separation has kept these inhabitants of the global village, whom the Germans also are, in history and on the earth and has given them a concrete meaning in the word *refugees*. There is nothing like it in France, where there was a complete difference *because there was Vichy*. As Vladimir Jankélévitch reminds us so well, the majority of the French went through the war without seeing it, or almost that. They ate garlic sausage while listening to Maurice Chevalier sing *Prosper et Yop la boum*; they danced to the rhythm of light music while so many other Europeans shed tears of affliction: "The entire paradox of the 1940 disaster is found in this derisive contrast between a political-military breakdown almost without precedent and the relative clemency of destiny toward a great part of the nation. . . . The French rump state of Marshall Pétain was viable. The trains ran. The bourgeoisie went on vacation and enjoyed their winter sports. Speakers gave their talks. . . . For it was the good time. Given a few more years, I tell you that Mr. Abetz, like everyone else, would have had his leftist intellectuals, metaphysical cafés, and avant-garde journals. The good times, I tell you. France was looking good. Hardly over its disaster, Pétain's France put on white gloves, shoulder belts, and white ankle socks."[23]

Today one calls it Vichy-the-Shameful, and we no longer know what kind of ceremony to have for France to confess and beg for pardon. But if the most outspoken Frenchmen against the France of the dark years were not, in spite of themselves, Vichy's heirs, they would not have removed themselves from reality and they would have been revolted by the present assistance their government gives Serbia. Had there not been any Vichy to let France step to the side of the Second World War, France would not have done the same thing for this war, and the trauma of history would have dispelled the charm cast on it by the word *tribe*.

Things changed when we learned, despite the care taken by the different chancelleries not to divulge the news, that there were concentration camps in the self-proclaimed Serb republic of Bosnia-Herzegovina. The pictures of dazed and half-starved people behind barbed wire resurrected yet other images. The revelations concerning the system of ethnic cleansing set up by Serbia in the conquered regions awakened the sentinels of memory from their torpor. Seeing not only the imprisonment of civilians in mobile places of detention, which could thwart any inspection by the Red Cross, but additional tortures on a grand scale, summary executions, systematic rapes, mass expulsions after the confiscation of all belongings, the obligation imposed on all non-Serbs authorized to remain in the area to wear an armband together with the prohibition on leaving their homes from four in the afternoon till six in the morning, to get together in cafés, restaurants, and other public places, to bathe in the local river, to drive a car, to use any means of communication other than the public telephone, to exchange or sell their houses without the permission of the local authorities – seeing all that, some newspapermen and politicians began to raise their voices, and some went so far as to demand a believable military intervention to stop and punish Serbia. Sharply dismissing the proposal, the president of the French Republic underlined the dangers of such an undertaking, repeated that the wrongs were on both sides, and recalled "the historic bonds between Serbia and France, and their solidarity in the two world wars."[24] But his argument was not convincing. His minister of humanitarian action tried in vain on his return from a trip organized to the concentration camps to say that atrocities were committed on both sides and that the prisoners in Sarajevo also did not look so great. He did not succeed in confusing the issue. Trying to wipe out the guilty party by diluting the fault failed. The *humanitarian exoneration of the crime against humanity* did not have the same result as it did during the first year of the war.

What did happen was that suddenly Europe stood accused. Electoral slogans that schizophrenically boasted European peace were turned against their promoters. The very idea that Europe had brilliantly passed the Yugoslav test by staying united and by neutralizing the wishes of its partners to intervene became obscene and damning. It was no longer possible to say with Alain Minc, "On Yugoslavia, I think Europe has played a discreet but major role as the reducer of follies. The Germans were headed for a kind of absurd historical 'trip' and the French, by reaction, for one that was just as absurd: the Germans were pro-Croatian, the French pro-Serb. And though historical, it was no less ridiculous. By making these two countries give up their historical weight, the European Community played an interesting role, if not an extremely important one. I would say that it functioned as a developed civil society. We need to realize that, by doing this, it put a stop to possible injustices."[25]

Certainly the famous "powder keg of the Balkans" exploded this time only in the Balkans and contagion was avoided. Sarajevo did not once again lead Europe into war. Yet how can we even rejoice in this when it has been at the price of Sarajevo's slow death? Before the formation of Europe, every local war tended, through the wager of political alliances, to become global. With Europe, local wars remain local, but where is there any progress if this means that these wars "under glass" can unleash in peace all their murderous effectiveness? And doesn't it push rather far the grand national ethnocentrism to pretend that, since we did not enter into war between Bosnians, Croatians, and Serbs, war has been avoided?

We can see, in light of the ethnic cleansing programmed and set up by Serbia, that Europe, born from the trauma of the Second World War, has in reality been conceived to prevent the repetition of the First World War, and that crime against humanity can return to European soil with impunity. To put it another way, what the so-called Yugoslav conflict has shown is that in political matters *unity makes for weakness*, and that this weakness is secretly desired by the states, which cast upon one another all responsibility toward the world and which compensate for their ineffectual action with humanitarian bustling about.

Caught in the act of being a Swiss isolationist, Europe has disappointed a number of its most sympathetic supporters.

The will to power has been quelled, but to the advantage of a *will of helplessness*, which itself causes appalling damage. On the cover of a large Parisian journal published in September of 1992, we could read that "Europe died in Sarajevo." This deception, however, will not change the course of things. Serbia will push its advantage and increase its destruction to create an irreversible situation before the American presidential elections take place. After the memorable party in Dubrovnik where a singer and a member of the government encouraged the besieged to be tolerant, France rejoiced over its new humanitarian gestures, which were as much in good taste as they were ineffective, all the while looking after the preservation of the essential interests of its old ally. Europe and the international community will continue to ignore the last plea of Alija Iztbegovic, the president of Bosnia: "Do not defend us, do not send your troops into my country, do not send any food: simply lift the embargo on weapons. We shall be able to defend ourselves and we shall be able to nourish ourselves." With the military intervention ruled out and the negotiations more than ever on the agenda with Messrs. Milosevic, Karadjic, and/or Cosic – that is, with the recognized promoters of memoricide and ethnic cleansing – the commission of inquiry that the United Nations Security has just formed will not lead to any prosecution of the guilty. It is not even certain that the guilty will ever be named: the system of annihilation by some has inevitably provoked among others exactions and revenge. There will be a great temptation to justify the world's laissez-faire attitude, and to address, in the name of the outraged world, a solemn reprimand to all the barbarians of the Balkans with, perhaps, as for Nuremberg, a special mention of Serbia.

And nothing lets us predict the end of Ideology's reign. For all those who had denounced all nationalisms the most violently, and *without* the benefit of an inventory, referred themselves explicitly to the fate of the Jews: once already, they would say, Europe as a victim of this drunkenness of borders wanted to exterminate the peoples who do not keep their place, the people who are both from some other place and from here. *Nie wieder*! "Never again!" was their answer to the liberation so desired by the little nations of southeastern Europe.

The planetary telecity inspired them with a certain disdain for any attachment to place, and they believed it was the meditation of the Shoah. Their "jet-modernity" made them poke fun at identities and lands, and they thought it was Chagall. They were the spokesmen for a world that abolished distance as proximity in the immediacy of the image, and they quoted Isaiah, "Peace, peace near and far." In short, at the very moment that they were congratulating themselves on judging history in light of the Jewish experience, they projected onto it the sweet weightlessness of universal consumerism and instantaneous communication.

The view they now have of the war in the Balkans has changed, but as long as the Jewish fate continues for them to be identified with the destiny of the *consumer without qualities*, the memory they proudly claim will remain a prisoner of Ideology.

NOTES

1. On 16 and 17 July 1944, roughly 4,500 French police rounded up 13,000 Jewish men, women, and children in Paris and herded them to the Vélodrome d'Hiver, a bicycle-racing facility also used in the thirties for political rallies. The detainees were kept in the Vél d'Hiv in atrocious conditions for several days, then shipped to Drancy and on to Nazi death camps to the east. The code name for the operation was Spring Wind. *Trans.*

2. Quote is from Edwy Plenel, "La République et l'oubli," *Le Monde*, 19–20 July 1992.

3. In April 1992. *Trans.*

4. "It" being the horrors of Nazis and the Final Solution. *Trans.*

5. Ilya Ehrenbourg, *La Russie en guerre* (Gallimard, 1968), 45–46.

6. Quoted by François Fejtö, *Budapest, l'insurrection* (Complexe, 1990), 22.

7. "L'Autre, une idée neuve: Un appel d'écrivains contre la xénophobie et le nationalisme," *Le Monde*, 23 Nov. 1991.

8. Paul Virilio: "Quand il n'y a plus de temps à partager, il n'y a plus de démocratie possible," *Le Monde*, 28 Jan. 1992.

9. Jean Chesneaux, *Modernité-Monde* (La Découverte, 1989), 48.

10. We noted this with the small "yes" vote for European Union. In France there are eloquent and fierce partisans of a certain republican idea of the nation. But, in the eyes of these patriots, only France fulfills the conditions for being a republican nation. When they say "Long live the nation!" they are defending universal values. When other people shout the same thing, they shy away from the universal idea and adopt the local idea, and leaving the idea of humanity, they embrace the region. So the *republicans* and the *democrats* whom everything opposes, as Régis Debray has brilliantly shown, have joined camps in the name of the citizen nation in one case and, in the other, for the purpose of going beyond nations in order to "tribalize" the aspirations to independence on the part of the peoples of the former Yugoslavia. Their solitude is therefore *without appeal* (See "What Is a Nation? – Second Episode," in part 2).

11. The *beurs* are French-born children of North African immigrants. The word is slang. This second generation has tried to have its own identity and not simply belong to the mixed group alluded to by Finkielkraut. *Trans.*

12. Claudio Magris, *Danube* (Gallimard, 1988), 407.

13. Edgar Morin, *Un nouveau commencement* (Le Seuil, 1991), 24.

14. "A real chronicle of an announced death, I myself heard the future president of Croatia, Franjo Tudjman, warn as early as 1990 that his country did not desire independence, that he would be resigned to it however for lack of a negotiated solution with Belgrade, but that, in the event of a break in the negotiations, Slovenia would become independent, and that Croatia could only follow suit and then the Serbs would attack. That is exactly what happened, with

the West putting no pressure at the time on Belgrade to seek a negotiated solution." Pierre Lellouche, "Le prix de renoncement," *Le
Figaro*, 31 Aug. 1992, p. 3.

15. Edgar Morin, *Transversales* 29, July–Aug. 1992, p. 14.

16. Edgar Morin, "Association ou barbarie" (Association or barbarism), *Le Monde*, September 19, 1992, p. 2.

17. Havlicek, quoted by Hans Kohn, *Le panslavisme* (Payot,
1963), 35.

18. Eric Weil, *Essais et conférences* (Vrin, 1991), 2 : 21.

19. "L'Autre, une idée neuve: Un appel d'écrivains contre la xénophobie et le nationalisme," *Le Monde*, 23 Nov. 1991.

20. Mirko Grmek, "Un mémoricide" *Le Figaro*, 19 Dec. 1991.
The designation of History as pseudo divinity is Hannah Arendt's,
in *Juger* (Le Seuil, 1991), 20.

21. *Globe*, Jan. 1992.

22. Aleksandr I. Solzhenitsyn, *The Nobel Lecture on Literature*,
trans. Thomas P. Whitney (New York: Harper & Row, 1972), 9–11.
*Zek* is Russian slang for a prisoner: *zackluchonny*. *Trans.*

23. Vladimir Jankélévitch, "Dans l'honneur et la dignité," in *L'im-
prescriptible* (Le Seuil, 1986), 84–86.

24. *Sud-Ouest*, 13 Aug. 1992.

25. Alain Minc, "A côté de l'essentiel" (interview with Thierry de
Montbrial), *La Revue des Deux Mondes*, Dec. 1991, pp. 16–17.

# PART TWO

# How Can One Be Croatian?

*Journal of a Disaster*

# 5

# A Death Announcement

*Le Monde*, 9 July 1991

*Le Monde* (LM): In your view, won't the demise of communism lead Europe into a vertiginous regression, brought about not through a nostalgia for the old order, but because the disorder created by the rise of new nationalities could generate new catastrophes?

AF: If there is a regression, it is *our* regression, which is to say a regression on the part of Western Europeans and of the French that we are. Look at Yugoslavia. Two nations, Slovenia and Croatia, declare their independence and in the same breath their Europeanness. What does France do? She ostracizes the two nations in question from Europe in the name of the territorial integrity of Yugoslavia and in the name of maintaining the status quo at all costs. This attitude testifies in the first place to an abysmal ignorance. Our government, along with a number of journalists and the majority of our intellectuals, discovered Slovenia on 25 June 1991.[1] Reasoning by analogies, approximations, and clichés, they imputed the disorder in the region to the secessionists. The opposite is in fact the case: the Slovenian declaration of independence, along with that of the Croatians, did not engender the chaos, but rather the chaos resulted from the final disintegration of Yugoslavia, and the increasingly real threat in the region of Yugoslavia's replacement by a military dictatorship provoked these acts of secession.

In Slovenia, everything began with the struggle for pluralism and democracy throughout Yugoslavia. Two newspapers having divulged a military plan to crush these efforts and to arrest the leaders responsible, the Federal Army responded by arresting the overly curious journalists and Slovenian soldiers accused of leaking the plan. In this fashion the idea took hold that there was no national salvation or democracy except outside the Yugoslav federation. The Slovenian population having voted by an overwhelming majority during the month of December in favor of independence, the democratically elected government of this republic gave the federal government six months to come up with a *joint* solution to the crisis. In the meantime, Serbia appropriated for its own purposes half of the nation's currency for 1991. Then Serbia prevented the Croatian Stipe Mesic from assuming his rightful turn as president of the Yugoslav federal government. Despite this behavior, as well as the occupation of Kosovo, French pressure was brought to bear only on the two secessionist *(souverainiste)* republics. The only chance to save Yugoslavia was ruined in this fashion by those who wished to maintain its integrity at all costs. The Baltic countries – Armenia, Slovenia, Croatia – for France, these smaller countries are guilty of sowing disorder in a newly liberated Europe. But freed from what if this new Europe doesn't have the right to be free?

LM: Aren't you troubled just the same by the fact that Slovenia is after all a creation of the Yugoslav Federation, and, moreover, that in Croatia one of the political currents emerging today was precisely the one in charge in 1944? Doesn't this "vengeful" aspect of Croatian nationalism nuance your analysis?

AF: Slovenia is not the creation of the Yugoslav Federation! It is a thousand-year-old country that, after the collapse of the Austro-Hungarian Empire in 1918, agreed to participate in what was originally called the State of the Serbs, Croats, and Slovenians, and from which it chooses today to divorce itself because all that remains of Yugoslavia is the double perspective of political dictatorship and the collapse of the economy. I interpret the word *nation* not in an ethnic sense but in the elective sense given to it by Renan: a patrimony and a project, a rich heritage of memories and "the consent, the desire clearly expressed, to share a life in common." Both of these dimensions are found in Slovenia and Croatia. The dark episode of the Ustacha state created by Hitler in 1941 does not make Croatia a non-nation. As to reducing the current form of Croatian patriotism to a resurgence of fascism, this is an essentialist perspective that obscures Croatian resistance during the war and which should have led us to erase Germany and Russia from the map. This being said, there is a temptation to revise history in Eastern Europe today.

LM: Isn't this tendency triumphing, or on the verge of doing so?

AF: No, but it is present in Romania among those who are nostalgic for the dictator Antonescu, in Slovakia among the admirers of Monsignor Tiso, and everywhere, in fact, where the catastrophe of Stalinism followed directly on Nazi Occupation. The temptation is to reinterpret, if not Hitlerism itself, at least collaboration with the Nazis, in an effort to defeat communism or to escape from its hold. The hatred of fascism used to nourish communism. Now the situation is reversed. It is necessary now to reflect on the two totalitarian experiences together instead of having them take turns relaunching each other. But this is not to suggest that until this is done we should cast a hostile eye on every emancipatory national movement in postcommunist Europe. We don't have the right to use the struggle against anti-Semitism to justify sustaining an empire or a military invasion. This is nevertheless the attitude of an entire antitotalitarian intelligentsia, which, in deciding that nationalism is the most dangerous of dangers, makes the small European nations pay for the crimes committed by the great continental empires. This intelligentsia chooses Gorbachev over Solzhenitsyn, even though the former, with all his qualities, uses force to flatten the Armenians and the second, with all his faults, pleads for the dismantling of the Soviet Empire. This so-called progressive intelligentsia also rejects any group's desire to have a state and a flag, except of course, the Palestinians.

LM: Isn't it out of fear of the Soviet Army that we cling to the status quo?

AF: The Soviet Union and Serbia depend on the West for their survival. It is therefore possible to get Gorbachev to compromise today just as yesterday it was possible to constrain the government in Belgrade to accept the transformation of Yugoslavia into a confederation of sovereign states. Instead of following this path, our president [Mitterrand] chose to perpetuate colonialism and injustice. He could say along with Metternich: "My primary moral element is immobility," except that in Metternich's case he knew he was fighting against liberal principles, while our president claims to be their defender. It is a bewildering form of diplomacy that comes down on the side of crushing small nations in the name of the struggle against nationalism. It is a strange republic that has only the word *différence* on its lips but wishes only to see one authority in Europe, which honors in its heart hip-hop culture but impudently ignores the existence of Slovenian culture. Long live rap! Down with Slovenia! The two chants go together.

LM: Isn't it so that, leaving France aside, it is Europe itself, the European Community, that seeks to avoid getting involved in a situation that before the war led to war?

AF: What leads to war is immobility and inaction. And, moreover, it was completely surreal to see Jacques Poos, a minister of the Lilliputian state of Luxembourg, demand of the minuscule Slovenians, in the name of the EC, that they renounce their aspirations to become a country. Perhaps tomorrow Prince Rainier of Monaco will demand of the Baltic nations in the name of Planet Earth that they be reasonable and accept, for just one more short century, that the Stalin-

Hitler pact hold sway! In any case, in this face-off between the European troika and Slovenia, the only Europe that counts, the Europe of democracy and diversity, was on the side of the Slovenians.[2] Today, by contrast, the European Community no longer speaks with a single voice: France clings to a conservative position, at the risk of favoring the invasion of Slovenia and of losing its prestige in posttotalitarian Europe to Germany. Out of fear, you say, that once again the Balkans will lead us into war – (but Slovenia is not part of the Balkan world; but the First World War was born of a conflict of empires; but Archduke Ferdinand was assassinated by Serb extremists . . .).

LM: It is necessary just the same to define for both economic and cultural reasons what models for the integration of minorities should be implemented. In the case of Yugoslavia, this is clear. The problem will come up elsewhere, in Hungary for example, where one third of the population is in the minority in neighboring countries.

AF: Let's not mix everything together. Slovenia and Armenia are not minorities; they are nations whose peoples are in the majority in their own territory, countries which aspire to regain their rights. The problem of minorities will never be resolved by falling back on the rights of peoples to control their own destiny.

LM: Don't you think that you're engaging in a dangerous game of subtle distinctions that is impossible to win unless one adopts as the most basic criteria that every national aspiration is legitimate that allows a group to leave communism behind? Are Slovakian aspirations to leave Czechoslovakia behind still legitimate, given that they have already emerged from communism?

AF: They are. Undeniably the Slovaks form a nation. As a consequence, they have the right to self-determination, unless you wish to argue that this right is no longer really valid or that in moving from communism to a "city hall" and democracy itself, peoples simply exchange one form of prison for another. It is true that the independence of Slovakia would pose insurmountable technical problems. But if in fact one wishes to preserve the bond between Czech and Slovak, it is necessary to recognize the legitimacy of Slovak patriotism. It is in the end necessary for the Czechs to say to the Slovaks: "Yes, you form a nation, with all the rights that that entails" if Czechoslovakia, perhaps in a somewhat different form, is to remain viable. But to say, as do our diplomats: "Long live the end of communism, and let nobody move!" – this is the path to catastrophe, not the means to avoid it.

LM: Your reasoning is interesting. Were you in fact in favor of recognizing Corsican independence?

AF: No.

LM: All the criteria you've enumerated apply to Corsica. So you're saying "don't move" to the Corsicans, in the name of a Jacobinism that you've just denounced in Yugoslavia.

AF: I'm not a Jacobin. I'm a Republican. And I see three major differences between the Corsican (and the Basque) situation and the situation facing the Slovenes. A cultural difference: French identity exists, and the Corsicans share in it. There is, by contrast, no Yugoslav identity. A difference which is both constitutional and historical: France is a republic both one and indivisible ("The Republic one and indivisible, our French kingdom," Péguy wisely used to say); Yugoslavia, on the other hand, is a federation of republics that have the right to secede. Finally, a political difference: Corsican and Basque separatists are in a minority and rely on terrorism in their struggle against democratic states. All the Slovenes wish for an independent country, and they are struggling by democratic means against a state terrorism. To judge Europe in the light of the Corsican problem is to pro-

vide indisputable proof of provincialism and French ethnocentrism.

NOTES

1. Slovenia declared its independence from Yugoslavia on 25 June
1991. *Trans.*

2. Presumably, in recognizing Slovenian independence. *Trans.*

# 6

# Words and War

*Le Monde*, 4 October 1991
Croatia is not the scene of a civil war, as is so often repeated at the moment, but of a military invasion. The navy, MIGs, tanks – in short, all the firepower – is on one side, that of the "federal" army.

This army is not really federal, but communist, to the degree that it is still attached to a particular ideology. Its officer corps consists of Serbs. It is not fighting a resurgence of Ustacha fascism in Croatia but rather a decision taken democratically by the Croatians to be masters of their own destiny. The latter no longer wish to support financially a hostile federal government, preferring instead to create a sovereign state of their own within the community of Europe. The "federal" army, for its part, is seeking not to protect a Serb minority within Croatia but is instead attempting to punish the Croatians through the destruction of their monuments and shrines, and in conquering their territories to the benefit of Greater Serbia. In this instance, the "antifascist" struggle against the Croatian "Ustacha" justifies the Serb power grab and serves as a pretext for the destruction of a people guilty only of the crime of aspiring to self-determination.

As to Serb "autonomists" of the Krajina region and Slavonia, they are undoubtedly legitimately concerned about their future, but they are not fighting for autonomy or for respect or to bolster their political and cultural rights. They are fighting so that all Serbs, wherever they reside, will be citizens of the same state. This is all that remains of the idea of Yugoslavia.

In short, in the current situation in Yugoslavia, we are not dealing with two archaic nationalisms struggling with each other but rather with an imperial power and a people seeking emancipation, as was the case in Budapest in 1956 and Prague in 1968.

In failing to report this situation as it is, the media are not informing public opinion but are rather putting it to sleep. If Europe sanctions this war of conquest and, tomorrow, grants itself a clean conscience in recognizing only a Croatia whose borders are established by its invader, this will mean that after forty-five years' interdiction, it is once again possible and acceptable to extend one's borders by force in Europe. If this occurs, it is certain that, sooner or later, others will follow Serbia's example.

# 7

# The President Gives a
# History Lesson

*Le Nouvel Observateur*, 12 December 1991
Invited by journalists of the *Frankfurter Allgemeine Zeitung*
to clarify the French position on the war in Croatia, President François Mitterrand stated: "What I know is that for a
long time Serbia and Croatia have been the scene of many
such dramas, especially during World War II, when large
numbers of Serbs were killed in Croatian concentration
camps. As you know, Croatia was allied with Nazi Germany,
but Serbia wasn't. After Tito's death, the latent conflict between Serbs and Croatians was bound to erupt. And that is
what has happened. I do not believe that Serbia is making
war in order to conquer Croatia but rather to alter its borders with Croatia and to gain direct or indirect control of
Serb minorities residing in Croatia."

I felt shame in reading Mitterrand's declaration and in noting that it did not provoke indignant responses either from
other French Socialist leaders or from opposition leaders so
quick to denounce our head of state in other circumstances.
After the destruction of Vukovar and before that of Osijek,
and while hundreds of thousands of Croatians have been
subjected to a forced exodus, the individual who speaks in
my name as a French citizen, and who controls the foreign
policy of my country, espouses point by point the racist and
misleading propaganda of the Serb aggressor. And no one
challenges him.

In the first instance, it is inaccurate to assert that Croatia
was in the Nazi orbit and Serbia was not. Yugoslavia was
invaded on 6 April 1941 by the Italian and German armies.

Capitulating twelve days after the invasion began, Yugoslavia, like France, fell under the control of the Axis powers. The country was then divided up. Ante Pavelic, a protégé of Mussolini, was brought to power in Zagreb, while in Belgrade, the Germans installed the regime of Anton Nedic, the strongly pro-German former minister of war in Yugoslavia. The same year, the Germans created a vassal state in Croatia, which they misleadingly labeled "an independent state," and restored Serbian statehood while keeping it completely under their control. If it is true that massive numbers of Serbs were savagely murdered at the Jasenovac concentration camp and elsewhere by the Croatian Ustacha, it is also true that we French, incorrigible preachers that we are, should not forget that there were more resistance fighters in Croatia than in France, and that, from 1942 on, Croatians were in the majority among the resistance.

As to the argument that Serbia wishes only to protect the Serb minority in Croatia, that argument holds as much water as the Nazis' claim that they only wanted to protect the Sudeten Germans in Czechoslovakia, at the time when Western Europe was abandoning Central Europe to its fate. As was the case yesterday in Kosovo, as will be the case tomorrow in Bosnia, and the day after tomorrow in Macedonia, the "protection" of Serb minorities is merely a pretext for a policy of territorial expansion.

At the heart of all these lies one discovers an essentialist manner of thinking that is especially astonishing when it is voiced by our president: Ustacha will always be Ustacha, and if the Croatians arrest the leaders of their own extreme right while the Serbs allow their outspoken fascists to prosper and proliferate, among the Croatians this is only a ruse for public consumption. They remain genocidal to the core. Their racism is hereditary, genetically determined, inescapable. This *racialization of racism* transforms into a legitimate act the Serb invasion of Croatia – for what can one do with people

culturally and biologically programmed to kill, except anni-
hilate them? What can one do but crush a genocidal people?

Apart from the unbelievable faux pas of informing the
Germans in that defending Croatia's right to self-determination they are defending a nazified people, France's adhesion to the theses of Serbia's rulers also sheds a frightening
light on the humanitarian assistance the media continue to
glorify. Under the pretext of coming to the aid of the victims, France contributes to the removal of Croatians from
wealthy regions that Milosevic has singled out for conquest.
French humanitarianism has contributed to making eastern
Slavonia *Croatenrein* (cleansed of Croats) in order to facili-
tate tomorrow a new alignment of national borders that will
be much more favorable to Serbia.

But why should we be ashamed? After sixty-five years elsewhere, hasn't the Davis Cup just returned to France? [1]

NOTE

1. Under the captaincy of Yannick Noah, the French won the
Davis tennis cup against the United States in 1991. *Trans.*

# 8

# "Ave Europa, Morituri Te Salutant"

*Le Figaro*, 10 December 1991
While the Twelve were discussing the future of Europe in downtown Maastricht, the Croatians were authorized to assemble at a stadium on the outskirts of the town. "Hail, Europe," said the Croatians, "those who are about to die salute you." "Ecu!" responded the echo.

The truth is there are two kinds of peoples in post-communist Europe: legitimate peoples who make history and for whom freedom is a right and then the useless peoples, the excess baggage, who fall outside of history and don't even qualify as tragic victims when they are massacred for seeking to be free.

In the past, because of the rivalries and alliances that held sway, every regional conflict risked degenerating into a world war. Now that "Europe" exists, this threat is no longer valid: mass murder takes place in a vacuum, protests occur in a stadium. The edifice of the European community certainly shouldn't be threatened by a simple ethnocide! Die, Croatians! Europe salutes you as well!

# 9

# A Dismissal of Charges

*Le Monde*, 25 April 1992
Quite recently the Croatians and Slovenians have been accused of succumbing to an ethnic madness and of dissociating themselves from a multinational Yugoslavia in order to remain exclusively among themselves. The Republic of Bosnia-Herzegovina is a multinational state both in the composition of its population and *in its constitution*, and yet it is criticized along the same lines as Croatia.

The Croatians are accused of wanting to infringe on the rights of their Serbian minority. It is equality with Muslims and Croatians that the Bosnian Serb militias, backed by the federal army, refuse to accept.

Are things clear enough? Have we finally come to understand that the universal condemnation of all the nationalisms in question amounts to a whitewashing of the aggressor, or, to be more precise, to a dismissal of the case against those who only yesterday systematically destroyed Vukovar and who, today, in the name of the same Serb state, within the framework of the hegemonic and terroristic policies, arrest Bosnian civilians, order them to drop their pants, and massacre those who are circumcised?

# 10

# Sarajevo

*Crimes against Humanity*

*Le Journal du Dimanche*, 10 May 1992
Taking their cue from the lessons learned from the trial of
Klaus Barbie and wishing to avoid banalizing the Shoah,
the members of parliament charged with preparing the new
French penal code have established two categories of crimes
against humanity. The first consists of genocide, defined as
the destruction of a people. The second category is defined
as "the deportation, enslavement, or the massive and systematic carrying out of summary executions; the roundup of individuals, followed by their disappearance; torture or other
inhuman acts inspired by political, philosophical, racial, or
religious motives organized and executed as part of a con-
certed plan to be carried out against a specific group within
the civilian population."

The war being waged by Serbia against Croatia as well
as against Bosnia-Herzegovina falls unquestionably into the
second category. Razed villages, villages destroyed by aerial
attacks and heavy artillery, the designation of hospitals as
military targets. Cultural sites and monuments erased from
the map, planned massacres, systematic rapes and throat-
cuttings, Muslims and Croatians chased from their homes
by the hundreds of thousands. All of these measures serve
to modify the ethnic composition of these two independent
republics in accordance with the implementation of a con-
certed plan of annihilation and conquest.

And the least that can be said is that our reaction to the
catastrophe is not commensurate with the events themselves. With few exceptions, the journalists are still looking

for the guilty party, the intelligentsia is sleeping, and the "Europhile" political leaders are impudently congratulating themselves for bringing peace to Europe through the Maastricht accords. In the meantime, their nationalist opponents are explicitly lamenting the fact that we caved in to German pressure in recognizing Serbia, Croatia, and Bosnia-Herzegovina.

Today France is making a great deal of the duty to memory. "Never again should 'that' occur!" the nation affirms, each time the leader of the National Front indulges in verbal outrage.[1] But when "that" occurs a few paces from our doorstep, the nation does not have eyes either to see or to cry. When crimes against humanity occur on European soil and their images are broadcast daily on television, the nation wonders anxiously if 1992 will be the year of Europe or the year of Germany. When on 6 April, the inhabitants of Sarajevo demonstrate peacefully for their freedom and the integrity of their republic, and decide, their backs against the wall, to defend themselves, our nation distractedly files them in the same category as those who are bombarding their city so as, at a later date, to feel more comfortable about partitioning the besieged city. The nation's "duty to memory" is thus just the latest version of French navel contemplation.

NOTE

1. Finkielkraut is here referring to the Shoah and, more broadly, to genocide in Europe. *Trans.*

# II

# Past—Present

*Libération*, 27 May 1992

"Slobodan equals Saddam!" chanted Belgrade's democratic citizens in March 1991. Now that Slobodan Milosevic's full measure is evident in the destruction of Sarajevo and Mostar, following that of Vukovar, now that corpses are rotting in the sun because it is unsafe for anyone to go outside to bury them, now that Bosnian Muslims are beginning to die of hunger because the enemy doesn't even give them the right to flee, geopolitical experts invited to speak on French radio and television are still blaming Croatian and Bosnian "nationalists" for having wanted independence too soon and for having thus led their people into a war in which, militarily speaking, they held the weaker hand.

In other words, Neville Chamberlain and Georges Bonnet were right in 1938 to follow the path of appeasement and, by the same token, Pétain was right in 1940 to adopt a policy of collaboration with Nazi Germany. Besides, the French, reasonable adults that they are, opted massively for the Pétainist line rather than the one proposed by De Gaulle, who was, after all, a fanatical and irresponsible nationalist.

But why stigmatize endlessly this episode in our history? What good does it do to express one's disgust over Vichy at the moment of the Touvier decision when, Vichyites in our dealings with the victims in Yugoslavia, we accuse them of collaborating in their own massacre and the destruction of their country as they choose to defy a cynical, lawless enemy.[1]

The same media – the same news and television – also announce that today there are over a million Yugoslav refugees, something that has not happened in Europe since the

Second World War. In the guise of providing hard information treated objectively, the media crystallize the ideology of this postideological age that we flatter ourselves unduly into believing we have entered. Because it is the Croatians and Muslims who are being chased from their homes by an army whose stated objective is not simply to conquer their territory but to "cleanse" these territories by displacing their inhabitants and by destroying their monuments – in short, by erasing every trace of their presence. To put it bluntly, these civilians are no longer Yugoslavs, and they are being punished for precisely that reason. They no longer wish to live in a Yugoslavia that, since Milosevic's accession to power, is merely the name used for what is in reality a Serb empire. Before they were refugees, these civilians were voters, and today they are paying for the crime of opting for self-determination. It is true that there are also Croatian-Serb refugees who have fled to Serbia, but many of these left Croatia after being informed by the federal army that the assault on Croatia was imminent.

In speaking in general terms of Yugoslav refugees, however, one doesn't speak of things as they are, one uses a red herring. In the place of the war of aggression that is actually taking place another war is substituted, an imaginary war, one into which nationalists in all the countries involved are supposedly throwing themselves, a war fought on the backs and at the expense of a population desirous only of living as before in a united Yugoslavia.

"Nothing that is human is foreign to me," affirm the proponents of humanism. "Nothing that is truly human interests me," asserts, to the contrary, the new humanitarian sensibility, which, the better to pity the refugees, strips them of their identities, their being, their raison d'être; that is to say, of all that which comprises their humanity. This new sensibility engenders passivity: one can react to an act of aggression, but what does one do except keep score, when dealing with these delirious inhabitants of the Balkans who are firing at each other from all sides? And let's not fool ourselves: Milosevic's extremism isn't nourished by the extremism of his adversaries but by our own passivity, which itself resembles our passivity of another period of history frequently invoked but never truly understood.[2]

After many months of failing to see things as they are, the United States seems at last to understand things. But our media experts, who know how to discern even the most carefully disguised motives, have discovered the real reason for James Baker's denunciation of "ethnic cleansing" in Bosnia-Herzegovina. The White House was simply getting back at Europe for emancipating itself from the American yoke. And these media experts will not fail to tell us tomorrow that we must let the events in the Balkans run their course or we will be capitulating to the United States. To each his own form of resistance.

NOTES

1. On 13 April 1992, the Paris Court of Appeals dropped charges against Paul Touvier of crimes against humanity for the execution of Jewish hostages at the end of the Occupation. The April 1992 decision shocked the nation and was partially overturned later the same year. Touvier eventually stood trial for crimes against humanity in March–April 1994. *Trans*.

2. Finkielkraut is referring here once again to the Vichy period. *Trans*.

## 12

# Sarajevo Twenty Days after
# François Mitterrand

*Libération*, 21 July 1992
It took guts and a real sense of timing to go and force the issue at Sarajevo, to secure the reopening of the airport through the weight of one's influence alone.

Undoubtedly our president was less alone than he appeared on the TV screen: his trip took place precisely seventy-eight years after the assassination of Archduke Ferdinand and the day before the UN ultimatum expired. This last event must have counted heavily in the decision of what are referred to as the Serb "irregulars" to allow the reopening of the airport. The fact remains, however, that Mitterrand came and saw, and after three months of no progress, a humanitarian breach, so to speak, has been opened in the siege of Sarajevo.

Somewhere between Moses and Cyrano de Bergerac, Mitterrand's accomplishment seemed nothing short of miraculous. It is only natural, therefore, that an editorialist, speaking with a pride legitimately shared by all Frenchmen, was able to write: "Two or three days after Mitterrand, the city so long cut off from the world was slowly able to begin living again and to receive aid brought in on the giant wings of cargo planes."

But where do things stand, some twenty days after François Mitterrand's visit? Planes are landing with impressive regularity in Sarajevo, the airport is the theatre of a remarkable humanitarian machine, but rather than the city coming back to life, those whose job is to sow death have regained control of the city. They gave the UN forces exactly three hours, and not a minute more, to enter the Dobrina quarter, distribute their care packages, and get out before the shelling resumed. And the Serbs also redoubled their attacks in the rest of Bosnia-Herzegovina and in Croatia in their stated aim of "purifying" and linking up the conquered territories. To put it bluntly, Mitterrand's miracle was a mirage; the presidential mission failed.

But this is certainly not François Mitterrand's fault. What is more, no one here seems to be aware of his failure. As if politics were solely a matter of images, most of the media continue to celebrate Mitterrand's panache ("Long live the France of Mitterrand in Sarajevo," reads the headline of a weekly magazine very much concerned with being up to date), and the president continues to find himself handsome in the mirror the media hold up to him. As for those supposedly succored through Mitterrand's efforts, they are loved as his foils, their applause is savored, their gratitude gives pleasure, their ecstasy is shared. But if they get it into their heads to request military intervention, as Slovenia, Croatia, and Bosnia-Herzegovina – all in dire straits – have recently done, their supplications move no one, and especially not France, which impassively proposes an international peace conference. In other words, the criminal Serbian actions of today will tomorrow become acceptable. They will also become the bases for negotiations. They will no longer be condemned. They will be discussed. Their interdiction will disappear in the process. In redoubling his efforts to conquer today, the aggressor proves that he has clearly understood the message.

Hasn't panache become in our democracies merely the window dressing our complacency toward brute force needs in order to make itself acceptable?

# 13

# The Boat Is Full

*La Tribune de Genève*, 31 July 1992

1108: that is the exact number of former Yugoslavians France boasts of allowing to enter the country to date. 1108, not one more, not one less. And not one of them can be counted as a refugee *stricto sensu* because French consulates deliver visas only to those who have family members already living in France. By way of comparison, one should remember that Germany is sheltering 200,000 persons uprooted by the war; Austria, Hungary, and Sweden about 50,000 each; and Switzerland about 20,000 persons.

The explanation for France's attitude has recently been given by the prime minister. "The solution to the problem at hand should be found on Yugoslavian soil," declared Pierre Bérégovoy. What does this statement have to do with the problem itself, and besides, who would contradict what Bérégovoy has asserted? Seeking asylum abroad is not what the victims of the war would want in the first instance. At best, asylum is only a temporary shelter one would seek while waiting for better days ahead. And what the Germans, the Swedes, the Austrians, and the Swiss are offering is not a solution but a resting place and temporary shelter. It is not a question of finding a "solution" but of making a gesture of hospitality. The High Commission for refugees certainly knows the difference, and so they are already at work on repatriation procedures for a time when a solution to the conflict has been found.

And if one were to reverse the situation and seriously seek a solution to the conflict, it is necessary, first of all, to furnish oneself with the means to bring about that solution. One must be ready to assume the political risks involved and stop the machine that functions so successfully in fabricating refugees, the Serbo-Yugoslav army. France, for one, has always been unwilling to consider a military response to the war and the ethnic cleansing that are ravaging Croatia and Bosnia-Herzegovina. At no time was the question even raised of sending arms to the besieged in order that they might defend their homes, or of assisting them through naval or aerial intervention. Reconstituting the Munich Axis, Paris and London took up Serbia's call for a peace conference, once ethnic cleansing in the conquered territories has been completed. The perpetrators of ethnic cleansing will themselves be participants in the conference. As a consequence, the chances of a repatriation of the refugees is nonexistent, and it is because France is aware of this that it hides behind closed shutters.

To put it bluntly, when one speaks of intervention, France responds by pointing to the spectacle of humanitarian aid to the region, and when a truly humanitarian gesture is asked of France, and not simply one fabricated by the media, the nation responds that the remedy is exclusively political. In effect, France tells the refugees to go and make themselves heard elsewhere and at the same time, through its own refusal to act in the face of Serb aggression, makes it impossible for them to remain in their homeland in the first place. Undoubtedly a nation has to be the land of the Rights of Man and of the Citizen to pull off such a feat.

# 14

# Bastards and Victims

*Le Figaro*, 3 August 1992

When the inhabitants of Sarajevo leave their basements to receive foodstuffs and other supplies brought to them by UN forces, their assembly in queues and their immobility while waiting in line make them easy targets for the Serb besiegers, who take advantage of the situation to kill even more people.

When these "beneficiaries of humanitarian aid" denounce the Serb attacks, General Mackenzie, the officer in charge of the blue helmets, accuses them of firing on themselves in order to project a more negative image of their adversaries.

When they fire back at their besiegers, Lord Carrington, in Belgrade, complains that they have violated the cease-fire more than is their fair share.

When in the place of the humanitarian sandwiches they receive and the military intervention that, to their chagrin, they are never offered, the besieged ask at the least for weapons with which to defend themselves, France responds by calling on them to attend a peace conference, the purpose of which is to renegotiate national borders and the status of minorities – which is to say, in reality, to accede to the demands of the aggressor.

When the new secretary-general of the UN, Mr. Boutros-Ghali, sees the faces of the refugees on television, he says they look fine to him and declares angrily to the Security Council that this "war among the rich" is getting too much attention and mobilizing too many resources.

This is certainly not the first time the international community is guilty of not coming to the aid of peoples facing death. But never before, perhaps, has hatred of the victims been expressed so freely.

Will it take twenty, thirty, or even forty years for our consciences to awaken at last and for the Committee for Bosnia-Croatia, composed of vigilant and prestigious intellectuals, to demand an international day of shame so that, at last, the world will express penitence for what happened and vow never to let it happen again?[1]

NOTE

1. The Committee for Bosnia-Croatia is presumably the Comité Vukovar-Sarajevo, which organized a public rally in the Latin Quarter on 21 November 1992. The committee was associated with the periodical *Esprit. Trans.*

# 15

# Insults and Abandonment

*Le Monde*, 9 August 1992

As time passes, it becomes more and more incomprehensible that the Allies did not think of slowing or halting completely the implementation of the Final Solution by, for example, bombing the railway tracks leading to the deathcamps. But at least the Allies were making war on the Nazis. Today, *the West wants to have peace*, and neither the destruction of Vukovar nor the horrific sieges of Sarajevo, Bihac, and Gorazde, nor the implementation of racial discrimination in all the regions occupied by Serbia, nor the existence of concentration camps in the self-proclaimed Serb Republic in Bosnia-Herzegovina, can dissuade the West from pursuing this primary objective.

In other words, the "peace" that the West defends is not, as it claims, a peace reflective of the progress of our civilization. It is the peace of "not bothering anybody," the peace of "leave me alone," with your sacked cities, your razed mosques, your babies assassinated by military irregulars, your burials bombarded, and your detainees paying for the sin of not being Serb while eating grass to stay alive.

In denouncing brute force in this instance, the European Twelve and the United States do not cite principles of law, as they usually proudly do. More prosaically, since their vital interests are not at stake, they respond to force with indignant protests and symbolic and humanitarian measures that have no dissuasive power over the aggressor and put those responsible for carrying them out at risk. Thus brute force continues *peacefully* in the accomplishment of its destructive ambitions. The combatants who are defending their liberty and thus have right on their side are even convened and asked to relinquish their arms. That is, they are asked to ratify a fait accompli of crime and conquest.

The television images of skeletal prisoners at Omarska Trnopolje have, it is true, forced the West to adopt a more strident tone – from now on humanitarian aid brought to Bosnia will be protected by military means. But the West's political objectives have not changed: in order for peace to come about, the West continues to insist that the weaker must in essence give in to the stronger.[1]

Despite the grandiose rhetoric surrounding it and the impressive diplomatic maneuvers it sets in motion, this political "realism" remains unpalatable. The West is therefore obliged to insist that *all* the belligerents are possessed of the same demon of hatred; the reality of the crime is dissolved in references to the "complexity" of the situation. The difference between besiegers and besieged is effaced by the expression "rival factions." One worries over the fate of minorities when it is the majorities who are chased from their homes, massacred, or starved to death in concentration camps. The Croatians are repeatedly accused of the same crimes as their aggressors, and in this fashion, an imperialist, ethnocidal, total war carried out by the Serbs in full view and with the full knowledge of everyone is transformed into an indiscriminate "Yugoslavian chaos." In short, the victims are insulted in order to justify their abandonment. And unfortunately, the "West," in this case, is above all France, its president, its Quay d'Orsay, its television, and its experts. If there were truly one ounce of a "duty to memory" in our commemorations, then the fiftieth anniversary of the Vélodrome d'Hiver would have dictated a very different comportment vis-à-vis the conflict in the Balkans.

NOTE

1. At the Serb concentration camp at Omarska Trnopolje in Bosnia, between three and five thousand Bosnian Muslims and Croatians were detained in horrific conditions. British journalists Penny Marshall and Ed Vulliamy visited the camp and revealed its brutalities. *Trans.*

# 16

# Let's Not Add War to War

*Le Figaro*, 18 August 1992

Having received a desperate message from Bosnian President Alija Izetbegovic comparing the situation of the inhabitants of Sarajevo to that of the fighters of the Warsaw Ghetto, François Mitterrand, listening only to his courage, rushed to the Bosnian capital accompanied by his minister for humanitarian aid.

Things having gotten worse since Mitterrand's visit in Sarajevo as well as in Gorazde and Bihac. Bosnia has asked the West to intervene militarily, or, failing that, to lift the embargo on arms to the region so as to reduce the arms imbalance that is currently so unfavorable to the besieged. This time, listening only to his "wisdom," the president of the French republic offered his response to Bosnia's request in the newspaper *Sud-Ouest*, asserting that one should not "add war to war."

At the same moment, General Mackenzie, who until recently commanded the UN force assigned to protect Sarajevo, declared in *Time* magazine that references to a possible armed intervention only lulled the government of Alija Izetbegovic with harmful illusions. As long as rumors of a military intervention circulate, the general implied, the Bosnians will continue to believe in the possibility that territories conquered by the Serbs will be restored to them, and they will thus continue to refuse to negotiate a cease-fire.

So the general and the president deliver the same message about the war in the former Yugoslavia: after a year of cultural vandalism and ethnic cleansing without equal in Europe since the time of Hitler, a humanitarian West calls for the immediate and unconditional capitulation of the aggressed. In other words, it does not defend right in the face of crimes; it wants peace, peace immediately, peace at all costs, even if it must be bought at the expense of what is right, if all this amounts to rewarding crime.

But France will always be France and "form" will always be its most precious trump card. Our president thus certainly possesses more eloquence than the Canadian general. "Adding war to war will resolve nothing" sounds a lot better than "Acknowledge your defeat, lay down your arms, and surrender!" It sounds so good that one is surprised that Pétain's speechwriters, known for their talent for translating dishonor into virtue, hadn't already whispered this masterful expression to the marshall years ago.

Following the publication of this article, a reader, whom unfortunately I cannot thank personally because he or she preferred to remain anonymous, sent me the following "communiqué":

COMMUNIQUÉ (1944)

We, the undersigned, Dwight Eisenhower, Supreme Commander of Allied Forces, and Bernard Montgomery, Commander-in-Chief of Land Forces, declare that while we understand the intentions of those who have stated their support for military intervention, we do not share their convictions. The nature of the terrain, notably in the landing zone comprised of Utah Beach, Omaha Beach, Sword, Juno, and Gold, as well as the power of the armaments possessed by the enemy would doom any military intervention. It therefore seems to us that the most prudent course of action under the present circumstances is a negotiated solution. The opposing army is ready for the fight and one would also run the risk of encountering resistance fighters or rebels. The proposed plan of attack known as Operation Overlord should, therefore, not be implemented since other means for obtaining a peaceful solution to the conflict are possible. A military assault against Nazi forces would prove to be a most difficult ordeal. To escalate the conflict, to add war to war, so to speak, would accomplish nothing. Efficacy, not military adventurism, must be our highest priority. Our soldiers should not be treated as so many toy soldiers. Finally, as concerns the camps of "ethnic purification," one should follow the line of the International Red Cross which affirms that, for the moment, there is no reason to believe they are extermination camps. If they were in fact extermination camps, it would of course be desirable to set up as quickly as possible an international commission composed of experts charged with the task, in the least amount of time possible, of finding synonyms for the expressions "concentration camp" or "extermination camp" that would be more palatable to European public opinion.

*Dwight Eisenhower, Supreme Commander of*
*Allied Forces in Europe*
*Bernard Montgomery, Commander-in-Chief of*
*Ground Forces*

# 17

# The French Exception

*Libération*, 1 September 1992

Everyone in France fears Germany. Some assert that the Europe of Maastricht is already a Germanified Europe. Others argue that if one wants to control, integrate, and Westernize German might, it is essential to ratify the treaty to create a European Union.

And it never occurs to anyone that there are reasons to be wary today of France. Only Germany, in the eyes of the French, is disquieting; only Germany is possessed of evil demons. This line of reasoning deserves scrutiny.

Certainly France, which no longer has the means for doing so, does not practice a politics based on force. Moreover, wherever possible, she gives in to force. There is even a specifically and inimitably French way of bowing to force in the name of justice while mobilizing fears of a renascent Pan-Germanism. All of this while playing along with the two active Reichs in the world of today, the Syrians in Lebanon and Serbia in Croatia and Bosnia-Herzegovina. Raymond Aron has distinguished fairly recently between two types of peace: peace through right and peace imposed by empire. In the former Yugoslavia, France has chosen the second option from the beginning of the conflict, through her call, borrowed from Serbia, for an international peace conference that would confirm the Serb victory while allowing for a few hollow concessions from the latter to keep up appearances. But, all noblesse oblige, France has disguised this disdain for rights as a concern for rights – the rights of minorities, to be exact, or to be even more precise, the rights of Serb minorities living in the newly created republics occupying the old Yugoslav space. As if the war itself had not been started by the Serbs to permit all Serbs to live in the same state; that is, no longer to be in the minority anywhere.

Thus France is legitimizing the return of wars of conquest to European soil, all the while repeating through the mouths of her president and foreign minister that international law does not recognize the borders of the new republics created on the soil of the former Yugoslavia. It is the French minister of education *and culture* who treats as "macho beach boys too fond of video games" his rare compatriots who are European enough to believe and to state that Europe can no longer condone, through its inaction, what the former mayor of Belgrade, Bogban Bogdanovitch, calls the "ritual massacre of cities" in Croatia and in Bosnia-Herzegovina. It is in France that Ideology has taken refuge in so-called expertise, and that geographers will explain to you, maps in hand, that Serbia needs access to the sea, or that the Serbs and Croats alike are in the process of dividing up poor Bosnia at the expense of the Muslims, who, for their part, wish to keep the country intact.

The idea of cantonizing the country on the Swiss model is a (bad) European idea, *and therefore also a French idea*. And yet the French persist in their errors, even though, in the Derventa region, Croatia does not come to the aid of ethnic Croatians in Bosnia because they fear offending world opinion, and the Serbs take advantage of this to chase out whole populations, raze villages, annex territory, and create a corridor that would tie together Serbia, the Serb Republic in Bosnia-Herzegovina, and the Krajina region stolen from Croatia; even though the Croato-Muslim city of Mostar, formerly an architectural jewel, is now a pile of ruins; and finally even though, despite the fact their interests and strategies occasionally diverge, the vast majority of Bosnian Muslims uprooted by the Serb army are welcomed in Croatia.

Europe, America, and the UN refuse all political assistance to the victims of Serb aggression, but it is France that refuses to "add war to war" when non-Serbs in Bosnia ask for access to the weapons that will allow them to remain where they are. When these non-Serbs ask for asylum in France, the door is closed in their faces and they are told to find a solution to the conflict that will allow them to remain at home.

It is this French line of reasoning, brutalized more than that of any other nation by humanitarian discourse, that, by subsuming in the same pejorative term *war* acts of aggression and the right to defend oneself, refuses to grant the victims of aggression the right to defend themselves. It is the same antitotalitarian elite in France that, succumbing to the technique of amalgamation after having tirelessly denounced it during the Cold War, transforms the practice of ethnic cleansing – put into effect and espoused by the Serbs – into just another symptom of an *interethnic* night where all cats are almost equally gray.

For almost an entire year, it was in France that news of the Yugoslav war followed sports news or, more precisely, the sporting exploits of the French. In other words, it is in France that one criticizes the national aspirations of others while simultaneously indulging in an exacerbated chauvinism.

It is in France, and nowhere else, that partisans of the European Union treaty proclaim: "Long live Europe so that peace will reign!" as if peace was reigning now and it was only a question of massaging this state of affairs! As if *hic et nunc*, at this very moment, on our continent, among us, a war wasn't taking place, and a criminal war at that. It is also in France that the opponents of Maastricht in their majority stigmatize the disappearance of the Yugoslav state and blame a German will to power for the outbreak of hostilities.[1] Jean-Pierre Chevènement and Philippe Séguin both affirm that if blood is now flowing in the region, it is because Europe recognized *too soon* the new republics that had voted in favor of their own independence.[2] And Europe acted thus precipitately, they continue, because Germany, true to its history, presented its partners, or more precisely its vassals, with a fait accompli and forced them to follow suit. The fact is that Germany recognized Slovenia and Croatia on 23 December 1991 – that is, *after* the destruction of Vukovar, *after* the bombardment of the historic center of Dubrovnik, *during* the siege of Osijek, and after the war against Croatia had already lasted six months, killing around ten thousand people and forcing another five hundred thousand Croatians to flee their homes. At a time when our former allies, the Serbs, are committing ethnocide with impunity in the Balkans, our two champions of "the French exception" are calling, through the intermediary of the Serbs, for a struggle against the hegemony of the hereditary enemy.

General de Gaulle once stated that "there is a very secular pact between the grandeur of France and freedom in the world." This pact was broken once by France a half century ago in betraying Central Europe. France is doing the same thing again today. But perched on the pedestal of her past glory, she continues to preach to the world. Offering cynicism and medicines – both of which serve Serb ends to a T while conjuring up a humanitarian smoke screen – France has become the land of duplicity par excellence.

"Right or wrong, my country" is not a patriotic motto. I love France, I love my country, but France has succumbed to the demon "impostor" and, until things change, she is more dangerous than Germany. And so if it is true that the European Union will weaken France's power to do harm, then it is necessary to say "yes" to Maastricht.

NOTES

1. Finkielkraut is here referring to Germany's recognition of Croatia in 1991. *Trans.*

2. Chevènement is currently minister of the interior in the Socialist government of Lionel Jospin, and Séguin is leader of the parliamentary opposition. *Trans.*

# 18

# What Is a Nation? – Second Episode

September 1992
"Europe," writes Milan Kundera, "is the maximum of diversity in the minimum amount of space." And, as if by echo, Ludvik Vaculik asserts: "The European spirit, as multiform as the contours of the continent itself, is born of contradictions and relativism. . . . Each one of us is defined not only by what we think of ourselves but by what others recognize in us."

Referring to this Old World uniqueness, certain French politicians claim that sacrificing these national sovereignties on the altar of economic power amounts to undoing rather than constructing Europe.

The argument has its strong points. But, mysteriously, in the eyes of these politicians, what applies to us Frenchmen – current members of the European Community – doesn't apply to the people of the former Yugoslavia. We are expressly invited to defend the treasure of our diversity against a driveling, reductive, and unifying centralism, while those who wished to shake off the yoke of Yugoslav centralism and give life to the idea of the diversity of nations are severely reprimanded and even accused of having provoked the war.

Why this different treatment? Why aren't the criteria applied equally in both cases? Because there are nations and there are nations, reply the French specialists of humanity, and because the Slovenians and Croatians, followed by the Macedonians and the poor Bosnia-Herzegovinians, opted for a retrograde ethnic concept of nationhood, as opposed to the progressive, emancipatory and republican model France has brought to the world and which is incarnated in *Yugoslav* patriotism.

We know that these two theories of nationhood – one ethnic, the other elective – opposed each other in Europe after 1870 and in the context of Alsace-Lorraine. The great German historians Strauss and Mommsen said at the time that since the two provinces were German in language, tradition, and culture, they belonged legitimately in the German empire – and so their return to a victorious Germany was dictated not only by historical fact but by right as well. To which their French counterparts Renan and Fustel de Coulanges responded that one could not ignore the opinions of the interested parties and that the "wish to live together," the explicit adhesion of individuals – in short, the sense of belonging to a nation – was the crucial factor in constituting one. Renan and Fustel de Coulanges did not deny that a nation was a cultural community as well as a community of shared destiny – "Man," affirmed Renan in his celebrated speech, "does not improvise himself." What they did vociferously condemn was the notion that one could brandish the cultural argument in order to deny to a people the right to choose their own destiny.

The successors of Renan and Fustel are now accomplishing a veritable tour de force in refusing to grant this right to the people of the former Yugoslavia. When the latter express this desire they are sent home from school with the following criticism on their report cards: "aggravated ethnocentricity." The French instructors invoke the principle "the desire to live together" in order better to denounce the legitimate desire of the peoples of the former Yugoslavia. Without shame, the French instructors pontificate on the elective model in order to denounce actual election results. They make reference to the lovely metaphor "plebiscite" in order to declare nul and void the referenda that vanquished the ethnolinguistic myths of Slavic unity and that put an end to the pseudo-federation this myth secreted. Indifferent as well to the *irreparable* cultural damage inflicted on their enemies by the Serbs, our French instructors proclaim that there is no future for Yugoslavia other than Yugoslavia, no destiny for these nations other than a few changes in the arrangement of their forced marriage: "Today, again," affirms one of the most fervent proponents of the French idea of nationhood, "peace is unimaginable if the renovation of the idea of Yugoslavia, even in a very flexible form, is abandoned. . . . France, which played a crucial role in the creation of Yugoslavia in the first place, is now in a position to act efficaciously in constructing a third Yugoslavia."[1]

And so here are the Slovenians, the Croatians, the Macedonians, and the Albanians of Kosovo condemned to a life sentence in Yugoslavia, as, in the past, were the Alsatians in Germany. The ethnic theory and the elective theory of nationhood are changing roles. Whether out of laziness or a misguided projection of the Jacobin idea onto a political reality to which it does not apply, or perhaps out of anti-German sentiment or an immutable fidelity to an alliance forged with Serbia in 1914, those French who are the most well versed in France's message, those citizens most proud of belonging to a European community that has championed a nation's right to determine its own destiny, those individuals have turned these doctrines on their respective ears to save an empire furious over its own dissolution.

NOTE

1. Jean-Pierre Chevènement, "De Maastricht à Sarajevo," *Libération* 2 (Sept. 1992).

# 19

# "If This Is a Man . . ."

*Le Monde*, 15 September 1992
Shocked a few weeks ago by the images coming in from the concentration camps in Bosnia-Herzegovina, certain of the most influential figures from the world of politics and the media spoke out in favor of measures that would at last be commensurate with the horror of the events themselves. Then, taking into account that these measures would not be realized and that the inertia of Europe risked chilling the pro-European ardor of a portion of public opinion, these same influential figures reproached themselves for not thinking before speaking out on the camps in Bosnia, and quickly tried to forget a reality that risked distracting public opinion from the Maastricht Accords.

In the recesses of their hearts, however, these individuals were not proud of themselves. They had guilty consciences. "Maastricht is certainly worth an ethnic cleansing" – this is surely a line of reasoning with which one feels uncomfortable, even in an occasional conversation with oneself. Hence the sense of relief when this elite learned that the Bosnians themselves had fired on a UN convoy and killed two French soldiers. The besieged thus revealed themselves to be as barbaric as the besiegers. No more good guys, no more bad guys: one could in all good conscience return to one's own affairs. But the camps, of course, remained open. Mr. Mazowiecki, the emissary from the international community, was denied access to one of the camps by a Serb commandant, who told him that the detainees were tired out from all the visits they had received from international organizations. Meanwhile, snipers continue to blow the heads off newborn babies in Sarajevo – but henceforth it is legitimate, and even recommended, *not* to be moved or affected by such horrors. Over there, they are just a bunch of assassins who kill each other between ambushes of UN soldiers of peace.

If you respond that the encirclement of Sarajevo is not the fault of its victims, or that the expression "soldiers of peace" is ludicrous in the present context; if you agree that the political strategy of the Bosnians in attacking UN soldiers is atrocious, evil, and inadmissible but also testifies to their despair at not being defended and their sense that foodstuffs are being distributed by international aid organizations so that they, the Bosnians, will die with their bellies full; if you are indignant at hearing General Morillon, second in command of UN forces, declare: "It is necessary that the international community clearly state that no military solution to this conflict is possible, only a political one, and the latter can only be worked out around a table in Geneva," because you know that this lovely expression "political solution" really means the capitulation of the besieged, which is to say the victory of the Serb camp commandant who defied Mazowiecki – know that your revolt is in vain. You have absolutely no chance of being heard by the important people who are in charge. Those who count, without having his reasons, resemble the French soldier interrogated in Belgrade just after the death of his comrades, who does not wish to return to Sarajevo to risk his life for "those assholes."

In the poem that opens his greatest book, Primo Levi writes:

> *You who live safe*
> *In your warm houses,*
> *You who find, returning in the evening,*
> *Hot food and friendly faces:*
> > *Consider if this is a man*
> > *Who works in the mud*
> > *Who does not know peace*

*How Can One Be Croatian?*

*Who fights for a scrap of bread*
*Who dies because of a yes or a no.* [1]

Sarajevo is not Auschwitz, nor the camp of Omarska. But if it is merely an "asshole" and not a man who dies according to someone's whim, everything becomes marvelously simple. There are no more reasons to argue with oneself when evening comes, nor scruples to live with in the warmth of one's house, one's country, or the European Community.

NOTE

1. Primo Levi, "If This is a Man," in *"If This Is a Man" and "The Truce,"* trans. Stuart Woolf (London: Sphere Books, Abacus, 1987), 17. *Trans.*

## 20

# The Perfect Crime

*Le Monde*, 15 October 1992

A year ago the Croatians were accused of breaking the back of the Yugoslav state. During the siege of Vukovar, they were judged guilty of the crime of exposing this town and its inhabitants to destruction by choosing to fight when they had no chance of winning. Today, they are accused of acting like thieves on the loose, along with the Serbs, in Bosnia-Herzegovina, where they are supposedly following the same expansionist ambitions as their Serb partners. First they were separatists, then they were fanatics, and now they are colonists.

The French media pay a great deal of attention to the tensions between Croatians and Muslims. The idea continues to circulate that Serbs and Croatians are in cahoots to destroy Yugoslavia, to dismember Bosnia, and to build at the expense of their Algerians or Palestinians their own little empires, one called Greater Serbia and the other Greater Croatia.

This is a very useful grievance because it allows the French, who hate to be disoriented, to approach what is new with their habitual categories intact and to justify their initial partiality. But this is an absurd grievance; it is not because the aggressor knew how to divide his enemies – not all Croatians, by any means – and play the interests of one group (those who sought an accord) against the interests of the other (those who wished to continue the struggle) that there are not two victims and one aggression. Under the same pretexts, the same devastating war of conquest spread from Croatia to Bosnia-Herzegovina, the same fire was started, the same tragedy occurred. And besides, if the Croatians of western Bosnia and Herzegovina – a region where they comprise 95 percent of the population – had relied on the Bosnian army to defend them, they would have been annihilated by Serb forces. Finally, the decision to let the fledgling Republic of Bosnia-Herzegovina die was not made by the Croatians but by the West, which, in a phenomenon unique in the annals of international affairs, confirmed the right to existence of this state and at the same time, through an arms embargo, refused it the right to defend that very existence. As complicated (or naive) as were the negotiations in Geneva, the diplomatic game continued while the ethnic cleansing of *Croatians* was reaching its final phase in Banja Luca. At Jacje, bombs were falling indiscriminately, while at Bosanski Brod, Croatians and Muslims were massacred and expelled from their pillaged town, having together futilely resisted Serb efforts to assume definitive control of the region linking Serbia to the Krajina by conquering the town.

Journalists and politicians who denounce Croatian aims are misunderstanding the war and letting the West off the hook for its crushing responsibility in the whole affair. And tomorrow, once Serb aggression has been sanctioned and the Bosnian Republic buried, when the Croats of western Herzegovina ask to be reintegrated into Croatia, the same journalists and politicians will exclaim triumphantly: "I told you so!" and assert that Croatia has shown its true face.

And so, real progress having been made since the days of Munich, the West will be spared the shame of its shameful conduct. The English call this a "self-fulfilling prophecy." In letting the imperialism of Greater Serbia have a free hand, the West will have done everything to let events transpire so that its own abdication will be transformed into a premonition. In this fashion, access to the truth will be forever denied.

# Writings on the Balkan Conflict,

## 1993−96

# 21

# Introduction to Part 3

Imprecation is not one of my strong points, and I am neither an expert in nor a specialist on the Balkans. In addition, since I lack any sentimental or family attachment in the region, nothing predisposes me to being called derisively "Finkiel-croate" as a consequence of positions I took during the recent wars in Croatia and in Bosnia.

Nothing unless, perhaps, the reading of an older text by Kundera, "Un Occident kidnappé ou la tragédie de l'Europe centrale" (A kidnapped West or the tragedy of Central Europe). Central Europe: in resurrecting this lost name, Kundera unsettled the perception shared by a waning progressive and a triumphant antitotalitarian thought; he repatriated, geographically to the Center and spiritually to the West, an entire world whose place in the East was no longer a problem for anyone.

This Europe, Kundera underlined, is not the Germanic *MittelEurope* but "the uncertain zone of small nations between Russia and Germany." And he defined the small nation in these terms: "The small nation is the one whose existence can at any time be questioned, which can disappear and which knows it. A Frenchman, a Russian, and an Englishman don't ordinarily ask questions about their nation's survival. Their national anthems speak only of grandeur or eternity. But Poland's national anthem begins: 'Poland has not yet perished'."[1]

If I could not bring myself to submerge in a vague tribal rage all the protagonists of the conflict that began with the entry of the Yugoslav army into Slovenia and that found temporary conclusion in the Dayton agreements, I owe it all to Kundera. Through the essays and speeches collected in this part of *Dispatches from the Balkan War*, I have tried to overcome the oblivion facing Central Europe and the prejudice against small nations. This has been useless, alas, even with those who have finally recognized the need to use force to stop Serb aggression. And I then discovered that arrogance was not the only thing at issue: in the eyes of most people, the word *nationalism* summarizes this century's evil. "Nationalism, that's the enemy," is what most of the large European countries concluded after two world wars. Combating it provides a solution to every problem. In this fashion they presume that memory lives on in them, but this supposed memory blinds them no less to past tragedies than to present-day reality. The war Hitler started in 1939 was an imperial war, a war that aimed at empire, as Raymond Aron demonstrated in 1943: "Among the ideas that, by definition, the Hitlerian empire and the justification of that empire had to aim to destroy, figure first of all the two related notions of the national state and of the right of nationalities, large and small, to enjoy self-determination. In effect, it is clear that a victorious Germany, unifying Europe under its law, would not let anything subsist that essentially made for a nation's political independence or cultural autonomy. Hence, against this mortal threat, the United Nations has taken up the watchwords of the last war, only because on the Continent, one resists the invader with the cries of 'Long live Poland!', 'Long live France!', and 'Long live Holland!' Free nations or tyrannical empire, that is the meaning, for Europe, of this European war."[2]

This meaning has been lost. In the name of "Never that again!" we have leaned for support on one catastrophe in order to authorize another. Hence the tormenting question that haunts these pages: how do we explain that a memory so obsessed with barbarity can be, at the same time, so fallacious? Of what use, then, has the twentieth century been?

*Alain Finkielkraut*

NOTES

1. Milan Kundera: "Un Occident kidnappé ou la tragédie de l'Europe centrale," *Le Débat* 27 (Nov. 1983): 15.

2. Raymond Aron, *Destin des nationalités*, War Chronicles series (Gallimard, 1990), 613–14.

## 22

# The Demands of the Day

*Le Monde*, 16 December 1992

It's because the situation is too complex in Bosnia-Herzegovina that the international community cannot do for the Muslims and Croatians what it does for the Somalians. This is what the recipient of the Nobel Peace Prize, Elie Wiesel, has just affirmed.

But where is the complexity? In response to the democratically affirmed will of the captive nations of Yugoslavia to win back their freedom, Serbia has declared war unilaterally, and its aim, vertiginous in its simplicity, is to conquer territories by emptying them in every possible way of their non-Serb inhabitants. As for the arguments used – "We are protecting our minorities; we are killing in order not to be killed; we are merely preventing measures against the genocides fomented against us by the Croatians in Croatia, by the Muslims in Bosnia, and by the Albanians in Kosovo" – they have an air of déjà-vu about them, and they come from a paranoia devoid of all mystery. All the grand persecutors of modern history have lived as though they were being persecuted; they have all exterminated *under the claim of legitimate defense*. Wasn't it the Jewish project to dominate the world and destroy Germany that the Nazis attacked?

The complexity invoked is the alibi of our defeatism. And the chasm never stops growing between the Yugoslav reality and the "anti-genocide system" that the new law of humanitarian support should constitute for its backers. The humanitarian system is in place in the former Yugoslavia, but the racial war is also and will be for another ten years, if we believe General Momir Talic, commandant of the first Serb corps of Bosnia-Herzegovina. Hardly more intimidating than the cameras whose dissuasive powers we praised not long ago; assistance helps . . . perpetuate the crime. Humanitarian aid merely notes the massive violations of the no-fly zone; it simply records the Serb refusal to allow the Croatians chased from the Krajina region or from eastern Slavonia to return home; it coexists with deportations, destruction, and massacres. For lack of any show of international or European force, which, contrary to what detractors say, could be limited to air strikes, the ambulance driver is condemned to working along with the assassin. Between the "all" of sending several hundred thousand men into Bosnia and the "nothing" of letting this "war among the rich," in the horrible expression of Mr. Boutros-Ghali, take its course, lies the necessity for some real aid to the besieged. For we can no longer get by with words alone: the charitable option, if it helps some victims, gives free rein to the butchers and reveals itself to be *much less humane* than the military option, to the detriment of which it has been chosen. The same General Talic is not mistaken when he welcomes the trip of President Mitterrand to Sarajevo as "a gesture representing a very great hope for peace in the region."

In order to have General Talic finally despair, in order truly to bring assistance to the peoples he is helping decimate, and for the peace to be something other than the realization of all the racist and territorial objectives of Serbia, humanitarianism is no longer enough. Only what Thomas Mann in 1935 called a "*militant* humanism," "a humanism that would discover its virility," is capable of breaking the present alliance of cynicism and sentimentality: "If European humanism is no longer capable of a burst that would make its ideas pugnacious, if it is no longer capable of being aware of its own soul, then it will perish, and a Europe will subsist that continues to bear this name in a historical sense only, and before which it would be better to seek refuge in the indifference of timelessness."

# 23

# Revisionism

*Le Monde*, 15 January 1993

The partisans and detractors of military intervention in Bosnia who are arguing with one another these days in the media seem to agree about one thing. They say that Europe has made the Yugoslav federation explode by recognizing Slovenia and Croatia too early. But this is to forget that in June 1991, when Germany had begged France and its other European partners to welcome into the society of nations the two republics that had just declared their independence after failing, because of Belgrade's intransigence, to reform Yugoslavia, Europe said no. France, with its will to preserve at all cost the status quo and its diplomacy of appeasement, won out over Germany. The Germans had to give in to French pressure, and not the reverse.

Certainly, recognition was finally given, but only seven months later, once Croatia's campaign was over. If we had then mobilized for Vukovar as we finally did for Sarajevo, we could have avoided the siege of Sarajevo and saved the Muslims of Bosnia-Herzegovina from the war of annihilation the Serbs explicitly planned for them.

So at no time can Europe be accused of having acted too hastily. From the recognition of the republics to putting pressure on Serbia, it has always decided too late, when the evil of conquest and ethnic cleansing was over. That's the truth. It is unbearable. But all the rest is revisionism.

# 24

# The Peacemakers

*The Dream of Peace without Intervention Ends Up*
*Prolonging the War*

*Le Figaro*, 3 February 1993

In 1945, it was necessary to defeat Nazi Germany in order to make peace with Germany and establish the basis for the construction of Europe. The military victory made the political solution possible.

In the Balkans today, we want peace without pain. We want to convince the aggressor rather than defeat or stop him, even though he has used methods that violate all the laws of war and do not even come close to ending his project.

Hence the significant return to a diplomacy carried out along a lake: the international community brings the besieger and the besieged together in Geneva without even requiring the first to suspend his ethnic cleansing or interrupt his bombing raids. And, as the refusal to resort to any threat of arms has deprived the international community of every means to threaten, it has proposed a plan that takes into account the military situation. To whit, in the field, the Croatians of Herzegovina have pushed the Serbs back and kept them from establishing their border on the Neretva, while the Serbs have crushed the Muslims to the north and to the east of Bosnia. Consequently Muslims are the big losers of the partition. Observing that the "new world order" easily sacrifices its principles to the fait accompli, they quite naturally prefer to try enlarging their territory by using force against the Serbs on the Drina and against the Croatians in central Bosnia, rather than signing what appears to them to be a capitulation.

The dream of peace without intervention therefore ends up with still more war. That troubles the partisans of this option, but it doesn't move them at all. On the contrary. "They are all savages!" is what they say triumphantly, now that the victims of Serb aggression are tearing each other up. There is no more crime for them, but universal guilt. Henceforth evil is everywhere; that is, nowhere. And so now, having enjoyed for over two years the total freedom to maneuver, those who have actualized the principle that "wherever a Serb boot has trampled the ground, there is Serbia" are now about to obtain their acquittal. After impunity, innocence. The peacemakers, one more time, will have merited the recognition of their fellow barbarians.

# 25

# Two Europes

Speech Given at the Conference at Osijek, February 1993
I would first like to thank you for attending this conference and tell you that I'm sorry so many of you can't be seated. So, in solidarity, I'm going to remain standing.

I hope that I'm up to your expectations. I'm not sure I am, because yesterday I left for Osijek and Vinkovci in Slavonia, and I have only just arrived from Vinkovci a half hour ago. So I ask for your indulgence, and I shall begin with this trip that is still fresh in my mind. So I went to Osijek and Vinkovci and, thanks to the goodness of the people who welcomed me in these two cities, I saw Osijek's theatre or what remained of it, Vinkovci's library, or what remained of it, and also what remains of its hospital.

Of course I knew that these cities had been hard hit by the war. I knew that the aggressors had particularly aimed for the hospitals and places of cultural interest, but there is quite a difference between knowing and seeing, between seeing something on television and seeing it for real.

So I was struck by the contrast between this horror written in stone and the coolness of France and Europe's reactions.

Then at Osijek and Vinkovci, I again asked myself the question I have been asking since July 1991: why this contrast, why this chasm between the horror and the indifference?

And then I thought about Stefan Zweig's book, which I have been reading and reread periodically. It's called *Le Monde d'hier: Souvenirs d'un Européen (The World of Yesterday)*.

In this book (which shows, moreover, what was for a long time Zweig's political naivete), he refers to an event in Europe in 1905: the pogrom of Kichinev. Today Kichinev is in Romania but it was then in Russia, and the pogrom that occurred there had been organized by the czar's police, and it made victims of between forty and fifty among Kichinev's Jewish population.

And Stefan Zweig says that the news of this pogrom was reported immediately throughout Europe, and it provoked shock and a universal sense of scandal. And from that point Stefan Zweig reflects and observes that Nazism's worst legacy has been, in some way, to dull the sensitivity of public opinion by raising the ante in scandal and horror.

This absolute horror in a way established a kind of record and, at the same time as arousing indignation, you might say it made public opinion demand more extreme reasons for becoming indignant. It needed more killings and more destruction than a simple pogrom. That's what Hitler's legacy has left us.

But I think that the civilization of images in which we live, far from making things better, aggravates them even more and allows us to follow Stefan Zweig's reasoning. Horror presented by television has become our daily bread, the individual's natural environment. A kind of mood music for his comfort. The same goes for horror – if I can throw out this risky and shocking comparison – the same goes for horror as for rock music. Rock, Milan Kundera recently remarked, is a music that has freed itself from melody to become a kind of continuous ecstasy.

This music of ecstasy, which we hear everywhere and can't keep from hearing, has also become the daily background for our weariness. We live a life that is always more routine and more regulated within the double environment of horror and ecstasy.

And thus do pictures at once sharpen our compassion and at the same time silence it because, in this kind of mood, in this environment of horror, we aren't able to distinguish between particular horrors. After Hitler, what – in our picture civilization – is the destruction of a theatre, or a hospital, or a library; what is the destruction of three-fourths of a village like Nustar? We need at least something like Sarajevo's destruction to get our attention.

We can say, it is true, that we who live in a world saturated with images and who live in this society, in this post-totalitarian, post-Hitlerian world, we are nevertheless Europeans, and this destruction of a theatre and a library of some eighty-six thousand volumes should have hurt our European conscience. And instead of wondering – with stupor, with condescension, even with repulsion – how one can be Croatian, we should have felt ourselves attacked in our own Europeanness by the bombs that touched our own heritage.

And if we haven't, if by a large majority public opinion has not reacted in this way, it's because of another effect or another damaging effect of this civilization of the picture.

On the one hand, I said that the continuous representation of horror dulls our sensitivity to horror; but on the other hand, the picture does give us a feeling – and it is this feeling that has changed everything, that has changed the world – the feeling of being equally situated in relation to everything.

That is why I think we can say, without fearing the solemnity of the statement, that television has introduced a veritable ontological break. Before television, man was in situation, to use an expression Sartre liked; since television, man is equally situated in relation to everything.

He sees the world from above. He has attained a kind of observation point outside the world, which lets him observe the planet. If you notice the credits for the television news programs in all the countries of the world, they show you the planet Earth. They show you the Earth as though you didn't live on the Earth. For the inhabitant of Earth, the Earth is not a planet, it is a land. And it is for the inhabitant of the Earth that the concept of situation has meaning. For the individual uprooted from the Earth, emancipated from his terrestrial condition by television, the concept of situation no longer has meaning because he is equally situated in relation to everything. Then he sees Osijek, Vinkovci, like the famine in Somalia, like the civil war in the Sudan, or like the civil war in India. He doesn't inhabit the Earth, he looks at the planet's convulsions. And from time to time when he is too touched or shaken by horror, he rushes, like Superman, to one of the places on the planet that seems to need his help.

The humanitarian action being developed today in our countries is, if you like, one of the consequences and one of the effects of this uprooting from the Earth. It is an action of men who no longer inhabit the Earth but who look at it from on high and who fly (the word should be understood in its proper sense) to help the victims, as in the Superman comic books.

And I think that this ontological break explains, in the end, the lack of comprehension and the misunderstanding between Croatia and the rest of the world. Because this television viewer's position, this fact of being equally situated in relation to everything, inevitably shapes people's political conscience and always modifies the very meaning of the concepts, values, and ideals to which they subscribe.

For the man who considers the Earth as a planet, who sees things from above, all borders are anachronistic and obsolete. He desires, he wants the real world, the political world, to rejoin the universe in which television and technology have him live. And if he celebrates Europe, it's not because of his past or because Europe is for him a community of destiny. All of that still refers to the old useless concept "situation." It is because Europe is a step in the right direction.

The right direction would be the total synchronization of an absolute coincidence between politics and technology – when in politics all men would also be equally situated in relation to everything.

In this perspective Europe would be good because it's big, because it's larger than what is too small. Because this perspective has taken over the concept of Europe, the Croatians have not been understood and were notably misunderstood when they claimed for themselves a European heritage and when they said to outraged Europeans: it is your heritage that they are murdering today. They were talking about a Europe before the ontological break; they were talking about a Europe with inhabitants on the Earth. They were talking about a Europe in situation, and that Europe no longer has any meaning for those who no longer live on the Earth but look at the planet. It's because an extraterrestrial mentality has become widespread that Croatians have been regarded by other Europeans as though they were Martians.

Now I don't want to stop here but would like to continue but do so in another format, if that meets with your approval. And, eventually, I would like to answer any questions and objections. But maybe it is now best to have a conversation with you since I am rather tired. I think we should distinguish between the political game of governments and the apathy of public opinion. I wanted to explain the reasons for this apathy in the brief exposé I have just made.

The governments that are still anchored on the Earth had other motivations. And this war was precisely the intersection of government cynicism and public indifference. As for the French government, I think its pro-Serb attitude can be explained by several factors. There is a tradition that goes back to the First World War and to the Treaty of Versailles. France conceives of Yugoslavia as its creation and doesn't want its plaything broken (when I say France, I mean the foreign policy traditionally made at the Quai d'Orsay). There was also (and that played a very important role) the desire to save the Soviet Empire at any price. At the beginning of the war, France had bet on Gorbachev.

# 26

# The Inadmissible Frontier

*Le Monde*, 18 March 1993
If Seville or Venice were bombed and not Sibenik or Zada, if Vienna or Brussels had known the abominable misfortune of Sarajevo, if Dutch, German, and French villages were being cleansed and not the small town of Czerska, the Europeans would immediately take up arms "for the protection of common values, fundamental interests, and the independence of the union," and the Americans would not merely drop medical supplies and food into the devastated zones.

Croatia's and Bosnia's misfortune is to be situated on the other side of a line of which the disappearance, only a little more than three years ago, was celebrated by all the inhabitants of the Old World. Western Europe, in effect, rejoices that Europe is no longer divided, but it refuses to accept any responsibility for what this new situation implies. The Soviet world has fallen apart, but Yalta remains.

To denounce the immobility or embarrassment of the Twelve, we have evoked Munich. This comparison is much too flattering. The "Munichois," at least, had the excuse of fear. But Slobodan Milosevic is not threatening any country of the European Community. His expansionist project takes Serbia up to the Adriatic but not beyond it. So it isn't fear that motivates our leaders but simply egotism.

But it's no longer the time for *sacro egoismo*. This attitude makes a mockery of the universalist and humanitarian principles to which Europe lays claim in all its speeches.

What do we do to get out of the situation? How can we justify such a cruel application of European preference? France, which hasn't any oil but is proud to have ideas, has resolved the problem.

After inventing the right of humanitarian intervention in order to camouflage political abdication before the invasion of recognized states and the elimination of undesirable peoples, France had the General Assembly of the UN vote for the creation of an international tribunal that would bring together the dual prodigy of not judging anyone, since it refuses to take the means necessary to stop the guilty, and of judging everyone – victims as well as aggressors – since, unlike the tribunal of Nuremberg, it will not have to make a judgment on the activities of a criminal state. Much more vaguely, and only in view of granting the amalgam some legitimacy, it must make a judgment on the violations of the rights of man during the war in the former Yugoslavia.

In that way Europe (of the Twelve) is able to maintain and consolidate its inadmissible frontier while flattering itself on having the world enter an era without borders, an era of solidarity and planetary justice.

# 27

# Bosnia-Herzegovina

## *Without Shame*

*Le Monde*, 21 May 1993
The other evening on television, Bernard Kouchner asked for a symbolic air raid that would strike both Croatians and Serbs, equally guilty of aggression against the Muslims of Bosnia.

More prudent than the man with a golden heart, current European leaders argue from the confused mêlée that the war in the Balkans has become that a military solution is to be rejected, and they consider extending to Croatia as well as to the Croatians of Bosnia the economic sanctions imposed today on the Serbs.

A confused mêlée? The Serbs refuse to ratify the Vance-Owen Plan, whereas the Croatians demand its application. Their hurry is without any doubt to be condemned. But it's because the international community refuses to give itself the means of stopping, and a fortiori of having retreat, those who have already conquered and "cleansed" two thirds of Bosnia-Herzegovina that the remaining bone of contention is so fiercely disputed. The Croatians are worried about the provinces that were given them, and the Muslims, who have almost nothing left, are trying to take from the Croatians a part of the territories lost to the Serbs. And it's because the embargo on arms has not been lifted, in spite of the terrible imbalance of force, that both sides want to gain control of the roads where the few convoys carrying equipment and munitions must pass.

Muhamad Sacirbey, the permanent representative of Bosnia-Herzegovina to the United Nations, wrote in a letter to the president of the Security Council: "The embargo on arms and the lack of basic necessities pit neighbor against neighbor. If the two armies had adequate means for defense and if the population of Bosnia had received sufficient humanitarian aid, the conflict between local leaders would never have exploded." After more than a year of unpunished and infernal aggression, everything – land, food supplies, guns, medicine – became sparse for the besieged. In this situation of sparseness, the other man appeared inexorably as an opponent and the other victim as an enemy. You couldn't imagine anything worse, but it's only in sentimental films that misery makes for beauty. You have to have lost all shame to transform into a reason not to intervene what is, in fact, the tragic consequence of our strange confusions and procrastinations.

# 28

# The Injunction of Buchenwald

*Le Monde*, 15 December 1993

FOR JACQUES DEFERT

In a work entitled "On the Common Saying: That May Be Correct in Theory, But Is of No Use in Practice," Emmanuel Kant wrote that the drama of human history must have a hidden meaning for us to be interested in it for long. For lack of a clear stake, noticeable direction, or visible solution, the actors continue to be enthusiastic because, Kant says, they are crazy, they are prisoners of their partial vision, but even the best-intentioned spectator eventually gets tired: "Even if the actors do not tire of it, because they are fools, the spectator does, when one or another act gives him sufficient grounds for gathering that the never-ending piece is forever the same."[1]

The spectator of the conflict in Croatia and in Bosnia-Herzegovina finds himself in the very same frame of mind Kant has described. Since the war over there has degraded into an interminable and indistinct mêlée, since everyone is fighting everyone – Serbs against Croatians and Muslims, Croatians against Muslims, Muslims against Croatians, Muslims among themselves, Serbs with Croatians against Muslims, Muslims against Croatians with arms graciously provided by Serbs – and since the aggressed have recourse in the fighting to the methods of their aggressor, enlightened opinion gives up. It isn't more misanthropic or less cosmopolitan today than it was yesterday. It is simply that the generalized confusion and the repeated horror have won out over curiosity. Kant writes, "To watch this tragedy for a while might be moving and instructive, but the curtain must eventually fall" [305]. And in spite of Sarajevo's suffering another winter without heat, water, and arms to respond to the Serb bombings, the curtain is now coming down.

In other words, strong as our temptation may be to denounce one more time modern frivolity and the speed of the news that turns all the spectators of the world into subjects who are both emotive and inconsequential, compassionate and forgetful, overflowing with sentimentality and totally insensitive, we cannot, in this case, stay with this explanation. Kant forces us to note the present weariness of the spectator.

But the same Kant, in the same work, allows us not to give this demobilization the last word. Drawing from his observation the conclusion that human history must have a meaning, he discovers what Hegel will later call the work of negation: "The need," he wrote, "arising from the constant wars by which states in turn try to encroach upon or subjugate one another at last bring them, even against their will, to enter into a *cosmopolitan constitution*; or else, if this condition of universal peace is still more dangerous to freedom from another quarter, by leading to the most fearful despotism . . . this need must still constrain states to enter a condition that is not a cosmopolitan commonwealth under a single head but is still a rightful condition of *federation* in accordance with a commonly agreed upon *right of nations*" [307-8]. This scenario imagined by Kant in 1793 was realized in Europe in 1945. In the days following Nazi capitulation, Europe committed itself to the construction not of a federated state (*Völkerstaat*) but rather, according to Kant's prediction regarding the federation of states (*Völkerbund*), to averting both the establishment of despotism and the return of war. And it is this model of alliance or its Scandinavian variant that the republics of Slovenia and Croatia have unsuccessfully tried to set up against Serbia's brutal seizure of the Yugoslav federation. At the time of the referendum organized in Croatia in May 1991, after Serb separatists massacred about ten Croatian policemen in Rorovo Selo (and after their bodies, which had first been cut up and recomposed differently, had been sent back in boxes to the Croatian Ministry of Defense), the voters answered massively and positively to a proposal worded thus: "Croatia as an independent and sovereign country guaranteeing the cultural autonomy and all the civic rights of Serbs and of members belonging to other nationalities living in Croatia, can with other republics join a confederation of sovereign states." The answer to this choice was war. Not civil war, as has been negligently said and mechanically repeated, but a war *against civil populations* "taken as enemies as such and attacked with the military means that would be adequate against another army" (Véronique Nahoum-Grappe).

This war violated all the laws of war and reintroduced into Europe the very thing that Europe born from Auschwitz and Buchenwald had sworn never to tolerate on its soil again. Those sworn to *Nie Wieder* reacted to this challenge by saying that the true enemies of Europe were not the aggressors but the secessionists because they chose the path of division rather than that of federation. They chose tribal regression against humanity's progress toward a *right of peoples arrived at in common*. That's how the president of the French Republic expressed himself. Misinterpreting Kant's legacy, many intellectuals followed in Mitterrand's steps and confused the legitimate demands of the cosmopolitan ideal with the hatred of nations. But it would be an insult to the culture of François Mitterrand and to his intelligence to accuse him of believing what he said. Didn't he recently affirm in Andorra that "the existence of small independent states" was "one of the riches of Europe"? It was not the fear of disintegration that led France and England to give Serbia free rein for as long a time as possible, but the fear of German power. It was thought in our chancelleries that it was better to have a Greater Serbia built with guns in hand than a Germany spreading its Mark zone and sphere of *MittelEuropean* influence thanks to the dismantling of Yugoslavia. A weakened Germany in a strengthened Europe was the result of our leaders' calculation.

The present European Union was supposed to take note of the definitive failure of the politics of the balance of powers, which Kant, in the work mentioned, said resembled "Swift's house that the builder had constructed in such perfect accord with all the laws of equilibrium that it collapsed as soon as a sparrow alighted upon it" [309]. In fact, this policy has not been repudiated by the Europe of Maastricht; it has been perpetuated within its borders. The result is that Europe, which has not given itself the means to punish the conquest, is in the process of supporting it. Might makes right, and since where the only law that rules is the law of crime, everyone becomes a criminal, we are today witnessing the discouraging spectacle of *the contamination* of the aggressed by the aggressor. Certainly this epidemic metaphor should not be taken to the point of exonerating the Muslim and especially the Croatian politicians. All the while proclaiming his attachment to a Bosnia of citizens, President Izetbegovic, at the time of the 1991 census, mobilized the Muslim population around the slogan "Our interest depends on our number," a slogan not quite compatible with the classical definition of citizenship. As for President Tudjman, he probably experienced real concern for the survival of the Croatian minority in a predominantly Muslim state, but the determining motives of his hostility toward the Bosnian cause come from something else. He believed, as a *candid realist*, that accepting Serb conquests in Bosnia would bring him the restitution of occupied territories in Croatia. As soon as the game began, he played the card for partitioning, and this choice could only lead to the violent constitution of three ethnically pure territories in Bosnia. But the responsibility of those present is damning, in every meaning of the word, and the destruction of the Mostar bridge by the Croatian forces is an attack against the beauty of the world. But some would not have been tempted to satisfy the beast and others, in order to survive, would not have felt obliged to take over central Bosnia if Europe had not itself indicated the way, making clearly known to the belligerents that it would not defend the integrity of Bosnia, in spite of its international recognition, and that each would receive as many territories as he could conquer. This Europe now denounces a game for which it set up the rules. It imputes to *their* delirium a Lebanonization that is, in fact, its own jurisprudence. It thus successfully accomplishes the feat of justifying by its very consequences the politics of abandonment that it has followed since the beginning of the war. "You see quite well," it conveys to a public opinion disoriented and wearied by the Bosnian imbroglio, "that the Balkans are not worth the bones of a single European grenadier!"

However, if those laying siege to Sarajevo see themselves as able to conduct yet another winter siege, and if Germany and France (now reconciled around the theory and practice of appeasement) succeed in convincing the international community to lift the embargo against Serbia in exchange for the restitution of 3 percent of its conquests, this would mean that in the Europe of *Nie Wieder* and protected from the commemoration of genocide, the realism we never wanted to experience once again imposes the absolute power of its spirit of concession to the arguments of brute force. We can't imagine any more perfect duplicity or more striking denial of the Kantian bet on the meaning of human history. Though faced with this spectacle, we cannot yield to apathy. For we are not spectators. We are Europeans and, as such, are implicated in the decisions of the Twelve.

That is the reason why, with Marek Edelman and Vitas Landsbergis, I participated in a meeting organized for Bosnia on 14 November in the Buchenwald concentration camp by the Association for Threatened Peoples. Certainly the same thing is not happening in Sarajevo as happened at Buchenwald. But the differences excuse nothing because Buchenwald is not only a place of memory. It is an injunction, and it must be repeated *tirelessly*, even if the chances for being heard diminish each day: for Europe, obedience to this injunction is a question of life or spiritual death.

NOTE

1. Immanuel Kant, "On the Common Saying: That May Be Correct in Theory, But Is of No Use in Practice," in *Practical Philosophy*, trans. Mary J. Gregor (Cambridge: Cambridge University Press, 1996), 305–6. *Trans.*

# 29

# Vukovar, Sarajevo

## *Hitler's Posthumous Victory*

*Esprit*, 1993

Marek Edelman, one of the last survivors of the Warsaw Ghetto uprising, declared the war in Bosnia to be the posthumous victory of Hitler.

It would be a groundless accusation against this member of the Jewish Resistance to say that he fell, so to speak, into the double trap of hodgepodge and banalization. More inclined to consider the Holocaust a catastrophe than to define it as a territory, Marek Edelman simply notes that the era in which "everything is possible" didn't end with the defeat of Nazi Germany, despite the fine declarations and grand promises that have produced the European Community. Less than fifty years later, a total war, a racial war, a war of conquest, a war against culture returns to the Old World, and it has been given a free hand. Why this complacency? Why this quasi impunity? Why has everything been granted to those for whom everything is possible, to those who stop at nothing, those whose violence knows no limits – because for them the world is will, and reality is to be molded?

Since Europe lies in its elegant and oratorical artifice – the only definition it really still possesses – truth came from the mouth of an American. Warren Christopher, American secretary of state, let the cat out of the bag in early June: "Bosnia," he affirmed, "is a human tragedy but it isn't a confrontation between the United States and Russia. Nor does it affect our vital national interests."

In other words, on the one hand there is a human aspect to the question, and on the other hand, there is the important aspect of the question. There are men and then there are those who have rights; there are local fires and then there are global tragedies. Of course, ethnic cleansing is a monstrosity. But to be our enemy you have to be more than a monster. On the contrary, to pursue a monstrous course unfettered, it's enough not to be our enemy. Milosevic's luck and his victims' misfortune was to inhabit a "no-man's-land" in the world order. That Greater Serbia should be born today by fire and sword won't change the face of the world much. That's what the strategists and a number of intellectuals think. For the philosophers of history who have replaced Marx with Tocqueville and the communist paradigm with that of the equality of conditions, the defeat of totalitarianism is consummated. However regrettable the events in the Balkans may be, they are only happening out in the suburbs, on the margins of Meaning. They neither constitute a true ideological challenge nor do they have the power to interrupt or hinder democracy's victorious march.

One can contest this view of the world and of what is not a part of it on one's own terrain. It's easy to foresee the disastrous consequences to us citizens of the Center, the new beneficiaries of History, of the lack of concern and stubborn *will to powerlessness* that our governments have shown during this war. Besides not seeing why the Serbs would limit to Croatia and Bosnia a politics of aggrandizement and purification that has to date been so advantageous to them, the idea that *crime pays* risks becoming *jurisprudence* and letting loose all the potential Milosevics that postcommunism has mastered the art of secreting. Finally, the abandonment of the Muslims risks aggravating the hostility of Islamic countries toward Europe. As the informed political experts Pierre Lellouche and François Huisbourgh have noted, "The proliferation of nuclear arms and ballistic missiles will give a certain urgency to this danger."

But putting political analysis aside, we can also remember

that the division between what is human and what is important has already caused considerable damage in Europe. After all, it was the fate of the Jews in modern Europe to be
exposed to anti-Semitism and *excluded* from History. They
were persecuted, but they were not part of the program.
What was essential took place elsewhere. The winds of history were not stirring where they were suffering, and during the Second World War itself, the Calvary they underwent
had no place in the war. Their tragedy unfolded in the background of the drama. That is why, moreover, the French ju-
diciary was able to exonerate René Bousquet in 1945: his participation as a zealous functionary in the Final Solution was
amply compensated for by the help he brought, at the desired time, to the Resistance; that is, to those who were making History. It took a good number of years for the Jewish
misfortune to come to the forefront. The injustice has now
been repaired: "The Allies haven't the right to consider this
war only from a military point of view [ . . . ]. We want an
official declaration of the allied nations stipulating that beyond their military strategy, which aims at assuring their victory, the extermination of the Jews forms a chapter apart.
Let the allied nations announce straight out, publicly, that
this problem is theirs."[1] The desperate message with which
the leaders of the Warsaw Ghetto had charged Jan Karski,
courier of the Polish government in exile, is finally heard and
understood. History has now incorporated the Holocaust.
But is this tardy remorse enough to declare innocent the very
concept of History? On the contrary, isn't thinking after
Auschwitz, as Adorno has written, to "address itself to those
things which were not embraced by this dynamic, which fell
by the wayside – what might be called the waste products
and blind spots that have escaped the dialectic." "It is the
nature of the defeated," he wrote, "to appear, in their impo-
tence, irrelevant, eccentric, derisory."[2]

With an ardor and virulence that the Serb aggression itself

never inspired in them, certain people condemned the poster campaign of Doctors of the World, which compared Milosevic to Hitler and the Serb concentration camps to Nazi camps. These people, of course, were right: the "Butcher of the Balkans" is not the Fuhrer; Omarska is not Treblinka. But they err greatly in being right: they believe they are defending the unique horror of the extermination of the Jews against the surrounding confusion, but, in effect, they are taking the side of the center against the margins. For the past to burn in us, in order that nothing attenuate the scandal of the absolute solitude and dereliction in which the Jewish victims of Nazism died, these people have now come to authenticate the present hierarchy of what is human and important. They consider themselves to be memory's guardians but they behave like the border guards of History, and they corroborate the prohibition against entering into it, a prohibition they should have been the first to want to abolish.

Warren Christopher, decidedly in a mood for geopolitical confidences, recently declared that Germany bore an overwhelming responsibility for the explosion of Yugoslavia and the escalation of the war, because it forced Europe rather prematurely to recognize Slovenia, Croatia, and Bosnia-Herzegovina. Lord Carrington, former mediator of the European Community, confirmed this analysis. And the president of the French Republic, François Mitterrand, certain as ever of his gifts for clairvoyance, had his entourage call into question the "unacceptable Germanico-Vatican pressures."

For the great of this world, in other words, the scandal is not, as it was for Marek Edelman, a European consent to the racial war perpetrated by Serbia. It is not – from the Brioni Agreements to the Washington Plan – the continued failure on the part of the West to keep its word. The scandal, as Serb propaganda states it, is Europe's and the world's submission to the combined demands of Hans-Dietrich Genschler and John Paul II.[3]

To this indictment of the Church and of Germany and their demons by the guiltiest and most compromised in the present circumstances, we must first answer with what used to be called factual truths. *The secession of the non-Serb republics is not the cause of Milosevic's imperialist politics but its inexorable consequence.* It wasn't the recognition of Slovenia, Croatia, and Bosnia-Herzegovina that provoked the explosion of Yugoslavia; it was the installation of a reign of terror in Kosovo in 1988 and all the measures that followed to reinforce Serb hegemony on the federation. Nor was it Croatia's reception into the community of nations that fired the powderkeg, since at the moment when this entry took place, Dubrovnik had already been bombed, Vukovar was in ashes, and the Krajina region had been occupied and emptied of all its Ruthenian, Czech, and Croatian inhabitants. Recognition intervened *after* the cessation of fighting and the signing of the Vance Plan. As to the assertion that the day after Vukovar's destruction was too early to recognize Croatia's independence, this is to imply that nothing happened at Vukovar. And that is precisely the view of those who divide geopolitical reality into what is essential and what is human. In history's *no-man's-land*, in the places not served by the high-speed train of globalization, death carries no weight and the irreparable has become meaningless. In short, what today we call the world is not the world; it is high society. *We have a worldly idea of the global world*; there are those who are *in* and those who are *out*, that is to say nowhere, and when they die, *they go from nonexistence to death*.

Still the indictment of Pan-Germanism and the pope, for and on behalf of Pan-Serbism and its European accomplices, would not have been accepted so easily by the press at large had a new war not broken out between Croatians and Muslims and had Serbs and Croatians not seemed to come to an agreement on dividing Bosnia-Herzegovina into three national entities. As a consequence of this Lebanonization and these intrigues, of this war within the war and the negotiation on the back of the weaker of the two great enemies, malaise and suspicion took hold of Western opinion: more and more people yesterday convinced of the necessity of a military intervention against Serbia told themselves today that the Balkans truly did not merit their solicitude or that, in any case, for the general good, we should never have opened the Pandora's box that was Yugoslavia.

Since the endless stream of continuous news has killed all historical continuity, and with each new event erasing the preceding one, we must, one more time, return to the facts. On 15 November 1991, or three days before Vukovar's fall, the newspaper *Le Monde* published an interview with the Croatian minister of defense entitled: "Croatia Warns against the War's Expansion into Bosnia-Herzegovina." Of particular importance was the Croatian minister Susak's statement: "We are perfectly aware that within the territory of Bosnia-Herzegovina there are three nations which are and which will continue to be obliged to find means of living together. That is only possible if Serbia is forced to abandon its ideas of territorial conquest. There are two possible outcomes: either the UN will quickly intervene or – and, unfortunately, it isn't a question of months or of weeks, but of days – the same thing will begin in Bosnia-Herzegovina as what is happening in Croatia." This warning had no effect. Three months later, on 2 January 1992 to be precise, when the Croatian minister of defense and General Raseta of the federal army met in Sarajevo to sign the accord for the implementation of the cease-fire, President Izetbegovic, in turn, urgently asked Cyrus Vance to deploy UN soldiers as a preventive measure in Bosnia-Herzegovina: "Vance doesn't follow up on it. Boutros-Ghali, who replaces Perez de Cuellar as secretary general of the United Nations, is extremely laconic on the subject. In his report of 5 January 1992 to the Security Council, he limits himself to saying that 'for the moment,' there is no reason to change the original plan, which is to send only observers to Bosnia-Herzegovina, and even then they will only be stationed in the regions which adjoin Croatia."[4] Thus, among those who distinguished between the essential and the human in order better to hand over the human to the agents of a limitless inhumanity, those who, like our president of the republic, generously exerted themselves to rule out every obstacle the international community might have been tempted to hold up to our friends the Serb nationalists-communists, those who conceitedly opposed Europe to the "savage tribes" or who affirmed with this editorialist of the *Daily Telegraph*: "The massacres are perhaps appalling, but neither Croatia nor Serbia is worth the death of a single vigorous English grenadier. Now that Yugoslavia has itself destroyed its tourist industry, I do not see anything over there that could interest us" – we have not found anyone to lend an ear to the warnings of Zagreb and Sarajevo. With Milosevic – from whom one can always expect the worst – aggression was therefore easily extended to Bosnia, razing cities and villages, destroying two hundred churches and six hundred mosques, provoking the new outbreak of typhoid fever in the heart of Europe, killing two hundred thousand people and making more than a million people seek refuge, of whom nearly three hundred thousand have been received in Croatia and seventy-eight in the Olympic village of Albertville. So there is no more Bosnia. And it is in this context that the Croatians of Herzegovina, against the Croatian church, the Croatian opposition, the Franciscans, and other Croatians of Bosnia but with the support of President Tudjman, have defended their territorial interests over the consolidation of the alliance with the Muslims. Violently condemned by the international community but encouraged de facto by its decision to let force have the last say, this policy could in the near future result in the temptation to ethnic cleansing of Mostar by all means necessary. One must denounce such an abomination *and the catastrophic choice that led to it*: I do so here without reserve, for I am no more an unquestioning supporter of Croatia than Montesquieu was the spokesman for the Persian empire when he was surprised to see his compatriots themselves surprised that one could be Persian.

But the deterioration of the war does not prove Warren Christopher and François Mitterrand right against Marek Edelman. And the condemnation by moralist-journalists of Croatian-Serb aggression against Bosnia's Muslims is no less stupid or out of sync than was yesterday's description of the invasion of Croatia in terms of a civil war based on ancestral hatreds. If the Croatians and Muslims negotiate with Slobodan Milosevic, it is because the international community has imposed him as an interlocutor. Because while it has never given itself the means to carry out its own decisions, it refuses to lift the embargo on arms destined for Bosnia and threatens the Croatians with sanctions if they suddenly want to retake Croatia's occupied territories by force. The Croatians, moreover, are not now creating a Greater Croatia in Bosnia-Herzegovina. They have in fact been expelled in the tens of thousands from regions that the Vance-Owen Plan had granted them. Two years of unpunished aggression have made the Muslims rely on themselves and enlarge, at the Croatians' expense, a territorial base that is constantly reduced by the Serbs.

It is not within our power to prevent Hitler's posthumous victory, but what we can and must prevent, with all our might, weak as that may be, is *the burial of the truth*. We must make sure that this war leaves some trace of itself. We must therefore continue to call a spade a spade, the gunners of the Pan-Serb state assassins, Europe a bankrupt enterprise, and France, par excellence, the country of the puffed-up chest and capitulation.

## Vukovar, Sarajevo

NOTES

1. Jan Karski in *Shoah* by Claude Lanzmann (Fayard, 1985), 186–87.

2. Theodor Adorno, *Minima Moralia: Reflections from Damaged Life*, trans. E. F. N. Jephcott (New York: Verso, 1985), 151. *Trans.*

3. Genschler was German foreign minister until 1992; the conflict is here in its early stages. *Trans.*

4. Henry Wynaendts, *L'Engrenage: Chroniques yougoslaves* (Denoel, 1993), 141.

# 30

# The Crime of Being Born

*Europe, Nations, War*

February 1994

*May 15, 1940.*
*No more Holland.*
*The number of small obsolete countries is shrinking in Europe.–*
PIERRE DRIEU LA ROCHELLE, *Journal, 1939–1945*

In the early summer of 1993, forty great writers, journalists, and university personalities, "preoccupied with the resurgence of antidemocratic currents from the extreme Right in French intellectual life," solemnly called for the establishment of a European committee for vigilance.[1]

The extreme Right, they explained in substance, had relinquished its sense of reserve and emerged from its traditional burrows. For some years, without fuss but obstinately, its most active ideologues had been weaving their web: they gathered unto themselves the most respectable signatures by having people believe they had changed. These contributions obtained by ruse allowed them to have us believe in the thesis of their repentance, and it also allowed them to penetrate, unrepentant, into places of legitimate thought. And so, masked, do they ever advance toward the reconquest of cultural power.

Since transparency is the imperative of public life, we should rejoice in being thus enlightened. And yet what might surprise us is the emphatic tone of this warning. Did the former New Right – since this is what we are talking about – warrant this resurgence of antifascist committees, and did its facelift merit placing Europe on maximum alert?

148

Isn't there an excess of honor in this excess of shamefulness? An excess of honor and a lack of moderation: if today the antidemocratic intelligentsia needs to appear acceptable, this is proof enough that conformism is no longer on its side and, unlike in the 1930s, the elites refuse to compromise with fascism. Whether they are credulous or distrustful, whether they advisedly or ill-advisedly grant pardon for past errors, the intellectuals are unanimous as perhaps they have never been in denying any rational foundation to racism, in saying that outside democracy there is no possible salvation, and in considering, with the forty vigilant members of the committee, that "the extreme Right's remarks are not simply ideas among others, but incitations to discrimination, violence, and crime." It is true that the economic crisis combined with large-scale immigration to resurrect these murderous ideas, but they prosper without any legitimacy and despite the disavowal of the show business community, churches, the media, writers, artists, and the academy – that is, the totality of moral authorities recognized in contemporary Europe. Each points to the infamy, but that doesn't make it go away. Whereas yesterday scientific racism protected, justified, and strengthened racial hatred, today science is absent, but hate does very well without its support, as it does, moreover, without the songs of poets or the blessings given by religious men and women. In short, what is troubling and paradoxical in our situation is much more the powerlessness of vigilant intellectuals to defuse the words that wound than it is the resurgence of this kind of discourse in our intellectual life.

But evil, for those who signed the petition in *Le Monde*, is not limited to these seductive schemes. The present "strategy of legitimization of the extreme Right," which they see at work and which in their view uses any means it can, "takes advantage of the multiple dialogues and debates about, for example, what is called at least flippantly the end of ideology, of the supposed disappearance of every political cleavage between the Left and the Right, and of the presumed renewal of the ideas of nation and cultural identity. This strategy is also nourished by the latest fashionable thesis, which denounces antiracism as being at once 'out-of-date' and dangerous."

Stated differently, naive people are not the only ones to play into the hands of the extreme Right – the unorthodox do it as well. To the unwilling accomplices we must add the objective ones, and the call for a vigilance committee is up against a double threat: it disillusions researchers or writers taken in by the tactical kindness of democracy's unrepentant enemies. It also denounces those who refuse to reduce the troubling plurality of the world to eternally opposed good or bad camps, to transform economic options into absolute choices, to revile the nation when multiethnic empires are falling apart, and to remove antiracism from all criticism on the pretext that it is packed with good feelings and that it is tirelessly tracking down the filthy beast. So watch out for hypocrites and heretics, for schemes and nuances. Yet vigilance is not enough: "Let us have the courage to be vulgar, let's sacrifice the spirit of finesse," as Nizan said.

Thus, having been invited to distrust, the addressees of the manifesto are instructed to toe the line and think correctly. Here they are at once informed and called to order, enlightened and watched over, informed of the threats hanging over them as well as of the threat of infamy if they do not adhere to the catechism of vigilance. What can we conclude but that, for the best of causes, a new orthodoxy is being set up in Europe? And *as though there were in communism infinitely more than mere communism*, this orthodoxy resurrects its procedures, categories, political absolutism, and Manichean simplicity in order to defend democracy against banalized fascism.

It wasn't fascists, moreover, but proclaimed democrats and irreproachable antiracists who qualified as *tribal* the avidity of the totalitarian empire's former colonies for recovering their identity and making their entry as distinct communities into the concert of nations. Europe or the tribes: this insulting alternative was declared not by the sly doctrinaires and astute extremists with whom the manifesto openly invites us to break off every relation but rather by the apostles of vigilance. At the time of the international colloquium held under this title at the Chaillot Palace in Paris on 27–29 February 1992, the intellectuals of the other Europe, who after forty years in purgatory were congratulating themselves on being able finally to rejoin Europe, could not get over being thus expelled geographically toward Africa and temporally into prehistoric times.

There must have been some misunderstanding: the new censors of the tribes did not talk from the heights of a superior civilization but in the name of a shared Humanity. They didn't picture the world as a ladder atop which they sat, but as a horizontal space threatened with fragmentation. They didn't defend culture against an unrefined nature, but the possibility of communication between men against the belief in their necessary and impassable division into hermetic entities. They were not the representatives of "evolved societies" confronted with "primitive societies," but the champions of hospitality before the fearful high tide of xenophobia. Their obsessive fear was separation and not backwardness, the disintegration of our continent into ever smaller nations and not the unleashing of the savage hordes onto the prosperous mother countries. In short, far from asking for an ethnocentric Europe, these frightened democrats called upon cosmopolitan Europe to fight against "the presumed renewal of the ideas of nation and cultural identity," that is to say, the ravages of ethnocentricity.

The word *tribe* was used, however, and it is not a neutral word: by placing the conflict between the nations of the former Yugoslavia deep into the heart of darkness and lodging all its protagonists under the same roof, it has had antiracist opinion pass over the first racial war Europe has known since 1945. And even the well-intentioned have themselves been contaminated by the racism inherent in this word, as witnessed by the reports of the few Bosnian refugees the French welcomed into their homes: "My hostess," begins one of them, "explained to me very seriously what a vacuum cleaner was used for!" . . . "And mine," said Dragana, "spoke at length about the advantages of a freezer." As for Fatima's family, they could not hide their disappointment on seeing that the young woman was not impressed by the big color TV in the living room! "It was only when one day I admitted having spent a few weeks in Monaco and on the Riviera that my family suddenly realized I wasn't primitive," remembers Nermina. Hadn't she been asked one day whether she had ever heard of someone named Picasso! "Come on, Madame," I answered, "his painting has been the subject of one of my year-long courses at school! In my country, painting and music are studied in the same way as physics and mathematics."[2] Men do not rule over language. The words they use have a past that escapes their command and, at times, fashions their judgment though they think they are well beyond it. It isn't enough to define tribal behaviors in terms of retreat and no longer in terms of backwardness so as to be free of the history associated with the word *tribe*. If Bosnian refugees have experienced some condescension at the very heart of hospitality, that is because, in the eyes of those Westerners most imbued with their superiority, European civilization is distinguished from primitive or barbarian societies by the freezer, the vacuum cleaner, and Picasso.

The problem, for all that, cannot be reduced to a question of words. In a philosophical-political editorial entitled "*Ex-Yugoslavie: Généalogie et conséquences d'un principe du droit inconditionnel des nations à l'indépendance* (Ex-Yugoslavia:

Genealogy and consequences of a principle of the unconditional right of nations to independence) and signed *T. M.*, as was done in the glory days, at the most critical moments of the Cold War and the war in Algeria, the members of the editorial board at *Les Temps modernes* applied the credo of vigilance to the Yugoslav catastrophe with semantic rigor, and they said what they wanted to say without resorting to an ethnocentric vocabulary.[3] The result is no less striking.

In the eyes of *Les Temps modernes*, the Slovenes are the people responsible for this atrocious war and, along with them, the "bards" of the small countries. By having identity override every other consideration, the Slovenes have imposed the model of ethnic homogeneity upon Yugoslavia (*Les Temps modernes* talks about "ethnically pure Slovenia"), and the bards have added to the barbaric refusal to mix ethnicities the democratic guarantee of the right of all peoples to self-determination. "Ethnic 'purification' (or 'cleansing') is not simply a consequence; in the search for homogeneity it has been present from the start as the only principle of unification and autonomy. . . . Did the birth of new nations merit such massacres, displacements, and hardships?"[4] Supported by the very powerful lobby of small nations, the Slovenes began a fatal process, which, in sum, the Serbs have merely carried out. The Slovenes and Croatians acted, the Serbs reacted or, more exactly, they *actualized* all the murderous potentiality of this initiative. The first made the decision, the second got caught up in the spiral of violence. The first transgressed a moral law, the others applied a mechanical law. Here causality, there responsibility: it's the same for the Yugoslav world as for the category of being in Cartesian philosophy. It is divided into two substances that cannot be reduced to one another: extension and thought. Inert and submissive like the bodies of the *res extensa* to the realm of passivity, the Serbs were moved from the outside, whereas the Slovenes and Croatians, like all that is spirit or *res cogitans*, initiated their own movement. So they can be blamed for all the crimes, in particular the destruction, massacres, expulsions, or rapes committed on order by their aggressor. For they provoked the shock and provided the momentum the automaton needed to get going.

When the Bosnians themselves secede so that they won't have to live in a federation where they would be in a tête-à-tête with Serbia, *Les Temps modernes* glorifies their fight . . . against the separatism of the other republics: "Bosnian resistance gives the lie to the principle that had presided at the breakup of the Yugoslav federation: that ethnicity is the foundation of the sovereignty and autonomy of small nations. . . . If the case of Bosnia is so exemplary, it is because it is the mirror of ex-Yugoslavia, a country where ethnic groups, languages, and religions have been mixed. For more than mere *coexistence*, it represented *the mixing* of peoples."[5] And when Bosnians call for a military intervention to save their state from the scalpel ("the scalpel, grand theoretician, philosophical leader of the twentieth century," as Vassili Grossman says), *Les Temps modernes* celebrates their will to live together while ridiculing the idea of intervention: you don't strike what is entirely determined, you don't take exception to the outcome of a necessary chain of events.

The vigilant are therefore wrong to worry: nothing threatens their catechism, not even factual truths. With an Orwellian and touchy zeal, *Les Temps modernes* is on guard against the dangers that the exacerbation and proliferation of national feelings weigh upon the very idea of humanity. All the historical data that could complicate this alternative are reduced to nothing. A *fanatical negationism* blurs Greater Serbia's plan as well as the steps necessary to its realization. To take such politics into account would be to recognize that, whatever the behavior of either camp, once the international community sanctioned the law of the strongest, the small nations of the Yugoslav space didn't have to choose between ethnic purity and mixing but between freedom and submission. It would mean giving credit to the secessionists for having fled not multinational Yugoslavia but Serb hegemony over Yugoslavia. Yet for vigilant Europe, this scenario linking freedom and identity is logically impossible: either you are free, in effect, and tear yourself away from what you are, you expiate through interbreeding the crime of being born, or you succumb to the temptation to cling to your identity, and then you perpetuate the crime.

In this case the crime is double: the identity politics of the small Yugoslav nations clashes with universal morality and offends truth. This ethnic homicidal madness is not only fierce; it is also fallacious. A heinous fable, a bloody fiction, folklore that is at once wicked and mythical: this is the way *Les Temps modernes* would characterize the feelings of identity at issue. The being who posits himself as different is moreover no one. For as unpleasant as it is, his claim is also "completely absurd because all, Slovenes, Croatians, Serbs, and Muslims (Slavs converted during the Ottoman Empire . . . must we be reminded?), are from the same historical origin: they are all Slavs from the South. Everything else (religion, one's belonging or not to the Austrian-Hungarian Empire, and so forth) is nothing but a smoke screen."[6]

Can you imagine an intellectual from Ljubljana dismissing the Franco-German wars that have punctuated European history with a peremptory and definitive "They are all Franks!"? The large nations – and this is just what defines them as such – are not subject to being told: "They are all – ." No one looks at them from on high, whence you no longer distinguish anything. For they occupy this very place. The aerial view is *their* privilege. By putting the small nations on trial, *Les Temps modernes* thinks it is condemning the division ad infinitum of our shared world. As the reference to "All Slavs of the South!" suggests, *Les Temps modernes* reiterates, in reality, the condescension the guardians of universal history display toward those who are no experts, and it ratifies the world's division into domineering nations and those that are undifferentiated.

Besides being arrogant, this indictment lacks all coherence. The same people are condemned both as racists and in the name of race. The twofold crime for which they must answer is, in fact, a terrible *double bind*. If they are always wrong, it isn't because they are twice culpable, it's because the accusers refer, in order to trip them up, to contradictory principles. "By being a group unto yourselves," they are reproached simultaneously, "you sacrifice the idea of humanity to ethnic belonging and true ethnic belonging to a pure fantasy." One confronts these separatists simultaneously with the real and the ideal. They are obliged both to be what they are and to tear themselves away from this essence. They must move beyond particularisms while not abandoning their racial bedrock.

Racial or vital. A sweeter and more widespread version of the argument consists in being astonished to see in the Balkans, in the Caucasus, or elsewhere people take up arms and kill one another although they "are all human beings"! What is today systematically opposed to the horrors of war is the immediate evidence of the species, the *biological* homogeneity of heterogeneous humanities, the empirical traits common to all men for all times and climates. Every person is born, consumes, is awake, sleeps, shelters himself, loves, reproduces, grows old and dies. All the rest is a smoke screen: "To affirm the fundamental unity of the human species precisely when every Serb is ready to jump on his Croatian, and vice versa, is not a negligible lesson," writes, for example, Gérard Dupuy in the newspaper *Libération*. The hyphenated Serbo-Croatian continues to unite peoples at war. From the point of view afforded by the species, they are not different, they are Siamese twins. There are no stakes in the conflict, it is simply ridiculous. You can see that this subdued version is as reductionist as the preceding one. "All Slavs of the South!" or "All human beings!": in both cases, nature is called upon to deny the plurality of destiny, situations, and styles. Going from the race to the species doesn't solve the contradiction. The anathema pronounced by the discourse of vigilance over the idea of nation perpetually oscillates between humanity as horizon and humanity as origin. Praise for the hybridity of identities is accompanied by the observation that all men are rigorously identical, and the call to transcend the given is imperturbably united to the affirmation of its *caractère indépassable*, its impassable character.

These two discourses are mutually exclusive, but they share a common element that explains their coexistence and, beyond illogicality, allows one to understand all their import. Both discourses conceive identity as a pathology and not as a category of the human condition. Not long ago we were *historical* beings: historicity meaning the commitment within a tradition and within an existential project. Today, however, inscription into a time and place is no longer a modality of our finitude. It is a sickness that vigilance attempts to cure with moralizing exhortations and references to biological evidence. Rome or Byzantium, the Austro-Hungarian Empire or the Ottoman Empire, Central Europe or the Orient of Europe – such oppositions are no longer relevant. They do not differentiate between worlds but rather reveal a culpable will to discriminate. "Why would it be necessary, moreover, to prefer Rome (Zagreb) to Byzantium (Belgrade)?" asks *Les Temps modernes*. "Why would one have more sympathy for deceased Cacanie than for this other part of Europe that was Ottoman for centuries? The one interesting attribute of the Austro-Hungarian Empire was precisely its nature as a multinational empire."[7] In other words, historical differences belong to humanity's prehistory, and the only thing to preserve from this long obscure period is whatever in it foretold our apotheosis: the reign of generalized exchangeability, the fact, celebrated by the worshipers of life as hybridity, that anyone could be anyone else.

The rejection of historicity does not mean the rejection of history. But, instead of feeling ourselves affected by the past or exposed to the work of history, we see the latter presented to us, just as Nietzsche had prophesied, as "the permanent festival of a universal exposition." We no longer live in history, we visit it. It no longer founds our being, it offers itself to our curiosity; we take from it as we think best, and the inclination that may attach us to any of its expressions comes from our discretionary power and not from its power upon us. To say it with some solemnity: in this era where technology suppresses all distances, man no longer exists as a being situated geographically and historically *but as a tourist* even within his own nation: "No longer sacrificial, funereal, and defensive, national feeling has become fun loving, curious and, one might say, touristic. . . . This is France à la carte – dining menu and Michelin map," writes Pierre Nora at the end of his monumental work, *Realms of Memory*. In effect, the Michelin Guide has dethroned the historian Michelet, and the debt toward the dead has been supplanted by the desire to travel and taste. No more "here," no more "there"; no more us, no more them: the world has overcome these ancient divisions. The event is immense, and it has not left one of our fundamental principles intact.

It is the renunciation of the absolute, the assent to finitude that, formerly, made possible tolerance, communication, and antiracism. To make place for the other, to need the other, to want to share the world with him, we need to know that since "the god Limit has set himself up as guardian at the entrance to the world," as Feuerbach has written, "nothing is realized without being realized as determined being," and that we cannot therefore occupy at the same time all points of view on the universe. The European Committee for Vigilance would like to inherit these threatened values, but what it defends, beset as it is with the logic of identity politics, is no longer so much the allocation as it is the malleability, the combinatorial freedom, the universal mix, the unlimited power to play with the data banks of the great world's hybrids that our traditions have become. Under the same name, the sense of limits has given way to the inebriation of total mastery: "The history of men is the long line of synonyms for the same term. To contradict it is a duty."[8]

So it is necessary to contradict the maneuvers on the part of *Les Temps modernes* and its apologia for ethnic mixing of the Bosnia cause. When the siege of Sarajevo had just begun, a Serb nationalist wrote at the very top of the main post office: "This is Serbia." "Idiot," answered an anonymous writer the following day, "This is the post office!" This marvelous joke reveals the political program of Sarajevo's inhabitants: to live together and maintain Bosnia's integrity. But this collective desire is itself anchored in memory and nourished by a particular tradition. What this joke expressed is more the fidelity to a particular past than the Yugoslav break with prior history. Since Bosnia-Herzegovina has conserved its unity under all the successive regimes it has known, a community of destiny was created, throughout the centuries, from the coexistence of communities and their intertwining. Of course it is a fragile, less than idyllic community, threatened by Greater Serbia's plan as well as by the separatism of the Croatians from Herzegovina, who unlike the other populations comprising Bosnia form a quasi-compact bloc and are, in addition, backed up against Croatia. However, Bosnia remains a community since a majority of its members clearly expressed the desire to continue, in Renan's words, to promote the undivided heritage.

Thus, contrary to the thesis espoused in the current climate and taken up by *Les Temps modernes*, *Bosnia is not a miniature Yugoslavia*. Yugoslavia is a chimera; Bosnia is a fact.

Yugoslavia has never truly functioned; Bosnia has practically never ceased to exist. The Yugoslav state is the recent and unfortunate embodiment of a grand ethnic illusion – that of the fraternity of Southern Slavs. The Bosnian entity is a legacy of history. The failure of Yugoslavia vividly illustrates that racial relationships cannot replace community; Bosnia's persistence reminds us that the nation is not the only possible form of historico-political community. In the first case, fusion is what violates the lived and concrete reality of the world; in the second, dismembering does the same thing. The *tabula rasa* mentality, the absence of scruples and the contempt for reality take on the form of *unitarianism* in Yugoslavia, and *partition* in Bosnia-Herzegovina.

European diplomacy neither knew how to nor wanted to take this delicate duality into account. All the while proclaiming its unwavering commitment to the integrity of a multiethnic Bosnia, it systematically confirmed Serb politics of the fait accompli. While it spoke loud and clear the language of rights, it granted the right of free speech only to brute force and crime. The Croatian partisans for the division of Bosnia took this as a sign of encouragement, and as a result all the protagonists are contaminated by waging war in the Serbian fashion.

As for a "vigilant" Europe, instead of opening itself up to the diversity of concrete situations and supporting the small nations as well as multinational Bosnia in their hopes for freedom, following the logic of "tourism" just described it played off *métissage* against national aspirations.[9] Then, following a more theological reasoning, it countered the original sin of origins worshiping with the mixing of ethnicities, and it defended democracy by dismissing the vote of homogeneous peoples as inherently flawed. So, at the very moment when resistance to the inhuman was vital, European diplomacy, taking its usual stance, capitulated, and antifascist Europe attacked all that remained, that was human, concrete, and historical in the human condition.

To those who, along with Drumont, attributed his birth to crime, Bernard Lazare answered one day, "I am Jewish, being born such. I don't care to change my name, or belong to a church, a temple, or a mosque. I have the right to remain as I am, and I shall uphold this right. Who can say I am wrong?" [10]

First among the Dreyfusards, Bernard Lazare had come a long way. Early in his career, confident in their promises of emancipation, he called on Jews to cease being *such* so as to be fully human. The persistence of hate made him become somewhat disillusioned, and he understood that this asceticism was doomed to failure. He also understood, beyond the context, that you don't win humanity but rather lose it when you seek to erase your different identities and uproot your particular determinations. Illusory, in the context of the hostility of the times, this behavior had something despicable about it: "The emancipated Jew conducts himself like an upstart, he forgets the miserable ancestor whose descendant he is." [11] Thus did Bernard Lazare fight on two fronts: against Drumont and against himself, against the intransigent disciple of the Enlightenment he had been and whose break with his poor Jewish ancestors was translated, in the guise of emancipation, by a dislike for poor living Jews: "What do these Russian moneylenders, Galician pawnbroker innkeepers, Polish horse sellers, resellers from Prague, and moneychangers from Frankfurt matter to me, a French Israelite? By virtue of what alleged fraternity shall I be concerned with measures taken by the Czar toward subjects who seem to him to have accomplished harmful work? By defending and supporting them, do I have to assume a part of their responsibility? What do I have in common with these descendants of the Huns?" [12]

Observing that anti-Semitism was irreducible and that uprooting was in fact humiliating, Bernard Lazare opted for the Zionist idea toward the end of his life or, at least, for its expression in the desire for a Jewish state: "The Jew who will today say, 'I am a nationalist,' will not say in a clear, precise and special way, 'I am a man who wants to reconstitute a Jewish state in Palestine and who dreams of conquering Jerusalem.' He will say, 'I want to be a man who is fully free, I want to enjoy the sun, I want to have a right to my dignity as a man. I want to be free from oppression, free from outrage, free from the contempt that others would heap upon me.' At certain times in history, nationalism is for groups of human beings the manifestation of freedom's spirit." [13]

Then, too, "vigilant" individuals were on the alert, and Bernard Lazare knew their objection: "'At a time when everything is becoming united,' you will say, 'you want to divide.'" But the progressive construction of a shared world no longer seemed to him to require the sacrifice of the world's diversity. What his own existence as a parvenu had taught him was that you don't come to the indispensable "moral unification" of humanity through uprooting and pure abstraction. [14] He didn't allow himself to be impressed: "Every human group is necessary, it is useful to humanity, it contributes to *putting* beauty into the world, it is a source for forms, thoughts, and images. Why would you make a little soldier out of humankind, why would you turn humankind over to a drill sergeant, why would you have it follow a canon from which it would never waver?" [15]

Sixty years later, when almost all of the intellectual Left of France reproached the Israelis for having betrayed both humanity by choosing the path to nationality and their miserable ancestors by becoming a kind of upstart state, *Les Temps modernes* refused to go along. With a certain courage, the journal resisted that conformism. Thanks notably to Claude Lanzmann who, before taking on the journal's editorship, would make Bernard Lazare's voice heard in *Les Temps modernes*. These discussions would keep in mind the link between the fighters of Tsahal and their ancestors from Prague and Galicia. While working for reconciliation with Arabs and for the rights of Palestinians, *Les Temps modernes* will never cease to remind its readers that Israel is a small nation – that is to say, according to Milan Kundera's definition, "a nation whose existence can at any moment be questioned" – and not merely a bridgehead for the American empire.

Well, the same people today see small nations as a supreme danger. They fiercely go after the peoples who don't want to die, and they condemn the right to self-determination with the very arguments Bernard Lazare refuted. Moreover, what is their "All Slavs of the South!" but the resumption of "All Semites!" – the vengeful formula that Israel's fiercest enemies used to deny both the reality of Arab anti-Semitism and the need for an independent Jewish state?

To defend the Zionist project and mobilize against the Slovenes the most hackneyed anti-Zionistic claims is an inconsistency made possible by the fact that, in the eyes of *Les Temps modernes*, to be Jewish is more than just being born such and wishing to remain so. Drumont and his disciples, in effect, don't blame Jews for being different but for not remaining in the space assigned for their difference. As Jankélévitch has shown, "anti-Semitism is aimed at another imperceptibly other; it expresses the disquiet that the non-Jew experiences before this other who is almost indiscernible from himself, the malaise he feels when faced by someone almost like himself."[16] Were there no Jew, the anti-Semite thinks, there would be no equivocation, no incertitude to mix up the essential division of humanity. Everything would be clear, and the world would be immediately understood. As opposed to the racist (though, of course, he can be both), the anti-Semite does not hate the other man *as other*, but the other *as man* and the challenge posed by the yet unfound difference of the Jew to desire to have done with the unity of humankind. "Whoever strikes a Jew shoves humanity down onto the ground," Kafka writes profoundly.

From this indisputable metaphysical specificity of anti-Semitism, *Les Temps modernes* implicitly draws a very questionable conclusion. The Jews were not being attacked as Jews, but as incarnations of the very idea of humanity. They are, so to speak, *directly men*; they don't need to justify their existence through uprooting and interbreeding. Their existence is already justified. The ethnic part and the ethical part of their being are not, as elsewhere, opposed but indissoluble. That is why *Les Temps modernes* thinks it impious to make any comparison between the extermination of the Jews and the atrocities of ethnic cleansing, and to refer to the first crime to clarify the second: "There is a specificity of historical situations, and what is happening in ex-Yugoslavia belongs to quite a different order."[17] In the first case, then, it is a question of killing Jews, this "antirace," in order to divide humanity into distinct races. In the second, the killings are the symptom of an already divided humanity where each being is reduced to what he is by birth. That is also why *Les Temps modernes* unhesitatingly grants its Judaeophile *nihil obstat* to Europe's abdication before Serbia. Vigilant people who meditate on the Jewish experience of history only to make a crime out of identity: could the fascism of our day hope for anything better?

NOTES

1. *Le Monde*,13 July 1993.

2. Annick Cojean, "L'Exil à vif des réfugiés réfugiés à Rumilly," *Le Monde*, 21 July 1993.

3. That is to say: Bernard Cuau, Roger Dadoun, Michel Deguy, Vladimir Fedorowski, Michel Giraud, Michel Kail, Claude Lanzmann, Jean Pouillon, Danièle Sallenave, Jean-Charles Szurek.

4. *Les Temps modernes*, June 1993, p. 104.

5. *Les Temps modernes*, 103–4.

6. *Les Temps modernes*, 104.

7. *Les Temps modernes*, 104.

8. Michel Foucault, one may remember, placed this sentence of René Char as an epigraph to the last two volumes of his *Histoire de la sexualité*.

9. *Métissage* means ethnic or racial mixing. *Trans.*

10. Bernard Lazare, *Juifs et antisémites* (Éditions Allia, 1992), 114.

11. Lazare, *Juifs*, 143.

12. Lazare, *Juifs*, 17.

13. Lazare, *Juifs*, 155–56.

14. Lazare, *Juifs*, 146.

15. Lazare, *Juifs*, 158–59.

16. Vladimir Jankélévitch and Béatrice Kerlowitz, *Quelque part dans l'inachevé* (Gallimard, 1978), 138.

17. *Les Temps modernes*, June 1993, p. 105.

# 31

# Intellectuals, Politics, and War

*Le Monde*, 16 September 1994

In an interview published in the spring of 1992 by the French journal *Commentaire* (Commentary), the former Polish dissident and historian Bronislaw Geremek pleaded with us Europeans of the West to show a little more comprehension for the phenomenon of nationalism. Worried about seeing the wall of misunderstanding survive the Berlin Wall, he cried out, "Don't fear nations!" Recalling that the victory of the civil community over totalitarian power had been accompanied in the other Europe with a victory of the nation over empire, he asked all democrats not to abandon "the defense of this strong and legitimate feeling of belonging to a natural community to the extremist movements of the popular-nationalist type."

Needless to say – but it is probably better to say it – that community Geremek sees as "natural" does not mean a community related by blood. There is no biological consideration in this reference to nature, no organicism, not even any naturalism, but this simple observation: we no more decide about our belonging to a group than we do about the language we speak, and these human creations – language, nation – are not, for all that, products of man because they do not belong to the category of things made. All our beginnings are marked with a passivity and an opaqueness that escape us. To live is to be already born into a condition that we have not chosen. "Language has been given to man so that he can testify to having inherited what he is," Holderlin says so grandly. In its red as in its brown version, the revolutionary passion of the twentieth century rose up against such a definition of the human. Affirming that everything is political, that is to say, that everything is possible, for being is will, it launched the freedom of man in the attack on his condition. By speaking of a "natural" community, Bronislaw Geremek, a survivor of totalitarianism, invites us to give back to a "given reality" its place on earth and to reconcile the freedom of man with his condition. Perhaps because the criticism of totalitarian regimes in Western Europe stopped short of the examination of their fundamental ambition, Geremek's appeal was not heard. And since he was himself, with the other former dissidents, too overwhelmed by the problems of the democratic transition in his own country to throw himself body and soul into the ideological battle over Yugoslavia, it was the first victims of the Serb aggression who paid for this disastrous deafness.

It was disastrous, in effect, because instead of defending the existence of a nation against nationalism, which elevates this existence to the rank of an absolute and ultimate value, we have continuously denounced the existence itself. Instead of condemning the systematic destruction of identities, we have found the source of all evil in their very perpetuation, to the greatest advantage of the ethnic cleanser or cleansers. Finally, instead of establishing cosmopolitanism as a value, as a requirement that all States, whatever their composition, must resolve (or at least soften, through a politics according to humanity) the contradiction between the particularity of the city and the universality of humankind, we have defined cosmopolitanism as a fact, as the privilege or the natural superiority of birth and of the essence of hybrid States over more homogeneous States.

Banish nature, and naturalism returns in full force and, with it, a strange inverted racism. To be cosmopolitan is first to know that cosmopolitanism is not of the order of being, that it is not a predicate but a horizon, that it is not a given but an ideal. That is what we have forgotten, to the advantage of a cosmopolitanism of identity, the most inconsistent, the most intolerant, the most stupid of all identities. That is how, during the first year of the war for a Greater Serbia, the fatal alliance of realism and idealism was formed, the alliance of calculation and principles, of the friends of force and the enemies of the tribes; briefly, of politicians and intellectuals.

Today this marriage is definitely over. But the simple fact that it could take place requires, before any new activity on the part of intellectuals, that each thing be returned to its place: the nation to its rank of carnal reality, cosmopolitanism to its rank of value and aspiration for nations. Once this task has been accomplished, intellectuals will be able to turn toward politicians and ask them to justify their actions. Ask them, for example, what became of the commitments they have made since the beginning of the war to create Greater Serbia. What have they done for the return of Croatian refugees to their homes, and for the restitution of the Krajinas to Croatia, stipulated in the Vance Plan signed on 2 January 1992? How did they react to the fact that the pseudo Serb parliament rejected the Vance-Owen Plan for Bosnia-Herzegovina? What became of the security zones created in May 1993 to compensate for the burial of that plan? What will they do tomorrow to obtain the effective retreat of Serb forces occupying regions given to the Croatian-Muslim Federation by the last plan now in force if not, because he looks so trustworthy, to lift the sanctions against the instigator of the war?

The attitude of Europe and of the international community in Croatia and in Bosnia-Herzegovina can be summarized as an uninterrupted series of unkept promises. The desire to embarrass Germany and the will to treat Russia with kid gloves clearly have their role in this politics of the unkept promise. But the essential lies elsewhere. Those who (we say) are in charge are torn between two contradictory responsibilities: on the one hand, they have to assume their participation in humanity and take care of the world as it works and as it doesn't; on the other, they must translate in political terms the modern promotion of life – and no longer of the world – and its place as supreme value or supreme good. In short, they want to make Europe into both a world power and a "bio-power." In the name of the first demand – to take charge of the world – they intervene in Yugoslavia. In the name of the second – to manage life, that is to say, first of all the life of those entrusted to them, the vital progress of the society they represent and administer – they intervene with blank cartridges. So they become referees without whistles, condemned to giving in to force, to accepting the fait accompli and to resorting to successive abdications through half measures, humanitarian cosmetics, and bad faith.

So our role, the role of European intellectuals, is not only to honor grand principles. We must reestablish the facts in their materiality and the belligerents in their differences. We must not let the victims of the European lie be called liars or agitators. We must always demand – at the risk of tiring the media – justice and freedom for Bosnia-Herzegovina, for Croatia, for the Kosovo that has been abandoned by everyone, and for Macedonia. Finally, we must remember that there were two and a half million refugees in the world in 1970, eleven million in 1983, and eighteen million in 1993. Faced with this progress of the inhuman, politics cannot be reduced to the pure management of life, unless we wish to accept the transformation of the world into an uninhabitable dwelling for all men.

# 32

# Will To Be Powerless

*Le Monde*, 29 November 1994

The European chancelleries, who want to be both realistic and human, advocate a *political* solution to the conflict in Croatia and Bosnia.

So they are angry because President Clinton, the day after his legislative defeat and in order to please a new majority that is both isolationist and pro-Bosnian, has decided – unilaterally – to abandon the enforcement of the embargo on arms into the former Yugoslavia. This indignation was kindly relayed, approved, and discussed by the majority of French editorialists. The media of this country that is so proud of its universality are, with few exceptions, so taken up by purely French matters that they cannot give any time or attention to the historic scandal of the Yugoslav policies jointly carried out by the French president and his minister of foreign affairs.

For this is certainly a scandal. And the war has not resumed in Bosnia because of the symbolic gesture of the Americans or because of the encouragement they would have given to the weakest, but because of the calculated hemming and hawing, and because of the implacable will to powerlessness that the international community has shown. Let's go back a few months. July 1994: the contact group gathering the United States, Russia, and the European Union, represented by France, England, and Germany, proposed a plan for the partition of Bosnia. This plan foresees 51 percent of the territories for the Croatian-Muslim Federation and 49 percent for the Serb "republic." It's a "take it or leave it" situation.

Milosevic takes, Karadzic leaves. Milosevic is immediately recompensed with a substantial reduction of sanctions against Belgrade. Karadzic is also rewarded since our diplomats are not content with closing their eyes to the supplying of men, arms, munitions, fuel, and provisions to the army of Pale. Forgetting their ultimatum, sabotaging their own plan, denying once again their solemn commitments, for fear of having to enforce them, the same diplomats tell the Serbs of Bosnia that they will be able to be a part of Serbia and let it be understood that it will be necessary to redo the non-negotiable map they had presented to the warring factions, so that the Serb part could be viable, that is to say, compact. On 17 October, the French minister of foreign affairs declared, "We know that the Belgrade authorities might accept abandoning every claim on Sarajevo in exchange for enclaves in eastern Bosnia." And Mr. Juppé added, "Several Muslim leaders might also consider this possibility, though with some regret."

In taking the offensive, the Bosnian army and the Croatian forces of Bosnia have only drawn the consequences of this new abdication. Traitors to their promises, the British and French governments have cried out treason in the name of the contact group. Then they let the Serbs punish this disloyal effort at liberation. They requested and obtained NATO raids on certain Serb positions in Krajina only to keep Croatia from entering the fight, and they waited for the fall of Bihac before giving the aggressor a look of reproach.

The evident moral of this tragedy is that the conflict can only be resolved by military force. No political solution can avoid a reversal of the power struggle, because as long as it is not forced to do so, the Serb faction will not negotiate. It will impose its conditions on the world, which is to say the establishment, by violence, concentration camps, and napalm, of a Greater Serbia ethnically pure and culturally cleansed of any non-Serb vestige, in Banja Luca as in Vukovar, conquered and entirely destroyed only three years ago.

Today, what the contact group defends is not, therefore,

the logic of peace against the logic of war, or the path of dialogue against a spiraling violence, but first its own preservation in the event of Russia's defection. Moreover, it defends the Serb conquest against the ill will of its victims and, even, sporadically and prudently, against the Serbs themselves when they seem to forget how far they can really go. And the complaint we should make to the United States is not to have tried to dictate its laws by planting its stars and stripes in the heart of Europe, as claim those touchy defenders of national independence who date the occupation of France from the moment the American troops landed. And it's not for having acted alone and deserted its camp but, rather, for having played but a symbolic role.

"One? Who is this 'one' who so reproaches everyone?" ask the intrigued chancelleries. Yet they only see activists and intellectuals; that is to say, in their eyes, no one. "The affair concerning one person has become an affair that concerns us all," is what Clemenceau said about Dreyfus. Unless the Bosnian affair does become the affair of all, there will be no political solution to the conflict.

# 33

# On the Uselessness of the Twentieth Century

*Le Monde*, 15 December 1994
We weren't always right to revolt. At least, revolt and indignation could at times disturb or perturb the order of things.

Now everything happens in one space, and everyone is subjected to the same pictures, commentaries, and verbal abuse. Even revolt is part of the spectacle. Moral posture is integrated into the circle of communication and is one of the expected ingredients. It even finds itself placed under the almost exclusive jurisdiction of a club of bad-tempered people whose code name is: intellectuals. These quick-tempered officers accompany the news from Algeria, Kigali, Bangladesh, or Bosnia with a kind of primal cry or with continuous vociferations, which tend to become the Muzak playing in the background of planetary news.

Faced with this undifferentiated vehemence, the Prince, his experts, and his ministers oscillate between condescension and annoyance. But, in any case, this vehemence serves them as a foil. Together they form the duo of Reason and Anger. And when they give homage to the warmth of emotion, our leaders take pride in knowing how, for their part, to keep a cool head. They may welcome or recognize the sincerity of those who adamantly work for justice, but only to congratulate themselves immediately afterward for remaining sober, resolute, and perceptive. The demonstration of intense feelings brings out, by contrast, their sound ability for analysis and anticipation. To the generous impulses they respect, they hold up the hard work of thought, less immediately sympathetic but infinitely more meritorious. To the lyrical infatuations, or violent outbursts provoked by the chaotic television spectacle of a world in convulsion, they answer with the necessity of staying on course, of clearly distinguishing the evils that depend on us and of those that don't. They insist especially on seeing the invisible – that is to say, on taking into account everything the picture doesn't show: the past and what is possible, causes and consequences, the historical depth and the far-ranging effects of the action.

It is precisely from this vantage of perception that Robert Schneider credits the president of the French Republic, in the chapter dedicated to the Yugoslav drama in Schneider's book on the last years of his reign: "History will probably be thankful to him for having had the courage – yes, the courage! – not to give in to pressure, however sympathetic, and to have had the wisdom not to take any measures that, at the time, would have earned him popular support." [1]

The confiscation of international citizenship by various blasphemers is deplorable on two counts: if we except the Algerian question – last bastion, in France, of classical commitment – it reinforces the apathy of opinion while reducing public action to a derisory and Olympian gesture. It comforts those whom Hannah Arendt called "the specialists of the solution for problems" in the idea that the less one is moved, the more intelligent one is, and that it isn't resistance to aggression, to occupation and ethnic cleansing, that makes great men but rather resistance to the desire to resist.

If it is probably too late to detach political commitment from the logic of the spectacle and the inexorable puppeteering of all things, we can still try to say that the king is naked and that the wisdom of experts is, where ex-Yugoslavia is concerned, the rationalization of a frightening fiasco.

Some time ago Pascal had already foreseen that "justice without force is powerless; force without justice is tyrannical. Justice without force is contradicted, because there are always some evil people; force without justice stands accused. So we must put justice and force together."

We have done exactly the contrary since the invasion of Croatia. We have carefully separated what we should absolutely have kept together. The result is that force has ridiculed the law and the law can now only sanction the conquests of force. How can we escape the shame of such an abdication? By no longer accusing the beast but the prey, by treating as mad extremists the very ones who accepted all the compromises and signed all the plans for peace that were proposed by the international community; in short, by transferring the guilt of force to its targets.

The strategists for the conflict and political analysts who today affirm that the cause of the conflict comes from a premature recognition of Slovenia and Croatia disregard chronology in order to avert or soften our debacle. And when they impute responsibility for recent fighting to Bosnian troops or to some bad outside genie who has thrown them to the wolves, they add insult to injury by blaming the victims they abandoned.

Failing being able to save men, the earth, and stones, it is important at least to defend factual truths against manipulation by officials and experts. It was not the secession of Slovenia and Croatia that brought about violence but Serbia's violent seizure of Yugoslavia that provoked the secession. The declarations of independence did not precede but *followed* the memorandum of the Academy of Arts and Sciences that denounced (like the grand paranoid programs of the century) a coalition against the Serb people and the suppression in Kosovo. The memorandum had proclaimed the boycott of Slovene products in order to have this coalition fail and thus announced the systematic refusal on the part of Slobodan Milosevic to reform the federal state. European recognition intervened *after* the destruction of Vukovar and the end of the war in Croatia. Likewise, the American decision to participate no longer in enforcing the embargo was taken several weeks *after* the beginning of the Bosnian offensive in Bihac. Was this a terrible strategic error? Perhaps, but we must not forget that since the month of May, of 138 humanitarian convoys sent into this so-called security zone, 132 had to turn back. As the Bosnian prime minister Haris Silajdzic has said, "With the approach of winter, the fifth corps tried to let supplies come through for a population that had been under siege for three years. Can one truly qualify as a bold offensive an attempt at survival that aims at breaking a siege?"

And this attempt would probably not have been condemned to failure had the Serbs of Bosnia not received reinforcements from their "brothers" of Krajina, deemed to be disarmed after the accords signed on 2 January 1992 under the aegis of the United Nations and which the UN soldiers were mandated to enforce.

As for saying that the war now going on under our eyes is a conflict between "Bosnian communities," according to the terms carefully studied and diplomatically chosen from the communiqué published on 25 November by the office of the president of the republic and the administration of the prime minister, we might just as well describe the uprising of the Warsaw Ghetto as a conflict between Jewish and German communities. On 6 April 1992 – the day the international community recognized Bosnia-Herzegovina – the demonstrators who walked peacefully through the streets of Sarajevo belonged to all the Bosnian communities. The shooters who then fired upon them were acting on orders from Belgrade and made no mystery of their final objective, to conquer as much territory as possible to annex it to Serbia. It is true that, because of our shameful retreats, the instigator of the war and of ethnic cleansing has since been promoted to the dignity of supreme recourse and keeper of the peace without ever having had to offer, in exchange, anything substantial.

But, and I already hear the objection, doesn't this replace the analysis with a mixture and criticism with a cry in comparing such incomparable things? Why this reference to Hitler? Why not accept this war in its Balkan specificity, even in it posttotalitarian newness? Because this apparent scruple shows a concern not to understand the horror but to reject its injunction. Because in so dispelling any reminiscence, we don't have to confront the truth of the present moment; we protect ourselves from it. Because, from our obsession with evil machinations to total war, the parallel is inevitable and blatant. Because if the tragedy of an earlier time had changed the spirit of our times we could not say, as Bernard Kouchner has just recently done, that given the resolve of the Serbs, Slovenia and Croatia should not have been recognized. Because if, beyond the incessant commemorations and unanimous antitotalitarian rhetoric, the names of Munich, Hitler, and Stalin truly evoke something and if the events these names refer to had truly been understood, it would not have been possible to raise up the resolve of brute force and pure will to power as an argument in favor of brute force, as a reason for giving in to power.

The day the French government appealed for "a settlement of a negotiated peace, the only lasting solution to the conflict of the Bosnian communities," one picture circulated the globe. It showed a soldier of the Serb forces of Bihac who obliged a Muslim prisoner to wear the fez and to sing, "Bosnia belongs to Serbia just as Moscow belongs to Russia." This was a racist gesture, an imperialist slogan, and an absolute humiliation. The coincidence between this muffled text and unbearable picture is damning. It proves that the twentieth century, which some say ended on 9 November 1989 with the end of Communism and the Cold War, has been a century for nothing. Looking at the increasing success of plot theories in the disintegration of Russian society, we can be fearful of everything in the postscript that began more than three years ago in Croatia and Bosnia.

NOTE

1. Robert Schneider, *Les Dernières Années* (Seuil, 1994), 134.

# 34

# Forgetting the World

*Le Monde*, 15 April 1995
The election campaign for the French presidency seems to have forgotten world affairs. They are absent from the programs and speeches, absent from the amiable exchanges among the different candidates, and also absent from the innumerable questions with which reporters daily assail candidates.

Three months after the resumption of hostilities and as a response to several stubborn intellectuals (*Le Monde* of 7 April), the candidates finally consented to discuss pressing international issues. But instead of making any concrete commitments on the issues, they made boisterous hollow statements, vague claims, and pious wishes, just as others had done before them.

To what do we owe this long silence? To an outburst of jingoistic fever? To a renewal of chauvinism? To an identity crisis? No, but to the fact that today collective life is understood only in its social and economic dimension. What is today called politics no longer mobilizes citizens but rather mobilizes workers and consumers, the social services recipients and beneficiaries we have become but which we were not when these questions still had meaning: "What purpose have we in the world? What can we contribute to humanity?"

The candidates are not neglecting the world for the nation. They are following *la pensée unique* [whereby no difference really exists between right and left] even as they denounce it, carried away as they are by a logic of production that is not only dominant but today exclusive of any other approach to reality. They don't give a fig about the role, the mission, the vocation, or the voice of France. Just as world affairs are no longer of prime importance, France's role as a nation has given way to concerns about social and administrative realities.

So neglecting the nation does not result in an opening up to the world but in forgetting it. And those who had no words harsh enough for the nationalisms of Eastern Europe, those who indiscriminately placed under this infamous label hegemonic will as well as desire for freedom, those very same ones were able, week after week, to campaign without proposing a reformulation of France's African policy in spite of what had happened in Rwanda, without making any reference to nearby Algeria, and without ever mentioning the names of Vukovar, Sarajevo, and Grozny, as though the war and the "urbicides" for which Europe is again the theatre had taken place on another planet and in no way concerned us French and Europeans.

It is important to remember the world and worry about the world in the face of politicians who have become nationalists without a nation, French patriots with no Revolutionary cap, and builders of a Europe that has no content. But so that some memory of the world can carry weight, so that the refusal to let politics sink into meaninglessness, and become absorbed entirely in economic regulations or reduced to the handling of social questions, so that this refusal might be something other than the intermittent and inoffensive racket of those assigned to grand causes, those who make that racket should know how to resist the angelic phantasm of an omnipotent morality.

We are not in the world as television pictures it. It's not that we can and must act everywhere at once because the images of evil and misfortune come to us from everywhere. There are limits to what a state, or even a group of states, can do. Let's not let the planetary village destroy in us a sense of the possible and an awareness of finitude. To lose this awareness and forget the limits inherent in every incarnate existence would be – while we are expected to exercise the moral convictions intellectuals are said to have – to give the providential gift of moral responsibility to men and parties who seek our votes while they wash their hands of all responsibility for the world.

No person is held to the impossible. But no one has the right to remove himself from his commitments. Noblesse oblige. Yet, since 1991, French and European policies in Croatia and Bosnia have broken their word several times when they offered ineffective guarantees, when they labeled areas safe zones by antiphrasis, and when they issued ultimatums forgotten almost immediately after their solemn proclamation. The Bosnian president said it with pain and dignity in Budapest at the time of the last meeting of the Organization for Security and Cooperation in Europe. Losing control, the French president then yelled at him with biting belligerence, as though by insisting on upholding the right to existence that the Serbs have denied him with repeated shellings, he were the guilty party in the war and thereby to be blamed for our own problems.

On that day François Mitterrand dishonored France. And we now realize that at the end of the twentieth century, and all things considered, those who govern us, far from feeling themselves obliged by the imperative voice of memory to implement a policy different from Munich's, answer brute force with a *try and try again* diplomacy. Like Chamberlain, they consider the war in the Balkans "a quarrel in a faraway land among people about whom we know very little."

None of the candidates for the office Mr. Mitterrand now occupies seems to have taken stock of this dishonor because for them honor has ceased to be a political category. If we accept this disappearance, we will be reduced to being global individuals and no longer European and French citizens worried about the world.

# 35

# The Kusturica Imposture

*Le Monde*, 2 June 1995

The audience that gave a standing ovation to *Underground*, the grand portrayal of Emir Kusturica depicting fifty years of Yugoslav history, and the jury that gave it the Golden Palm award at the Cannes Film Festival have, without any doubt, experienced the heady certitude of killing two birds with one stone. At the same time as celebrating an artist endowed with all the exterior signs of genius, this frenetic audience and its fervent jurors showed their indignation before the carnage of Tuzla and their solidarity with the victims of the war. The homage they paid the Sarajevan filmmaker quite naturally included his compatriots. They brought together these two imperatives that are so often contradictory: esthetic demand and the urgency to be committed. In their enthusiasm, the beautiful was confused with the good, the love of art with their participation in History and the admiration for the formal audacity of a work of art with the compassionate zeal for the unfortunate.

According to its author, *Underground* is nevertheless a nostalgic adieu to Yugoslavia. "There was once a country" is what the subtitle clearly lets us know. And for Kusturica, the destruction of this country cannot be imputed to those who, from the time of the occupation of Kosovo, showed their intention to make a "Serboslavia" of it. The responsibility rests with all the nations who have chosen independence to escape from their foretold spiritual death.

In October 1991, that is to say, during the first months of the conflict, Kusturica wrote, "There are many things I didn't know as a child. Now I know. The Slovenian has always dreamed his Slovene dream, the dream of an Austrian squire. But it was our ancestors who, during the First World War, saved this same Slovenian from the shit of Vienna" ("L'acacia de Sarajevo," *Libération*, 21 October 1991).

Four years later, several dozens of thousands of dead and some urbicides later, Kusturica persists, and thus gives substance to his remarks, "The archives used in the film show Nazi troops entering Slovenia where they are welcomed as though at home . . . , something that is still the case today, for Slovenia has always been conceived as a Germanic advance into the orthodox world . . . then they are in Zagreb where the same thing happens. And when they enter Belgrade, you see no one in the streets . . . they are on foreign soil." And, revolted by the support that certain intellectuals have been able to bring to a Bosnia in flames, Kusturica concludes: "You have to be stupid to refuse to understand that the fall of the Berlin Wall has completely shocked these very fragile places, and especially all these little satellite countries of the Nazis, like Slovenia, Croatia, Hungary, . . . and Bosnia! There is a completely stupid term that one hears everywhere, that of 'Greater Serbia.' How can a country of nine million inhabitants be qualified as 'great?' At the same time there is a united Germany, with eighty million inhabitants and which is truly great, and no one notices it" (*Les Cahiers du cinéma*, June 1995, p. 70).

Nazification of the victims of ethnic cleansing, denunciation of the Fourth Reich, defense of the Serb David in his heroic fight with the Germanic Goliath, covering up of all the crimes presently being committed revive the memory, itself doctored up, of the Second World War. What Kusturica has put into music and pictures is the very discourse that the assassins use to convince and to convince themselves that they are in a situation of legitimate defense because they are dealing with an all-powerful enemy. This moviemaker, known for his outrageousness, therefore capitalizes here on the suffering of Sarajevo as he takes as his own the stereotyped arguments of those who are organizing a famine in Sarajevo and who are besieging it. He has symbolized a suffering Bosnia while refusing to call himself Bosnian, and he goes into a holy anger when one dares call Slobodan Milosevic a fascist or the Serbs aggressors.

In recognizing *Underground*, the Cannes jury thought it was honoring a creator with a thriving imagination. In fact, it has honored a servile and flashy illustrator of criminal clichés. The Cannes jury praised to high heaven a version of the most hackneyed and deceitful Serb propaganda. But it is a rock version, one that is postmodern, disheveled, totally cool, Americanized, and made in Belgrade. The devil himself could not have conceived so cruel an outrage against Bosnia nor such a grotesque epilogue to Western incompetence and frivolity.

# 36

# Don't Let the Image of the Dead Bury the Dead

*Libération*, 16 June 1995

After the pogrom in Kichinev, which in April of 1903 claimed some forty people dead, protest meetings were held in New York, London, Paris, and Berlin. There was then no global village but there was already, as Péguy said, "*an opinion of the inhabited earth*," and it had not yet become bored by the monstrosities of the twentieth century. It had a rather rudimentary practice of dialectics; it had not learned the naive opinion that you don't make an omelet without breaking some eggs. Like Engels – yes, Engels! – horrified by the bomb attacks perpetrated by the Irish republicans at Westminster, this public opinion thought that a war ought to be fought against soldiers, not against civilians. Finally, unlike today's television viewers, it was not subjected to the continuous flow of planetary violence.

Today, we let the pictures of the dead bury the dead and, swept from accidents to catastrophes, we haven't time for anything, not even for the massacre in Tuzla where seventy civilians, mostly adolescents, were killed by a Serb bomb while they were seated outside a café. And this bomb did not fall there accidentally. For the political authorities of Pale, it served as a protest against NATO, which in its presumptuousness had thought itself authorized to respond with the destruction of an entire warehouse because of the repression and pillaging that had resumed in Sarajevo.

Don't let the pictures of the dead bury the dead: that was the basic raison d'être for the protest march that on 6 June led hundreds of demonstrators from the Panthéon to the

National Assembly. While Alain Juppé, solemnly flanked by his minister of foreign affairs and his minister of defense, was presenting the main lines of French politics for the former Yugoslavia before a parliament almost empty (because of the municipal elections then being held), demonstrators on Boulevard Saint-Michel chanted the ages and names of Tuzla's victims: Mehinovic Amira, twenty-one years old; Cajic Sanja, eighteen years old; Fatusic Muris, fifteen years old; Jojkic Damir, twenty-eight years old, etc. Going against frenetic current events and busy activity within France, the demonstrations of commemoration were aimed at inscribing the massacre of Tuzla in history as an unforgettable event and recording it in politics as an infamy requiring reparation. For Greater Serbia's zealots and enforcers did not become criminals, bandits, or terrorists the day they took several hundred United Nations soldiers hostage. They took these soldiers hostage because they are terrorists, as has been shown these last four years by the fate reserved for the monuments and inhabitants of Dubrovnik, Vukovar, Osijek, Sarajevo, Gorazde, Zepa, Srebernica, Bihac, and Tuzla. Until General Mladic's troops attacked us, we treated the aggressors and the victims as nationalists, with a neutrality Lord Owen ostensibly regrets having lost. So what name do we give to these humanitarian supremacists who continuously take pride in their solicitude but who talk about crime only when it touches their own people, and of belligerence when the objects of their compassion have become targets for snipers and bombs? There cannot be two humanities: one that counts and another that doesn't, the untouchable humanitarian humanity and facing it, or beneath it, a kind of human magma composed of interchangeable and featureless beings.

Besides, it is in no way illogical or illegitimate to defend multiethnic Bosnia while taking note of Yugoslavia's dismemberment, contrary to what strategic or geopolitical experts claim. They continually flatter themselves that they know more than the "Parisian moralists" and are cool headed when faced with the emotive dictatorship of the image. For Bosnia is not a small-scale version of Yugoslavia, and if those who are nostalgic for the former order deny thus fiercely Bosnia-Herzegovina's right to exist, that's because they don't at any cost want to swap a state where the Serbs would be able to exert their hegemony over the other nations for a republic that is authentically multinational. Consequently they conceive of no other alternative to this hegemony than that of ethnic cleansing; that is to say, not only *"where there is a Serb, there is Serbia,"* but where Serbia is, there can be no place for anyone else. War did not break out in the Banja Luca region where Serbs are in the majority, and yet Croatians and Muslims, who want to be safe, have no other choice but exile, and their places of worship – mosques, churches, and monasteries – are dynamited one after the other.

The idea of humanity will be undermined for a long time in Europe if those whom we call terrorists today have only to let their hostages go free in order to be reinstated into civilization and reap the fruits of their racism and crimes.

# 37

# The King with No Clothes

*Télérama*, 26 July 1995
Desperate jokes are the most beautiful and I know some time-less ones that truly make you sob.[1] This one, for example, which circulates between Sarajevo and Zagreb: "What do you have against the Serbs?" "Nothing effective."

Nothing effective: this has in every case been the slogan the great powers have used since the beginning of a conflict that has already lasted longer than the First World War. From the United Nations to contact groups, from large international organizations to ad hoc committees, the various arbiters who have been to the region have applied an unparalleled constancy at being turncoats and confirming the law of the strongest.

A simple negative vote by the parliament of the Serb Republic of Bosnia, this illegitimate and tiny country, was enough for the international community to abandon, without encountering any opposition, the Vance-Owen Plan for Bosnia, and to compensate for its defeatism with the creation of security zones. Since these very same enclaves blemished the beautiful Serb territorial continuity, a number of Western diplomats whispered privately (Oh! the whispers of diplomats . . .) that a decision would have to be made to get rid of them in order to have a durable and effective peace. Mr. Clean, who has quite good hearing, then began to scour, rub, and clean with all his might. And the stains are disappearing one by one. Serbia will soon be impeccably clean. Soon we will be able to lift all sanctions.

Faced with the collapse of every principle, only the sorry consolation of sarcasm would have been left had the president of the French Republic not suddenly spoken out, had he not found the right words to denounce the unqualifiable and to censure the eagerness of the big powers to lower the flag. Such statements warm the heart. But should we believe them? After all, three years ago, when the situation of the civilians detained by the Serbs in Bosnia was made known, our then minister of foreign affairs had caught all the warmongers short by exhorting the French army to liberate the camps! It didn't occur to Roland Dumas to carry out such a swell, booming idea. He simply speculated on the versatility of the newsmen and, rather than cringe with the hope of better days for his Serb friends, he chose to serve up, and thus satisfy the emotions of the moment, a scenario that was as beautiful and stupid as a Sylvester Stallone film. This cynicism paid off: the former Yugoslavia was soon snatched up into the buzz of daily news and no one, in France, held it against Roland Dumas that he was making fools of us all.

Certainly, unlike the former president and his closest minister, Jacques Chirac never accepted the arguments that Serb nationalists developed to justify their aggression. He didn't say that the borders between the republics were *administrative*. He didn't say that this war had been started to protect the threatened rights of Serb minorities. He didn't impute Yugoslavia's breakup to a Vatican-German conspiracy. So much the better for him, since these three positions were so many lies. By creating the second Yugoslavia, Tito had reestablished within their historic borders its diverse parts; the Serbs were not fighting for their rights as a minority but for the right not to be a minority anywhere on Yugoslav soil; finally, it was not John Paul II allied with Chancellor Kohl who engaged Slovenes, Croatians, Bosnians, and Macedonians on the path of dissociation, but the iron will shown by Slobodan Milosevic to restore Serb hegemony upon the federal state.

Nevertheless, Jacques Chirac's grand gesture comes rather late. Silent at the time of the Tuzla massacre, furious to see the Bosnian offensive to raise the siege of Sarajevo trouble the agenda of the Halifax Summit, not very combative after the liberation of our own UN soldiers, during the first two quite agitated months of his presidency he kept to a rather classic approach to the problem. To reestablish peace, he substantially said, we must remain neutral, refuse every military intimidation, and play Milosevic's card against those whom Chirac, in order to convince himself of their isolation, called the "Bosno-Serbs." Confronted by intellectuals enamored of the greatness of their causes, he justified all the choices giving rise to the Western fiasco with the need to reach practical results.

We can't keep from thinking that this conversion to firmness, too late to be true, makes France look good and saves not its honor but its image at a time when any idea of collective security is collapsing in Bosnia.

It remains however that a king, a king and not an intellectual, has said: "the king is naked." A head of state and not some intellectual mentioned the conversations between Chamberlain and Daladier and implicitly reminded us that already in 1938 there was a question of threatened minorities and of wild tribes. Lord Runciman, the Lord Owen of the day, had made known to the British cabinet his "sympathy for the Sudetens' case," and observed on the part of Prague certainly not an active oppression but "a lack of tact, a mean unwillingness to understand, intolerance and discrimination." Such contempt for the small nations of Central Europe aggravated, on the other hand, the fact that we didn't keep our word or abide by our alliances, precisely because it was used as a justification for these betrayals. Echoing Marshall Goering, who directly attacked this "little portion of Europe" without mincing his words, this "miserable race of Pygmies without culture" who made "life unbearable for Humanity," there is the hardly euphemistic remark of Stéphane Lauzanne, a famous Parisian editorialist of the 1930s:

"France does not have to run to help this or that amalgam of unknown races in the Balkans."

The false French note in the grand concert of renunciation will probably not change the order of things. At least it will have made us face this unbearable truth: Munich is not a deplorable accident of History, but rather the congenital attribute of our democracies.

NOTE

1. Finkielkraut begins with an allusion to Alfred de Musset's poem "La Nuit de Mai": "Les plus désespérés sont les chants les plus beaux, / Et j'en sais d'immortels qui sont de purs sanglots." The three preceding lines are: "Rien ne nous rend si grands qu'une grande douleur. / Mais, pour en être atteint, ne crois pas, ô poète, / Que ta voix ici-bas doive rester muette" (Nothing makes us so sublime as a sublime grief. But, in your stricken state, do not believe, O poet, that your voice here below must stay silent.) William Rees, *French Poetry 1820–1950, with Prose Translations* (New York: Penguin Books, 1990), 106. *Trans*.

# 38

# Of Men and Angels

*Le Monde*, 20–21 August 1995

So all that was needed was a victorious offensive for this simple idea to win out in the complicated Balkans: they are all horrible and putrid; they are all the same! The newspapers proclaim the end of contradictions; observers, international mediators, and the best known commentators of the media return to their original aversion for all the protagonists of what they continue to call the Yugoslav imbroglio. Their severity, sparing no one, is nevertheless unleashed with particular virulence against the Croatians, these henchmen who have taken us for a ride, these perfidious purifiers, these clever assassins, these conquerors who have been disguised as victims for much too long a time. To the "good souls" who have supported them or who have simply denounced without denting Serbia's resolve to solve all political problems with violence, an angry editorialist goes so far as to promise revenge to the people who have been fooled: "One day," he threateningly wrote, "public opinion will demand an explanation."[1]

Rather than pleading guilty or hiding yourself while hoping for better days, try risking going against the wrath of this popular media justice by reminding them that the Croatians, only after three fruitless years of diplomatic efforts with the Serbs and the United Nations to obtain the peaceful reintegration of Slavonia and the Krajina of Knin, did not conquer but rather liberated territories vital for their economy and situated within their own borders. You will then see the media look at you with the very same stupor that, in the seventies, was painted on all the world's progressive faces when, defending the right to independence of the Palestinians, you dared evoke the fragility of Israel and the danger of death that loomed over this country.

If you don't let yourself be discouraged by this first rebuff, and you indicate that the Croatians answered the pressing call of the Bosnian government and saved, with Bosnian troops, the Muslim enclave of Bihac, which was surrounded by the Serbs, deprived of everything, and sacrificed – like all the other zones of security – by the international community, they will make fun of your stupidity. They will answer you, with that tired Humphrey Bogart look of one who has been around the block several times and who does not allow himself be taken in, that this operation could not have been conducted without the support of Slobodan Milosevic. They will even advance, while whisking out – as one might pull a rabbit out of a hat – the map providentially drawn by Franjo Tudjman in London on a banquet table, that the taking of Knin is only the prelude to the grand partitioning of Bosnia-Herzegovina between Croatia and Serbia.

In other words, even though the Croatians have apparently changed their politics, they continue to pursue clandestinely the same end. They may well sign and apply military accords with the authorities of Sarajevo but it's Belgrade that remains their privileged interlocutor and their unchangeable accomplice. When appearances overwhelm the Croatians, as happened at the time of the conflict eternally symbolized by the ignominious destruction of the Mostar bridge, we don't need to look much farther. On the other hand, when appearances favor Croatia, we fall back, in order to dismiss them, on the theory of a plot and on the inexhaustible resources of secret diplomacy. In this game where we always recover our stake, concrete reality is true when it confirms our initial theses and it is a lie when it seems to invalidate these. This means that Croatians are devoted to hatred as

Jews are to business, Mexicans to their siesta, and Blacks to sports.

In its revengeful indignation, the international press gives itself the luxury of reproaching the president of this incorrigible people for wanting – *horresco referens!* – to divide Bosnia. Have we already forgotten that all the peace plans proposed these last three years are, unfortunately, plans for partition? Don't we have eyes to see that, once total liberation has been excluded by the world's cynicism, the division into a Croatian-Muslim federation and a Serb entity is much better than the partitioning into three blocks that was favored for so long by the major powers even though the latter solution pushed everyone toward crime and handed over to fundamentalism what remained of Bosnia?

If, finally, you affirm that the Serb exodus from Krajina was not due to a systematic politics of ethnic cleansing, you will be told that a refugee is a refugee and that, whether it was systematic or not, only the result counts: the Krajina region was emptied in a few days of nearly all its Serb inhabitants. A de facto ethnic cleansing has just taken place in Croatia. This lexical innovation of the international observers – "ethnic cleansing" – marks a watershed in the history of criminal accusations.

Since the mysticism of the race prevails in Serbia over the concept of nation, the Serb war leaders have themselves given the name of ethnic cleansing to the massacres, to the expulsion of all non-Serbs and to the leveling of every cultural trace of their presence on the land that has fallen into Greater Serbia's control. For four years, this methodical vandalism was given free rein in the Krajina of Knin. In Drnish, a village that was 80 percent Croatian, the inhabitants were chased away, the Catholic churches were sacked, and weeds now grow where houses once stood. In Otavica, the mausoleum of the sculptor Ivan Mestrovic, the Croatian Rodin, was destroyed, his tomb opened, and his bones scattered.

However repugnant, on the other hand, the exactions committed against the Serb refugees by a part of the Croatian army rabble or by some civilians, the motorized procession heading toward Belgrade has nothing in common with the horde of old people, women, and children without baggage who arrived in Sarajevo or in Tuzla after the taking of Srebernica. Their departure had been organized by the Serb army, after the selection and imprisonment or massacre of all the healthy men and adolescents. The Serb refugees, by order of their own leaders, left before the entrance of the Croatian army. And even though we could regard with suspicion the pleas to return that were repeatedly made by the religious and political authorities of Croatia, it remains that to speak of de facto ethnic cleansing is to have contempt for the law, in the very language of law. If the crime, in effect, no longer defines itself by the intention or by the act but by its consequences, then, since all men are mortal, Death is this perfect and total genocide in relation to which the Hitlerian enterprise itself appears as the work of an altar boy or some wise guy.

But why do we find it so difficult, confronted by this war, to respect the distinctions, the subtle gradations and criminal hierarchies that tradition has left us and that the twentieth century should have forced us to refine yet again? Paradoxically I have found the beginning of an answer to this haunting question in the international bestseller of Nicholas Negroponte, *L'Homme numérique (Being Digital)*. An enthusiastic champion of the information highway and other miracles of the videosphere, the author certainly doesn't know what to make of the conflict in the former Yugoslavia. But he writes this in answer to all the technophobes worried about the joint progress of the computer and ignorance: "Most American children don't know the difference between the Baltic and the Balkans; they don't know who the Visigoths were and don't know where Louis XIV lived. Well, why should it be so important? Didn't you know that Reno is west of Los Angeles?"[2]

This work, written while the conflict in the Balkans was already raging, has the merit of putting its cards on the table. Here ignorance is not only claimed but rightly established. What good is there, in effect, in taking into account dates and places, why burden oneself with the useless questions of where and when in the era of the electronic address and of the abolition of time and space by telepresence? Man was vernacular; now he is planetary; he was rooted, now he is wired in; he was situated, now he is weightless; he was from somewhere, and now he can be everywhere at once thanks to universal and instantaneous communication; he was inscribed in a world, but henceforth the world is inscribed on his screen; he was geographical and historical, but now he is numerical – that is, angelic, equipped like the angels with the gifts of ubiquity and weightlessness. And for this inhabitant of the immaterial, heaviness is at the origin of every barbarity. For this technological angel, ethnic cleansing comes naturally and directly from being stuck in a particular reality. For this citizen of world vision, violence is born from belonging; war comes from the prenumerical opposition between here and elsewhere. In short, Evil is the spirit that, instead of exploding, crashes and becomes flesh. Evil is incarnation itself.

Angelic humanity has distanced itself from earthly humanity with such maddening speed that today it imputes inhumanity, of which the former Yugoslavia is the theatre, to incarnation, that is to say, to the human condition. Croatians are the present victims of this monstrous ontological amalgam. But since history is not about to end, we can bet that moralism will have many other occasions to kill morality and that the anger of the angels is destined to cause even more damage.

NOTES

1. Jean-François Kahn, "Ex-Yougoslavie: Vers l'épuration ethnique généraliséé," *L'Événement du Jeudi*, 10 August 1995, p. 10.

2. N. Negroponte, *L'Homme numérique* (Laffont, 1995), 245.

# 39

# Race in Opposition to
# the Nation

*Frankfurter Allgemeine Zeitung*, 8 September 1995

"The stranglehold on this city must stop once and for all, and not just temporarily. The noose must be taken off and not just left on its shoulders." So ran a communiqué of the Atlantic Alliance the day following the first massive air attacks against Serb positions around Sarajevo. In the city itself, no one thought the UN would ever display such a clear or fierce resolve. One had believed in it for a long time, and then had ended up believing instead that the powerful were impatient to ratify what had already been done. It would be useless to wait for "the cavalry" (to use Warren Christopher's expression), for the cavalry was never going to come. Sarajevo's inhabitants left little by little; those who stayed, by necessity or choice, plunged into despair.

Hence, today, their feelings of disbelief, relief, and gratitude – but also of bitterness. NATO's military intervention is a sorrowful and divine surprise. Why sorrowful? Because the event that provoked it – the bombing of the Markale market place – is nothing exceptional. This carnage alone did not cause the war to degenerate into terrorism. It has been terrorist since day one. From the outset, enough was enough and the crime known. The Serbs – let's give them credit where credit is due – have never hidden their game or beaten around the bush. For them the enemy has never been the opposing army, but *the people* accidentally killed while accomplishing the most elementary tasks of daily life. In short, it is not the conflict that changed in nature on 18 August 1995 but rather the international community, which agreed to change its attitude only after four years of atrocities documented by innumerable analyses, reports, and witnesses. The truth up to this date clashed with two dogmas that seemed unassailable: the dogma of Serb invincibility and that of necessary diplomatic neutrality. "Intervention? Three hundred thousand men. . . . Choose a side? That's the luxury of an intellectual. A leader who wants to remain credible must try to keep an equal balance among all the parties involved." That's what, until most recently, was repeatedly stated in very high places when anyone pleaded for a less ambiguous discourse and for greater firmness.

The edifice of misguided assumptions began to reel with the Croatian offensive in Krajina and with the American diplomatic initiative. The Croatians have done justice to the myth or to the alibi that has allowed a little winter ski station to keep the world at bay and to make fun of its ultimatums to lay down arms. By plunging into this "window of opportunity" the Americans have shown that no political solution was possible without a reversal of the military situation. The dogmas collapsed – one could fight. This was accomplished thanks mainly to the determination of France's new president. After initially succumbing to a policy of appeasement – like everyone else – Jacques Chirac finally seized the opportunity to break with his hieratic predecessor and return to France a little of its lost honor. This was certainly an improvement, but it came very late in the game.

To the combination of joy and melancholy that this quick but tardy reaction evokes is added a feeling of perplexity before the blindness of the observers: how could so many editorialists of the French and Anglo-Saxon press interpret the Serb rout in Krajina and Bihac as the indubitable sign of a Serb-Croatian plot against Bosnia? How could they see in the American initiative the cynical officialization of this infamous scheme?

"Lying is stronger than the truth because it satisfies one's expectations": these words of Hannah Arendt's point to an answer. What can we expect of nationalism, in every situation and on every occasion? Hatred of the Other. This hatred must then be expressed in the same way and against the same victim in Croatia and Serbia. The rumor of the plot hatched behind the scenes or in back rooms was stronger than the event itself, since it fulfilled everyone's expectations . . .

If we now want to return to the real world, that is to say, to understand it instead of overinterpreting it, we must first let the Other have some rest. We must deprive ourselves of the facile hermeneutics given by the capitalized concept of the Other and grant it a sabbatical leave amply merited after years spent, without balking, serving philosophers and psychoanalysts. A lazy abstraction, a catch-all category, or more precisely a catch-all for everyone, the Other takes the place of the others. Under its edifying aspects, this substitution presents the twofold political and ontological disadvantage of conjuring human plurality and of closing the mind to the diversity of situations and historical data.

On 31 December 1991, the singer Barbara Hendriks, who had come to celebrate New Year's eve in the bombed and besieged city of Dubrovnik, introduced her tour with a memorable profession of faith. "I have a dream," she said, echoing Martin Luther King, and this dream that she sang out with sweet conviction was the great antiracist dream of tolerance, openness to the Other, and universal harmony. In short, the horror of the aggression was reduced to the problem of exclusion. The figure of the Other hid the enemy, and the besieged were encouraged to extend a warm welcome to this pious image that held them at gunpoint. As early as 1940, the writer Jacques Chardonne preferred the delicacy of hospitality to the coarseness of resistance: in an article published by the *Nouvelle Revue Française*, he imagined this answer of a wine grower to the German colonel occupying his land: "I would have preferred to invite you . . . but I can't change the situation. Enjoy my cognac which I generously offer you."

"Comparing doesn't make you right," would likely be the response of the singer as well as of all those who have sung the same song for so long. During the Second World War, ideologies and even philosophy, in conformity with Nietzsche's prophecy, confronted each other for world domination. On the other hand, no common name can be put on the proper names that fight for the control of Krajina or eastern Slavonia. The conflict between Serbs and Croatians does not engage one with ideas but with identities. And when identities bicker, isn't the only idea that must be upheld that of tolerance or reconciliation?

This apparently faultless demonstration clearly does not do justice to either of the two events it confronts. As Georges Bernanos understood early on, the world, between 1939 and 1945, was the theatre of a merciless war fought in the name of Race against the nations. "If there is international law," he remarked, "there is not, there never will be an interracial law." What other mission, in effect, could race assume in the world "if not that of destroying everything that does not resemble it? For everything that does not resemble it threatens it and is a threat to its integrity, to its purity." A mission and a program that Hitler confirmed in these terms: "We can only undertake the Germanification of the earth, not that of men." The war in the former Yugoslavia follows the same logic and reveals – at a level that is, of course, local – the same ultimate stake: race or nation. A stake that the humanitarian singer and many intellectuals did not grasp because, in their eyes, it is by raising oneself above one's allegiances, in tearing oneself away from one's particular convictions that humans attain freedom. This is why they preach the virtues of cosmopolitanism to all the nations who, worried about their identity, jealously guard their borders. Clearly, cosmopolitanism attests to the idea of humanity itself. But the cosmopolitanism they invoke is no longer a broadening of curiosity but a swelling of subjectivity. It is no longer care for the world; it is a globalization of the self. Originally it was a bond established or to be established with other men. It has become the quality inherent in the finally realized planetary man. Thus the famous sociologist Pierre Bourdieu calls himself European in the sense that it is for him "a degree of superior universality, in the sense that it is already better than being French." Following this principle, the sociologists, philosophers, and artists who had remained neutral during the first year of the war sided with Bosnia, not only because it was the country that suffered the most but especially because being Bosnian in their eyes was already better than being Slovene, Croatian, or Macedonian. To them multicultural Bosnia appeared to be a place elevated above every place. In it they saw the fatherland of planetary man. Useful and even beneficial, this commitment depended, nevertheless, on a quid pro quo. For the people who live in Bosnia are not immaterial forms or beings free from this modern sin of the flesh known as belonging or rootedness. If, in spite of the forces of disintegration, they do indeed have a common soul, this soul is carnal, anchored in a world, located in a land, born of a unique history; and it must be defended even more unconditionally since its disappearance from history and its obliteration from the earth have been preordained.

Does the constituting of two autonomous entities (one Serb, the other Croatian-Muslim) make this disappearance inevitable? Does a looming *pax americana* announce a final dissection? That's possible, and it is worth worrying about it. But we must not forget that a tragedy has taken place. For us, tragedy is a big word; for Bosnians it is an irreparable event. In it we see terrible images; Bosnians see the unleashing of unlimited violence. We would lose sight of the difference between them and us were we to believe that the war over there could be ended like a parenthesis and could give way, without any transition, to an idyll. Perhaps it will be necessary to pass through a transitional separation in order to let some tissue of common life come about. In any case, Bosnians are not the telespectators of their own sufferings. Whatever happens, therefore, these sufferings are not about to disappear.

# 40

# President Tudjman, Europe, and Bosnia-Herzegovina

*Le Monde*, 5 October 1995

In an interview that appeared on the day of his visit to France, President Tudjman affirmed that the role the powerful nations assigned Croatia was that of integrating Bosnian Muslims into Western civilization. He declared himself ready to meet the challenge and, with the help of the European Union, to take on this difficult mandate. While defending himself against the accusation of being paternalistic, he confirmed these remarks during the press conference held at the end of his visit. So he probably had the feeling of perpetuating the ancestral vocation of his country: yesterday *Antemurale Christianis* (rampart of the Christian world), today Croatia became the frontier of Western Europe confronted with the recomposition of an Eastern European civilization.

The Westernness of Bosnia is, we mustn't hide it, a stake that is already crucial. I was in Sarajevo in the beginning of August. In spite of the rigors of the siege, the activity of the snipers, and the bombing everywhere and at every possible moment, the city was not talking about the war but about the resignation of Prime Minister Haris Silajdzic. Talk also centered on the constitutional amendment that Alija Izetbegovic had just put to a vote to transfer the election of the president of the republic from the Collegial Presidence to the parliament. The prime minister resigned to protest the ever-increasing power of the SDA, the majority Muslim party, over the executive body and more particularly over the management of financial aid to Bosnia. Due to pressure from foreign capitals, the government has refused to accept his resignation, but he has obtained no satisfaction. As for the constitutional amendment, the sitting president has explicitly proposed it in order to avert the risk of having a successor who would not be from the SDA. The presidency is, in effect, multinational, whereas the SDA holds the majority in the parliament by a large margin. All the lay intellectuals of Sarajevo saw in these two events the confirmation of their fear for the European and democratic future of Bosnia.

So the problem does exist. But far from solving it, condescension can only aggravate it. What the democrats of Tuzla and Sarajevo need today is clear support for Bosnia and not some ambiguous protection.

And then it was not Muslims but Croatians and particularly – and this is of capital importance – Croatians from Herzegovina who destroyed the Mostar bridge. Today one only has to walk in this city to understand that the action was not an accident.

The spirit of Mostar constitutes a threat to European civilization that is more present and real than the spirit of Sarajevo. One has been able to think that this threat had been done away with by the creation, in March 1994, of a Croatian-Muslim federation. But in the reconquered cities, thanks to the implementation of this alliance, the slogan of "everyone for himself" seems to prevail. And flying in Jace is the flag of Herzeg-Bosna, the Croatian entity that was supposed to disappear in the new federation.

Certainly the worst is not always bound to happen. What is certain, on the other hand, is that were the spirit of Mostar to win out, it would be a disaster for the truth. The truth would be definitively buried under amalgams, contempt for facts, and the deafening remarks made against the tribes by the racist detractors. It would also be a disaster for Croatia and for Bosnia-Herzegovina, who can win the war as well as peace and democracy if they are united. It would, finally, be an unhoped-for gift to the ethnocidal aggressor of these two countries, at the very moment when the West finally consents to stirring from its long political lethargy and humanitarian cynicism. But then this is not the mission President Tudjman received.

# 41

# The Politeness of Despair

*Libération*, 14 September 1996
Invited to Sarajevo in October of 1994, with other writers from Ljubljana, Drago Jancar talked to President Izetbegovic about a linguistic curiosity used in the former Yugoslavia, where he had been a citizen. The Slovenes, he basically said, had long maintained the practice of ending a discussion or any reasoning with the formula, "Peace in Bosnia!" It was like a melancholic amen, a set way to conclude everything by referring the last word to an improbable future. For nothing had less of a chance of being established in Bosnia than some picturesque paradise.

A city that is authentically cosmopolitan, a vertiginous array of faiths, calendars, feast days, and architectures, Sarajevo has never for all that constituted the multicultural paradise that some, moved by sentiment and solidarity, thought to have discovered in it. Despite its true art of living and undeniable urbanity, this place of intermixing has also remained, throughout history, a place crossed by invisible barriers. And communism has not helped things with its treatment of differences by the system called "the national key." While the daily paper *Oslobodjene* was once printed on alternate days in Cyrillic and then in the Latin alphabet, the distribution of positions followed draconian rules everywhere: the assistant director of a publishing house, for example, had to be Croatian if the general manager was Serb and the business manager Muslim. Set up so that each nation would have a role to play, this procedure actually sharpened tensions, frustrations, rivalries, and fears.

Consequently, what we ought to have defended in Bosnia was not a social model (largely imaginary) but a civilized way of getting out of crises and resolving conflicts. After all, contemporary Europe was not founded on the tourism promise of a world where all styles of life would be available to everyone but rather on the political refusal henceforth to solve differences by recourse to war. Well, for its first appearance as an actor on the international scene, the European Union has proudly departed from the very principle it once held to be sacred. Serbia appeared, without any political protector, as the only stabilizing force in the region, and one has done everything to give it free rein. And this "one" is, in first place, France. This country, and *not Germany* – as so many experts and diplomats have repeated – led the European Ball up to the time of François Mitterrand's trip to Sarajevo and its miraculous result: the reopening of the airport for humanitarian purposes in exchange for a guarantee of nonintervention.

Brute force has therefore been given the chance to reshape Bosnia. Aggression suffered a sharp check *after* the irreparable was achieved. A tragedy took place that is not the same for those who lived it as for those who saw it from their window. This is why, manipulated or not, the elections will carry into power the nationalist parties that were already victorious before the war. Nothing can be done about it: no electoral campaign, however much in conformity with democracy's demands, can erase the trauma of the extreme violence or undo its toll. Whatever the constitutional framework to come, it is too late for aggrieved and aggressors to return to a common life.

What is still possible – and this depends to a large extent on the Europeans – is the rescue of the Croatian-Muslim federation in Bosnia. We can and we should use Croatian aspirations to join Europe against Mostar's ultras. It is incumbent upon us not to abandon to their mafiosi or to their religious extremists those whom we have already, for four decisive years, handed over to their assailants.

In any case, post-Yugoslav Bosnia is a far cry from the desired Europe. The dream is dead. What remains is humor, notably this joke that Drago Jancar brought back from Sarajevo. A Croatian, a Muslim, and two Serbs find themselves on the moon. "Look at these stones!" the Croatian says. "It's Dalmatia." The Muslim doesn't agree. "No," he answers. "There is only one place as rocky as this one: Bosnia-Herzegovina. Our republic!" Then one of the two Serbs takes out his gun, shoots his compatriot, and says, "It's a Serb cemetery; it's Serbia."

# 42

# Leaving the War

*An Interview with Alain Finkielkraut*

*Politique Internationale*, September 1996
*Politique Internationale* (PI): The Italian jurist Antonio Casese, president of the International Tribunal of the Hague for the former Yugoslavia, underlined that there could be no true peace, that is, a peace that would not just be an end to the fighting, without justice. Do you think that this is the sine qua non condition for every effort at reconciliation?

AF: What other means, in effect, than justice to get out of the infernal cycle of revenge? Obviously no tribunal is able to wipe out, let alone repair, the suffering undergone, but only the trial and punishment of those responsible for the "ethnic cleansing" can effectively counteract the pernicious and spontaneous idea of Serb collective guilt. We should therefore continue to demand the arrest of Radovan Karadzic, the mastermind of the crime, and of Radko Mladic, the first to carry out his orders. The problem is that despite having a clearer mandate than the now defunct UN Command had, the IFOR wants above all to refrain from arresting the Serb leaders, for fear of reprisals.[1] Since we see all this as spectators, it would be indecent to reproach the democracies for their obsession with a "zero death count." But we must also note that the international peacekeepers, however powerful they might be, find themselves at the mercy of their most pathetic prey when it is sufficiently determined.

We can pretty much bet that justice will not be done. If that is the case, law cannot replace politics. Even in the most improbable case that Serbia would hand over some of its most undesirable criminals to the Hague Tribunal, the conditions for reconciliation would not all be present.

Let's compare, since the creation of an international tribunal entices us to do so, the psychological situation of Germany at the end of the Second World War with that of Serbia today. Between 1933 and 1945, Hitler had plunged his people into the implacably coherent and completely fictional world of a fight to the death against a supernaturally wicked enemy, judaeo-bolshevism. Hitlerian propaganda combined megalomania and a persecution paranoia. But this fiction faded with the defeat; the paranoia didn't survive the shock of capitulation and the discovery of the concentration camps. With the collapse of the Third Reich, the objectivity of the real world dissipated the ideological fog. Well, the first difference from the German case is that the Serbs have not lost the war. NATO's intervention has definitely put a stop to their progress, but the Dayton Accords have also ratified their conquests. Their nationalism has not been shattered by the reality principle. They can also leave the war in the mental state with which they entered it – that is to say, with the certainty of having fought a world conspiracy that thwarted their complete victory. And we can bet they would consider the handing over of Mladic and Karadzic to be an act of treachery, an inadmissible concession to the international Enemy. In other words, the TPI can be explicitly placed in the tradition of Nuremberg, but it isn't the Germany of 1945 that today's Serbia conjures up but rather the Germany of 1918 with its feeling of innocence and its obsession with having been stabbed in the back.[2]

PI: Doesn't reconciliation also imply that each community judge its own criminals, not in order to absolve them but, on the contrary, to begin a real examination of conscience about one's own responsibility?

AF: Given the impunity that the aggressors now enjoy, it

is difficult to ask the aggressed to judge or hand over their own criminals. We must, however, insist and even force in every way possible the governments involved to keep their commitments. If anything is more scandalous than to pigeonhole all the Yugoslav "tribes" together – and tantamount to a kiss of death – it would be to spare Croatians and Bosnians from any examination of conscience, notably after the horrible war that has made them enemies.

Since the reconquest of Krajina, a climate of national exaltation and infatuation reigns in Croatia and it could threaten democracy. The exercise of justice would demystify the conflict that has just taken place and introduce into the relationship that Croatians have among themselves a necessary element of doubt, worry, and nonreconciliation.

PI: Whoever does not exorcise his past is condemned to relive it, as has been shown by the example of the former Yugoslavia, where the horrors of the Second World War have been repressed in the name of a feigned Yugoslav and communist fraternity. Don't you think, in the light of this event, that historical inquiry is crucial?

AF: The problem, clearly, exists not only for the former Yugoslavia but in all the European countries that have freed themselves from a totalitarian hold. As François Furet reminds us in *Le Passé d'une illusion (The History of an Illusion)*, the communists brought about and succeeded at an extraordinary O.P.A. on antifascism: "With this word 'antifascism,' all is said about what is going to make communism flourish after the Second World War. The communists, moreover, have not been mistaken in continuing to fight under this flag, more than under any other. They have never wanted any other political territory for their action than this space with two dimensions, or rather with two poles, one figured by the 'fascists,' the other by themselves."[3] This lie died in 1989. So we have the present difficulty, experienced by all the countries of Central Europe, of distinguishing antifascism from the intemperate use propaganda has made of it. Half a century of rigging things, inflated numbers, and extravagant accusations have succeeded in turning off many Croatians not so much from Ustachism as from its denunciation. That will not lead them to be reconciled with this horrible period of their history, but it makes any inscription of the truth upon the collective memory and any clear analysis of the past very difficult to accomplish.

PI: Isn't the resurgence of national frustrations and repressed irredentisms shared by all of Europe?

AF: The memory of fascism in Western Europe has not been completely confiscated by ideology, and it can still be used as a safeguard. Certainly, with the advance of the National Front, the discourse on the inequality of human races finds, in France, a front seat. Nevertheless, it remains that the left failed in its will to divide the right into those who ally themselves with the devil and those who refuse to lose their soul in order to win the elections. It was impossible to make Jean-Marie Le Pen's movement into the Communist party of the right because we live on the base of a common memory. Well, in what was once called the other Europe, this memory is corrupt. How can we heal memory of its decline or ideological perversion? That's the problem for the Croatians, but also for the Slovaks, Hungarians, and Romanians.

PI: In the wars of national liberation, as opposed to wars between states, the first step to reconciliation is the acknowledgment of the existence of the other, as the Israeli-Palestinian conflict has shown.

AF: Reference to the Israeli-Palestinian conflict is very enlightening, for it shows that in certain cases reconciliation can only come about through separation. No one in Europe thinks about any renegotiation of Jerusalem's status that could end up with its political and administrative partition. And, in addition, there is an important Arab minority in

Israel that could, one day, combine Israeli citizenship with Palestinian nationality.

To accomplish the political gesture and yet avoid the disentanglement of populations is the twofold requirement that, having been valuable in the Israeli-Palestinian conflict, should also, quite logically, have inspired the politics of the international community in the former Yugoslavia.

PI: You say that separation is a fundamental step. Is this because it is impossible to recognize the other as long as he is in you?

AF: To recognize the other is to recognize his freedom. With regard to nations, freedom functions through the constitution of distinct and sovereign states. There is no contradiction in working simultaneously for European Union and for the Yugoslav breakup. Contrary to what the unfortunate maxim "association or barbarity" would have us believe, marriage and divorce are in this instance the two faces of the same freedom.

PI: Recognition of the other is at times something extremely slow and difficult to attain, a dialogue of deaf people. The Palestinians say, "We don't have to pay for the Holocaust." The Israelis answer, "The Arabs are all the same" or "All they have to do is go and live in some other Arab country."

AF: You say it's a long and difficult process. In effect, it is necessary to have lost one's common sense and to forget the details of what has been seen and lived to speak of immediate reconciliation after a war. It's true for the Middle East and even more so for the Balkans: Croatia and Bosnia-Herzegovina have not been the theatre of a dispute, or even of a scuffle between hot-blooded Slavs. The survivors of extreme cruelty are not mixed in with those who destroyed Vukovar, laid siege to Sarajevo, and massacred the male population of Srebernica. It's because we have only been the television spectators of the confrontation that it seems to us quite natural to see yesterday's enemies patching things up and that we impute to the influence of unscrupulous politicians their obstinate rancor. Now we can only think about the *normalization* of relations. This word is colder than *reconciliation*. But it is also more precise, more political, and finally more moral because it accounts for the horrors committed and all the torture that has been endured.

PI: In the passage from war to peace, why are gestures so terribly important?

AF: The handshake between Rabin and Arafat was not just a great photo-op for the media. It truly constituted a moment that was both moving and essential for the Israeli-Palestinian peace process. Why? Because it was not easy, because Rabin did violence to himself, because he took it upon himself, because he was neither smiling nor relaxed, but worried and tense, and so the majority of the Israelis were able to share with him in this gesture. What gave the handshake great symbolic meaning was the fact that it required a visible effort from everyone. Moreover, it created an unforeseeable bond between these three *tired* men, Rabin the old general, Pérés the old diplomat, and the old leader Arafat. Perhaps this was the beginning of true reconciliation. I say perhaps, because this bond was broken, and the fatigue of both Pérés and Rabin left a place in Israel for Netanyahu's energy. The gestures are over; to hell with the fatigue: international pressure will perhaps prevent the worst, but it alone will never bring about peace.

PI: In Greece as in Spain forty years will have been necessary to heal the wounds of civil war. Reconciliation within nations seems to be a long and complicated affair.

AF: In this regard, it seems useful to dwell on what is going on in Croatia today. In 1972 President Georges Pompidou, when questioned about Touvier, declared, "Are we going to care eternally for the bleeding wounds of our national disagreements?" Today President Tudjman wants to care for the wounds of the Second World War, overcome old rifts, and in some way have Croatians love one another again.

Invited in June 1995 to Zagreb to speak about the shocking theme of *national reconciliation*, I contested this attitude in showing, in light of Vichy, the even more abominable crimes committed by "the independent State of Croatia." Why did the French leaders at the time insist on organizing themselves the roundup at the Winter Velodrome? As Henry Rousso has shown, this initiative comes less "from the desire to get rid of the Jews, presented in 1940 as elements of 'the dissolution of the national fiber,' than from the will to affirm that Vichy was capable of policing itself and thereby of demonstrating its autonomy and legitimacy."[4] In other words, it was a question of keeping, at whatever cost, the royal privileges of the French state. The obsession with sovereignty led to crime and aggravated the enslavement. Applying the same analysis *mutatis mutandis* to Pavelic's state, it would be disastrous for the truth and for the future to want to reconcile Croatians by distinguishing between the Ustachis' rightful desire for independence and their disastrous participation in the Final Solution. It was because their will for independence was closed to every other consideration that the Ustachis lent a hand in the extermination of the Jews and Tsiganes and that they engaged in extermination, using the Nazi model, of a large number of Serbs and other Croatian opponents. The general lesson that should be drawn from the episode of Collaboration is that the state cannot, in any case, be justification unto itself.

PI: To summarize, we can't place on the same plane victims and executioners?

AF: No, that's not exactly it. The partisans also committed massacres. At Bleibourg they killed not only Ustachis but dozens of thousands of enlisted men and civilians who did not share Pavelic's ideology. It is also true that the extermination camp of Jasenovac continued to function during the first years of the communist regime. It is therefore legitimate for us not to be content with a partial memory and to want to reconcile Croatians with the truth while keeping each of the two totalitarian traumas from covering up the other.

PI: What do you think about the desire of the present Croatian government to create a monument in Jasenovac in honor of all the victims?

AF: I questioned Tudjman about this. What he told me was much less scandalous than what I had read in the press. He said he didn't want to mix the dead but, in separating them, to create a place of memory shared by the victims of all totalitarianisms so that all their heirs who gather to pray for their martyrs could not avoid thinking about the crimes perpetrated by their own camp. Was he sincere? In any case, I don't think it is for the Croatian president to decide about the memory of a crime that concerns all humanity. Perhaps it would be good to create in Jasenovac an international scientific committee, as was done in Poland after the fall of communism, for the Museum of Auschwitz.

PI: Another problem of the Eastern nations today is whether it is necessary to reveal everything and open all the communist archives? In Germany, the disclosure of the Stasi dossiers was rather traumatic, even for some of the families. On the other hand, in the Czech Republic, Vaclav Havel has thought it better not to do so. What balance can be found between the necessity to shed light on past crimes and that of turning the page?

AF: In almost fifty years of communism, no one has been able to remain totally outside the system. So then everyone is suspect. And in wanting to put communism on trial, we risk perpetuating one of its most stifling aspects, people informing on one another and eternal trials. That explains Havel's reticence.

PI: Where do we place responsibility? Should we situate it at the level of the position occupied in the hierarchy, limit it to individual and concrete facts?

AF: I wouldn't know how to decide. I do believe that in what concerns communism's exit, it's better to choose the path of history rather than that of a trial, if only to break truly with the climate of the totalitarian period.

PI: Desmond Tutu, who headed the commission of reconciliation in South Africa, said, "Justice only exists because we live in an imperfect world. The only true possible way is pardon." Do you agree with that?

AF: Yes, but first one clarification. You can only grant forgiveness to someone who asks for it and, in the case of extreme violence, only once justice has been rendered. How do we pardon a torturer drunk on his impunity and certain of his right? It's true that Archbishop Tutu is referring to a quite different situation, that of South Africa, which has just freed itself peacefully from apartheid and has courageously chosen the path of democracy rather than that of revenge. And he is right to grant a preeminent place to pardon – this "revolutionary inversion of our vindictive tendencies."[5] As Hannah Arendt has remarked, "The discoverer of the role of forgiveness in the realm of human affairs was Jesus of Nazareth. The fact that he made this discovery in a religious context and articulated it in religious language is no reason to take it any less seriously in a strictly secular sense."[6] For acts are irreversible. What has been can no longer not have been. So "without being forgiven, released from the consequences of what we have done, our capacity to act would, as it were, be confined to one single deed from which we could never recover; we would remain the victims of its consequences forever . . ."[7] Without pardon, the faults of the past would be suspended like the sword of Damocles above every new generation.

PI: Pardon, however, does not erase the irreversibility of the act; it only makes it more acceptable.

AF: We must be careful, in effect, not to confuse pardon and forgetting. Pardon is the gift of going beyond commutative justice and returning good for evil. This gift can only be exercised knowingly. Forgetting is not a gift; it is a process. As Jankélévitch has said, "the present, that is to say, the ambient dailiness attacks us from all sides and never ceases to invite us to forget things that have happened; it is the pressure of every moment. . . . Forgetting doesn't need to be hurried, and it is quite useless to recommend it to men. There will always be swimmers in the waters of Lethe."[8]

But this distinction between the act of pardoning and the natural force of forgetting is still insufficient. However, there are crimes that are so terrible and radical that no one has the power to pardon them. For these the category of crimes against humanity has been created and we have declared them to be unpardonable. Only one man, to date, has admitted to the massacre of Srebernica and described to the Hague Tribunal the part he took in it. He was a Croatian enlisted in the Serb army. His deposition is all the more impressive since he was not seeking absolution. He did not reason according to the principle whereby a sin confessed is half pardoned. I thought, while looking at his face and reading his testimony, about this meditation of Simone Weil, "Punishment is a vital need of the human soul . . . . Just as the only means of showing respect to someone who suffers from hunger is to give him something to eat, so the only way to show respect to someone who has placed himself outside the reach of the law is it reintegrate him into the law by submitting him to the punishment it prescribes."[9]

NOTES

1. Under the Dayton Accords, IFOR was the military peace-keeping force organized by NATO and responsible for issues relating to the military parts of the agreement. *Trans.*

2. TPI stands for the Tribunal Pénal International, the International Tribunal of the Hague. *Trans*.

3. François Furet, *Le Passé d'une illusion* (Laffont–Calman-Lévy, 1995), 400.

4. Henry Rousso in *Esprit*, May 1992, p. 29.

5. Jankélévitch, *Le Pardon* (Aubier, 1967), 198.

6. Hannah Arendt, *The Human Condition* (Chicago: University of Chicago Press, 1958), 238.

7. Arendt, *The Human Condition*, 237.

8. Jankélévitch, *Le Pardon*, 74.

9. Simone Weil, *L'Enracinement*, Folio Essais series (Gallimard, 1990), 33.

# Source Acknowledgments

Parts 1 and 2 were previously published as *Comment peut-on être croate?* © Éditions Gallimard, 1992.

Part 3 includes the following previously published articles:

"Les Exigences du jour," *Le Monde*, 16 Dec. 1992.

"Révisionnisme," *Le Monde*, 15 Jan. 1993.

"Les va-t-en paix," *Le Figaro*, 3 Feb. 1993.

"Deux Europes," un discours prononcé à une conférence à Osijek, Feb. 1993.

"L'Inavouable frontière," *Le Monde*, 18 Mar. 1993.

"Sans vergogne," *Le Monde*, 21 May 1993.

"L'Injonction de Buchenwald," *Le Monde*, 15 Dec. 1993.

"La Victoire posthume de Hitler," in *Vukovar, Sarajevo . . .* , Éditions Esprit, 1993.

*Le Crime d'être né*, © Arléa, 1994.

"Les Intellectuels, la politique et la guerre," *Le Monde*, 16 Sept. 1994.

"Volonté d'impuissance," *Le Monde*, 29 Nov. 1994.

"De L'inutilité du XXè siècle," *Le Monde*, 15 Dec. 1994.

"L'Oubli du monde," *Le Monde*, 15 Apr. 1995.

"L'Imposture Kusturica," *Le Monde*, 2 June 1995.

"Ne pas laisser l'image des morts ensevelir les morts," *Libération*, 16 June 1995.

"Le Roi est nu," *Télérama*, 26 July 1995.

"Des anges et des hommes," *Le Monde*, 20–21 Aug. 1995.

"Race contre Nation," *Frankfurter Allgemeine Zeitung*, 8 Sept. 1995.

"Le Président Tudjman, l'Europe et la Bosnie-Herzégovine," *Le Monde*, 5 Oct. 1995.

"La Politesse du désespoir," *Libération*, 14 Sept. 1996.

"Sortir de la guerre," entretien avec Marc Semo, *Politique Internationale*, Sept. 1996.

# Index

Alsace-Lorraine, 106
anti-Semitism, 29, 73, 141,
    162–64
Arendt, Hannah, 174, 200, 218;
    on Jewish identity, 37–38; on
    totalitarianism, 13–14
Aron, Raymond, 101
Association for Threatened
    People, meeting at Buchenwald
    of, 138
Attali, Jacques, 10
Azéma, Pierre, xxii

Babic, Milan, 17
Badinter, Robert, 16, 44
Baker, James, 89
Balkans, 3, 6, 89, 131, 140, 192, 196
Bauer, Otto, 18, 26
Bérégovoy, Pierre, 92
Berlin Wall, 16, 48, 166
Bernanos, Georges, 3, 201
Bibo, István, 10, 23
Bihac, 96, 98
Bolshevism, 11
Bonnet, Georges, 87
Bosnia-Herzegovina, 3, 108, 118,
    120, 131, 132, 133, 139, 186–87,
    202, 204; and concept of na-
    tionhood, 105–6; and expan-
    sion of war in, 143–45; and
    idea of community, 159–60;
    and identity, 52, 55, 84, 96; and

minorities, xxii, 44. *See also*
    Yugoslavia
Bosnians, views on war of, 202–3
Bourdieu, Pierre, 202
Bousquet, René, 141
Boutros-Ghali, Boutros, 94, 119,
    144
Bruckner, Pascal, xix, xxiii
Buchenwald, meeting at, 137–38

Camus, Albert, 15
Carignon, Alain, xxii
Carrington, Lord, 94, 142
Casese, Antonio, 210
Chamberlain, Neville, 6, 87, 190
Chardonne, Jacques, 200–201
Chéreau, Patrice, xxii
Chetniks, 6, 30
Chevènement, Pierre, 103
Cheysson, Claude, 13
Chirac, Jacques, 189–90, 199
Christopher, Warren, 139, 142,
    146, 198
Ciliga, Anton, *Pays du mensonge
    déconcertant*, 29–30
Clinton, Bill, 170
communism, collapse of, 15
Cosic, 65
cosmopolitanism, 167
Croatia, 3, 25, 55, 84, 85, 215; and
    causes of war, 175–76; declara-
    tion of independence of, 44;

Croatia (*continued*)
ethnocentrism in, 58, 71; and
expansion of war, 143–45; history of, 17–19, 21; role during
World War II of, 81. *See also*
Croatians; Yugoslavia
Croatians: concept of nationhood
for, 105–6; diplomatic efforts
of, 192–93; as instigators of
war, 153; nonreconciliation
among, 212; and question of
identity, 50, 54; self-determination of, xviii–xix, xxi, 8, 52, 78,
82, 83; as viewed by Europeans,
127; and the Vance-Owen Plan,
131. *See also* Croatia

Daladier, Edouard, 190
Dayton Accords, xxiv, 211
Decoutray, Cardinal, xxii
democracy, 27; survival of, 33, 52
Djuric, Ivan, 40
Dreyfus Affair, xvii
Dubcek, 28
Dubrovnik, destruction of, 58,
104, 143, 186
Dumas, Roland, 189

Edelman, Marek, 137, 139, 142,
146
Ehrenbourg, Ilya, 47
Eisenhower, Dwight D., *Communiqué* (1944), 99–100
embargo, on arms, 131–32, 170
Engels, Friedrich, xxvii, 185
ethnic cleansing, xxii, 46, 93, 140,
153, 194, 210
ethnocentricity, 64, 151

European Committee for Vigilance, 148–64
European Community, xx, 42,
44, 46, 64, 74–75, 105
extreme Right: and European
Committee for Vigilance, 148–
64; rise of in Eastern Europe,
26–27. *See also* fascism

fascism, 47, 213. *See also* extreme
Right
fatherland, concept of, 51
Ferro, Marc, xviii
Finkielkraut, Alain: and defense of
Slovenian and Croatian claims to
independence, xviii, xxiii, xxiv–
xxv; on Jewish identity, 37–38
Fontenay, Elisabeth de, 29
France: ethnocentrism of, 77; extreme Right in, 148–50; indifference of media to conflict in,
5; penal code of, 85; politics of,
101–4, 105; 1995 presidential
campaign in, 179–81; and relations with Croatia and Slovenia, 71–72; and relations with
Serbia, 63–64, 127
French intellectuals: attitude toward Poland of, 13; on war in
former Yugoslavia, xvii–xxx
Fukuyama, Francis, 33
Furet, François, xviii; *Le Passé
d'une illusion*, 212
Fustel de Coulanges, Numa
Denis, 106

Genschler, Hans-Dietrich, 142
Geremek, Bronislaw, 23, 166–67

Glucksmann, André, xix
Goering, 6, 190
Gonzalez, Felipe, xix
Gorazde, 96, 98
Gorbachev, Mikhail, 73–74
Greater Serbia, xx, 7, 44, 46, 55, 78, 140, 154, 159, 168, 183, 186. *See also* Balkans; Serbia; Yugoslavia

Haldnik-Milharcic, E., 23
Halifax Summit, 190
Handke, Peter, 6–8
Havel, Vaclav, 48, 217
Havlicek, Karel, 19, 56
Hegel, George Wilhelm Friedrich, 14, 134
Heine, Heinrich, 24
Hendriks, Barbara, 200
Hitler, Adolf, 124–25, 177, 201, 211
Holocaust, 139, 141. *See also* Jews: extermination of
Huisbourgh, François, 140
Hungary, 1956 Revolution in, 47

Ideology, in France, 57–58, 60, 65–66, 102
intellectuals: attitudes of, 173. *See also* French intellectuals
Ionesco, Eugene, xix
Israeli-Palestinian conflict, 213–15
Izetbegovic, Alija, xxiii, 33, 65, 98, 136, 144, 204, 207

Jancar, Drago, 207, 209
Jankélévitch, Vladimir, 61–62
Jasenovac. *See* Ustachis

Jews: discrimination against, 163–64; extermination of, 142, 216. *See also* Holocaust
John-Paul II, 142, 189
Joseph of Arimatheia, 20–21
Joxe, Pierre, 10
Juppé, Alain, 186
justice: and forgiveness, 218; in relation to force, 174–75

Kant, Emmanuel, 133–37
Karadjic, Radovan, 65, 170–71, 210–11
Karski, Jan, 141
Kichinev, pogrom in, 124, 185
Kotchovitch, Bogoljub, 31
Kohl, Helmut, 189
Kosovo, 8, 107, 143, 175, 182
Kouchner, Bernard, 131, 177
Krajina, 78, 102, 168, 176, 194, 199, 201, 212
Kravchenko, Viktor, 15
Kriegel, Annie, xx, 24–25
Kundera, Milan, 105; and defense of Slovenian and Croatian claims to independence, xviii; and definition of nation, 163; "Un Occident kidnappé ou la tragédie de l'Europe centrale," 115, 124
Kusturica, Emir, 182–84

Landsbergis, Vitas, 137
Lanzmann, Claude, 162
Lauzanne, Stéphane, 6, 190–91
Lazare, Bernard, 161–63
Le Goff, Jacques, xviii
Lellouche, Pierre, 140

## Index

Le Pen, 6

Levi, Primo, 109–10

Lévi-Strauss, Claude, 106

Lévy, Bernard-Henri, xix, xxiii–xxiv

liberalism, 25–26, 34

Maastricht Accords, xxii, 86, 101, 103–4, 108, 136

Macedonians, and the concept of nationhood, 105–6

Mackenzie, General, 94, 98

Magris, Claudio, *Danube*, 53

Malraux, André, xxiii

Mann, Thomas, 119

Martel, Frédéric, xviii–xix, xxi–xxii, xxiv

Marxism, 26

Mazowiecki, Tadeusz, 108–9

Mesic, Stipe, 72

Mestrovic, Ivan, desecration of tomb of, 194

Milosevic, Slobodan, xxi, 82, 87, 88, 89, 129, 140, 142, 145, 146, 170, 175, 184, 189–90, 193

Milosz, Czeslaw: *Une autre Europe*, 19–20; *La Pensée captive*, 14

Mitterand, François, 135, 142, 146, 181; on Serbian aggression, 45–46; trip to Sarajevo by, xxiii, 90–91, 98–99, 208; on war in Croatia, 80; on war in Yugoslavia, xx, 42–44, 74

Mladic, Radko, 186, 210–11

Mommsen, Theodor, 106

Morillon, General Philippe, 109

Morin, Edgar, xxi, xxiii, xxix, 55, 58

Mostar, destruction of, 102, 137, 145, 193, 205

Muslims, in Bosnia, 87, 131, 133, 140, 143, 145

national identity, 27

nationalism, xix, 25; criteria for, 23–24; as Europe's enemy, 116, 166–67

nationhood, 105–6

NATO, military intervention of, 198, 211

Nazi Germany, 121

Nazism, xxvi, 11; and anti-Semitism, 29, 47

Nedic, Anton, 81

negationism, 134, 154

Negroponte, Nicholas, *L'Homme numérique*, 195–96

Nietzsche, Freidrich, 58, 158

Nuremberg, 130, 211

Omarska Trnopolje, 97, 110

Osijek, 80, 104, 123, 126, 186

Pan-Germanism, 34, 101, 143

Panic, Milan, 19

Pannekoek, Anton, 26

Pan-Serbism, 143, 146

Pan-Slavism, 18–19, 56

Pascal, Blaise, on justice and force, 174–75

Pavelic, Ante, 28; regime of, 31–32, 81, 216

peace talks, failure of, 121–22

Péguy, Charles, 7, 16; *Notre jeunesse*, 32, 76, 185

Pétain, Marshal Philippe, 87

Polanski, Roman, xxii

Pompidou, Georges, 215

Poos, Jacques, 74

Prague Spring, 21–22, 28

Raseta, General Andrija, 144

Renan, Joseph-Ernest, 106

revisionism, 120

Ricoeur, Paul, xxii

Rocard, Michel, xxiv

Rorovo Selo, massacre in, 135

Rousso, Henry, 216

Runciman, Lord, 190

Russia, 172

Sacirbey, Muhamad, 131–32

Sarajevo, 96, 108, 109, 110, 129, 145, 159, 186, 207; in film, 183–84; humanitarian aid to, 94; after Mitterand's visit, 90–91; siege of, 120, 137, 198, 204, 214; suffering in, xxviii, 185

Sarajevo-Vukovar Committee, xxiii

Schneider, Robert, 174

Scholem, Gershom, 37

SDA, 204–5

Séguin, Philippe, 103

Semprun, Jorge, xix

Serbia: aggression of, 18, 24, 85, 93, 121–22, 141–42, 144, 146, 175; as compared to postwar Germany, 211; as a stabilizing force, 208

Silajdzic, Haris, 176, 204

Slavonia, 78, 201

Slovakia, right to independence of, 75–76

Slovenia, 75, 143, 175–76; declaration of independence of, 44, 71. *See also* Yugoslavia

Slovenians: desire for self-determination of, xviii–xix, xxi, 8, 76; and nationhood, 105; as viewed by *Les Temps modernes,* 153

Solzhenitsyn, Alexander, 22, 59, 73

Springtime of Peoples, 10, 24, 25

Srebernica, 214, 219

Stalin, Joseph, 20

Suarès, André, *Vues sur l'Europe*, 11

Sudetens, 190

Susak, Gojko, 144

Talic, Momir, 118–19

Terray, Emmanuel, 6

Tito, Josip Broz, 8, 189

Toubon, Jacques, xxii

Touvier, Paul, xxvi, 45, 87

tribalism, in Europe, 40, 51, 57

Tudjman, Franjo, xix, xxi, 31, 136, 145, 193, 204, 206, 215, 217; *Déroute de la vérité historique,* 29–30

Tutu, Desmond, 218

Tuzla, 182, 185, 186, 189

UN. *See* United Nations

*Underground* (film), 182–84

United Nations, 17, 65; Command, 210; military forces, 109, 144, 176, 198; refusal of assistance, 102

United States: diplomatic efforts of, 199; foreign policy of, 89, 102, 172

## Index

Ustacha, xx, xxi, xxix, 6, 28, 30–
 32, 47, 73, 81, 216; Jasenovac
 camp in, 29, 81, 217

Vaculik, Ludvik, 105
Vance, Cyrus, 144
Vance-Owen Plan, 131, 143, 146,
 168, 188
Vargas Llosa, Mario, xix
Vassiljevic, Alexandre, 32
Vél d'Hiv. *See* Vélodrome d'Hiver
Vélodrome d'Hiver, commemo-
 ration of, 42–43, 97
Vichy government, xxvi, 42, 46,
 49, 62, 87
Vidal-Naquet, Pierre, xxii
Vinkovci, 123, 126
Vukovar, seige of, xviii, 40, 45,
 49, 58, 80, 84, 87, 96, 104, 111,
 120, 143, 144, 176, 186, 214

Weil, Eric, 56
Weil, Simone, 219
Wiesel, Elie, xix, xxi, 10, 32, 118
Wilde, Oscar, 20

Yugoslavia, 16, 18–20, 72, 105,
 136, 145, 169, 170, 175, 189, 212;
 as compared to Bosnia, 159–
 60, 186–87; consequences of
 the demise of, 58; history in
 film of, 182–84; as a political
 concept, 53, 55; and politics of
 identity, 76, 78, 155, 80–81; and
 refugees, 87–88, 92–93

Zagreb, 145
Zerjavic, Vladimir, 31
Zola, Emile, 10
Zweig, Stefan, *Le Monde d'hier:
 Souvenirs d'un Européen*, 123–24

In the *European Horizons* series

*The Consecration of the Writer, 1750–1830*
By Paul Bénichou
Translated and with an introduction by Mark Jensen
With a preface by Tzvetan Todorov

*A Modern Maistre: The Social and Political Thought of
Joseph de Maistre*
By Owen Bradley

*Dispatches from the Balkan War and Other Writings*
By Alain Finkielkraut
Translated by Peter S. Rogers and Richard Golsan
Introduction and chronology by Richard Golsan